SAGE was founded in 1965 by Sara Miller McCune to support the dissemination of usable knowledge by publishing innovative and high-quality research and teaching content. Today, we publish over 900 journals, including those of more than 400 learned societies, more than 800 new books per year, and a growing range of library products including archives, data, case studies, reports, and video. SAGE remains majority-owned by our founder, and after Sara's lifetime will become owned by a charitable trust that secures our continued independence.

Los Angeles | London | New Delhi | Singapore | Washington DC | Melbourne

SURVIVING
ON THE
EDGE

Thank you for choosing a SAGE product!
If you have any comment, observation or feedback,
I would like to personally hear from you.

Please write to me at **contactceo@sagepub.in**

Vivek Mehra, Managing Director and CEO, SAGE India.

SURVIVING ON THE EDGE

Psychosocial Perspectives on Violence and Prejudice in India

Edited by

SHOBNA SONPAR
NEERU KANWAR

Los Angeles | London | New Delhi
Singapore | Washington DC | Melbourne

First published in 2019 by

SAGE Publications India Pvt Ltd
B1/I-1 Mohan Cooperative Industrial Area
Mathura Road, New Delhi 110 044, India
www.sagepub.in

YODA Press
268 AC Vasant Kunj
New Delhi 110070
www.yodapress.co.in

SAGE Publications Inc
2455 Teller Road
Thousand Oaks, California 91320, USA

SAGE Publications Ltd
1 Oliver's Yard, 55 City Road
London EC1Y 1SP, United Kingdom

SAGE Publications Asia-Pacific Pte Ltd
18 Cross Street #10-10/11/12
China Square Central
Singapore 048423

Published by Vivek Mehra for SAGE Publications India Pvt Ltd, typeset in 10.5/13 pt Bembo by Fidus Design Pvt Ltd, Chandigarh.

Library of Congress Cataloging-in-Publication Data Available

ISBN: 978-93-532-8314-8 (HB)

SAGE YODA Team: Amrita Dutta, Sandhya Gola, Arpita Das, Ishita Gupta and Tanya Singh

Contents

Part I: Violence and Prejudices: Mapping the Landscape

Part II: Impact and Intervention

Acknowledgements

A special note of appreciation for the erstwhile editors of *The Journal* who so very patiently and persistently nurtured writers to regularly contribute to it. It made our work much simpler as many of these articles had been edited in a meticulous manner. The main editors were Jose Parappully and Sadhana Vohra. The others who assisted sporadically were Madhumita Puri, Nimmi Hutnik, Radhika Chandiramani and team, 'Tarshi', Rachana Johri, Reena Nath, Reenee Singh, Shalini Anant and Shobna Sonpar.

Acknowledgements

A special note of appreciation for the erstwhile editors of *The Journal* who so very patiently and persistently nurtured writers to regularly contribute to it. It made our work much simpler as many of these articles had been edited in a meticulous manner. The main editors were Jose Parappully and Sadhana Vohra. The others who assisted spiritedly were Mathumita Pan, Nimmi Hutnik, Radhika Chandiramani and seem, Tarsh, Rachna Joht, Neera Nath, Reene Singh, Shalini Anand and Shobha Sengar.

A Tribute to Dr Vimala Lal

The obituary of Dr Vimala Lal well describes who she was!

The Lal, Kapoor and Gupta families

Dr. Vimala Lal,
wife of (Late) Col. S.B. Lal, passed away on Thursday, February 11, 2016.

To celebrate the life of our revolutionary Aunt, Friend, Counsellor & Benefactor, there is a prayer meeting on Sunday, February 14, 2016 from 3pm-4pm, at the Malcha Marg Community Centre (off Dharam Marg/Malcha Marg, Chanakyapuri).

Surviving on the Edge is dedicated to the memory of the late Dr Vimala Lal, who passed away in 2016. Several of us have been thinking of a fitting tribute to her outstanding contribution to the development of psychological services to Delhi and the National Capital Region. She was the founder of the Psychological Foundations Trust and the moving spirit behind the publication of a professional magazine focusing on contemporary issues relevant to clinical psychology and the field of mental health. This was *Psychological Foundations: The Journal*, a bi-annual publication (1999–2011). We think that reprinting selected articles from the journal in a book that would be available to a wider public and a newer generation of readers would be a contribution to psychological theory and practice in India, would please Vimala enormously.

VIMALA'S EARLY YEARS

Vimala was born in Burma on 8 August 1931 into a large family of eight siblings. Her father was a civil engineer, and her mother a home maker.

The first ten years of her life were spent in this idyllic place, the land of pagodas, beautiful people, fragrant flowers, languid lifestyle and exotic food. During this early time in the Chin Hills, she took away a sense of wonder at the mysteries of the natural world. Family life was significant in offering her a sense of security. 'The regularity, sincerity and the commitment with which my parents provided us the basics, the little ups and downs, the simple pleasures, jokes and stimulations, undoubtedly this has contributed to my trust in myself,' she once wrote.

When Vimala was two years old, her maternal grandmother passed away in India. Her mother's unresolved grief affected her relationship with little Vimala, alternatively pushing her away and then commenting on similarities between Vimala and her dead mother. An understanding of the complexity of this early experience moved Vimala to an empathy for depressive reactions, the processes of forgiveness and acceptance of parents as imperfect care givers. She believes that her 'observing ego' gave her the coping mechanism for the process of growth and determined her choice of becoming a clinical psychologist and a therapist.

At the age of 11, in the background of the Second World War, and the invasion of Burma by Japanese forces, Vimala's quiet life was thrown into disarray as suddenly the family fled back to India, without her beloved father. The next two years were spent shuttling between Delhi and Ghaziabad, under the care of her mother. By 1944, the family, now reunited with father, moved to Dehradun.

Sheila, her elder sister, described Vimala during these years as very sensitive to situations and easily moved to emotional responses, though not seeking social engagement. She was hardworking and engrossed in her studies, extremely disciplined and methodical in her work. Studies provided the anchor during this uncertain time and her success in school was a source of self-esteem.

Choosing Psychology as a Career

During the final examination of the undergraduation degree, prior to the Psychology paper, Vimala had a bout of exam anxiety and broke down crying saying I cannot give my paper! Her elder sister Sheila narrates that they did not know how to calm Vimala. In the end Sheila went to meet Vimala's professor who came home to counsel her. His intervention made an impression on Vimala and she sat for the exam with Sheila sitting outside the examination room to give Vimala the emotional comfort she needed. In line with expectations, Vimala did exceptionally well in her exams.

Vimala had set her heart on continuing with Psychology as a career. Her father was very supportive of all of his daughters' education plans, even with limited resources. However, at this time a dispute arose between Vimala and her father, who admitted Vimala to Isabel Thornbell College, Lucknow much against her wishes; she was resolutely set on going to Patna which boasted of the best faculty for Psychology in India.

After a week in Lucknow, Vimala rebelled and quit the college. She took a train to her uncle in Allahabad and requested him to send someone along with her to Patna University after which she would look after herself.

Her uncle, after some initial hesitation (as he would be acting against the dictates of his elder brother), sent one of his office peons with Vimala to Patna. There, she went to the residence of Professor Maithi and told him about her wish to study under him at Patna University.

Professor Maithi, after giving the matter some thought, accommodated Vimala in the MA Psychology programme and also gave her a small room in his house to live in. Vimala on her part, to thank the Professor for his support, took tuitions of his children in lieu of monetary payments for the accommodation extended to her.

Her courage and perseverance, risking her father's displeasure and venturing alone far away from home in the India of the 1950s, was unusual. It marked her maturity as an autonomous and strong-minded adult. Given her commitment, she topped the University with a Gold medal in 1953. In 1954, she left for the US with the coveted Fulbright and Smith-Mundt Scholarship for her PhD at the University of Kansas. There she enjoyed the opportunities of many different experiences which widened her world view. After her studies, she continued to work as a Clinical Psychologist with the intent of returning to India at the earliest. In the early 1960s, she did return to India but could not get a job as the general employer response was that she was quite overqualified for the job. Disappointed, she went back and established a good practice in Vancouver, Canada, finally returning in 1971. Initially, she taught at SNDT College, Bombay, and later in Delhi, she worked at Holy Family Hospital and Sir Ganga Ram Hospital. After that, she started an independent practice as a Clinical Psychologist.

PERSONAL LIFE

Vimala grew up in a large and close family. In addition to her eight siblings there were uncles, aunts, cousins and extended family surrounding her. Even though she lived as a single, independent, successful professional for many years and thrived on that experience, she dearly cherished her relationships with family.

During her earlier visit to India in the sixties she was introduced to Col. S. B. Lal in Bombay. Col. S. B. Lal took Vimala out for coffee one evening. Much to her annoyance Col. Lal had his Bhabhi accompanying them, to which Vimala took offence saying I am marrying Col. Lal and not his Bhabhi! On that India trip, nothing materialised but both Vimala and S. B. Lal kept in touch, both remaining single until 1971 when they were married in a simple court wedding in Bombay.

While Vimala maintained a busy and full professional life, she was attentive to the relationships between her extended family network and that of her husband. She shared her life with generosity in spirit and resources in time and wealth with many people, some of whom she helped at critical stages of their life.

She was also a diligent philanthropist, examining carefully the many charities that she supported. Always large-hearted and giving, any request for any support from the numerous NGOs that reached her was never returned empty-handed.

About Psychological Foundations

Vimala had strongly felt the need for a community of mental health professionals. 'I need much more peer support, a forum to communicate, and to clarify my subjective and real experiences. This is a beginning,' she wrote. In order to facilitate the work of psychologists and other mental health professionals in clinical practice and to build a cohesive and sustaining professional body, Psychological Foundations was set up as a private trust on 7 October 1993 with Dr Vimala Lal as Founder and Chairperson. The vision was further developed on a rafting trip that Vimala, intrepid adventurer that she was, went on with some of her colleagues. On the banks of the Ganges, they talked about the stresses of their work, feeling isolated with clients in therapy rooms, without professional support, risking burnout. Thus, the Psychological Foundations Trust came to provide peer support and professional support through a number of initiatives. Monthly discussion meetings of academic and clinical issues and access to networking with professional colleagues helped provide much-needed peer support. In addition, professional support was offered through membership to a free library, Manojigyasa, which housed some of the latest books in psychology and clinical practice as well as psychological test materials that clinical psychologists, fresh in the field, could borrow. Professional support was offered through access to supervision as and when needed and through research grants to psychologists. *The Journal* was one of the most important contributions of Psychological Foundations. It was a publication that focused on contemporary issues in psychology practice in India. It was unique in character as the only Indian journal that provided space for clinicians to narrate, and clients to dialogue upon their experiences of mental health clinical work. It was multidisciplinary, inviting other disciplines to share their perspectives. The other trustees of Psychological Foundations at various times were Ms Radhika Chandiramani, Dr Jose Parapully, Dr Neeru Kanwar, Dr Sadhana Vohra, Dr Shobna Sonpar and Dr Vinita Kshetrapal.

Other Professional Involvements

Vimala was a pioneer of early intervention for learning problems and mental disability and highly regarded for her comprehensive, reliable and child-oriented assessments. Among others, she was associated with Aanchal, a school for children with mental disability. From the start, she realised the importance of engaging the caregivers of children with special needs and also the caregivers of persons with chronic mental illness. She understood their emotional needs and the stresses with which they coped and reached out to them with compassion and helpful guidance. She was frequently invited by schools to address and guide parents and to provide training to teachers in Special Schools. Under the aegis of Psychological Foundations, she, along with Neeru Kanwar, undertook the translation into Hindi of a guidebook produced by John Hopkins Hospital for parents of hearing-impaired children, an initiative much appreciated by the community of parents who received the copies.

Vimala was an active and enthusiastic member of the Indian Association for Family Therapy from its inception in the early 1990s. She was eager to learn at a time in her career when many other professionals were resting on their laurels. She attended every training, participating as an equal with therapists who were at the start of their careers. She was both warm and very straightforward. Her comments could be disconcerting in their honesty. Yet there was a reassuring quality that one could be equally honest with her. She questioned her knowledge and shared her insights and struggled with social constructionism and systemic theory as did all of us. This openness to learning coming from a respected professional who was the most senior member of our discipline profoundly impressed many of us.

In whatever forum she attended, Vimala initiated an open dialogue of examining orthodoxy, especially when that orthodoxy came dressed up as the received wisdom of the majority. She spoke her mind, and her mind did not accept clichéd thinking. In 1998, she attended an International Family Therapy Association conference in Dusseldorf, Germany. The theme of the conference was peace amongst conflicting people and nations. On the first day at the plenary, our small contingent from India was very diffident because the Indian government had chosen that day to explode the first Indian nuclear bomb. As speaker after speaker deplored India's decision to join the nuclear countries, we sank lower and lower in our seats with shame. Not Vimala. During a pause she stood up, dignified as ever in a cotton sari, grey hair in a tight knot, and confronted the speakers, saying that they were learned systemic therapists trained to see different viewpoints, and what was preventing them from seeing the trial nuclear bomb as an expression of pride from a former colonised and poor nation? There was a long and thoughtful pause. Vimala's intervention had reminded them that blaming instead of understanding does not bring peace, it just sets off more violence.

Remarkable in so many ways, Vimala helped psychologists and clinicians of whatever background when they came to Delhi. Her office was the first stop for so many. She would guide, suggest, share contacts, mentor, give information to help them start a practice or get a job or choose the next study programme. She single-handedly did more for creating a community of mental health service providers in Delhi during the 1990s than anyone else.

In later years Vimala reduced her professional commitments while retaining her zest for life and new learning such as becoming computer-savvy, and a new engagement with Buddhist practice. She encouraged young mental health professionals to shoulder the responsibilities of continuing the work of Psychological Foundations, but when she saw that this was becoming increasingly difficult, she pragmatically decided to dissolve it, trusting that the mental health community had increased in numbers and had the strength to grow in new ways. But for those of us whom Vimala and Psychological Foundations had nurtured and supported for 20 years it was a sad time of loss. During her last days, her preferred pastime was making Skype calls to her family, reading and drinking a glass of wine with close friends. She passed away on 11 February 2016 after a brief hospitalisation.

Introduction

The very diversity of our society makes for a richness that is sadly vitiated by challenges to harmony arising from contestations over issues of resources, power, and identity. Instances of intergroup violence are rising amidst loud proclamations of the superiority of one's own group and the devaluation of other groups, even as traditional social hierarchies of gender, caste, class and ethnicity are being challenged and technological, scientific and social changes are happening apace.

Violence occurs on a continuum spanning prejudiced beliefs about some other social group and norms for conduct towards them that are discriminatory, devaluing and exclusionary at one end, to acts of physical violence on the other. Stereotypes and prejudices that make up the base of the violence pyramid are often culturally congruent and normalised and therefore not acknowledged as forms of violence. Yet such prejudiced beliefs do often lead to verbal and non-verbal behaviours that are violating to the spirit if not to the body. For instance, in the case of violence against women, social attitudes that are misogynistic, favour male entitlement and prescribe rigid gender roles, form the base of a pyramid that peaks in acts of murder and rape. In between fall acts like sexist jokes, restrictions on women's mobility, forms of social exclusion, sexual harassment and abuse and so on.

Prejudice may be simply defined as 'bias that devalues people because of their perceived membership of a social group' (Abrams 2010). Theories of prejudice are several. One of the earliest forged in trying to make sense of the beliefs that led to the Holocaust is that people who display high levels of prejudice had an 'authoritarian personality' (Adorno et al., 1950). Altemeyer's (1998) concept of Right Wing Authoritarianism is a more recent version. The main characteristics of these personality types is conventionalism, belief in aggression towards those who do not subscribe to conventional ideas or are different, respect for submission to authority, need for strong uncompromising leadership, and a tendency to project feelings of inadequacy, rage and fear on scapegoated groups. The Social Dominance Theory (Pratto et al., 2006) also holds that people differ in the extent to which they desire and seek superior status and power over others. People who demonstrate higher levels of social dominance tend to be more prejudiced towards other groups believing their own 'in-group' to be superior.

Social psychologists have tended to look at prejudice as a phenomenon having to do with group membership rather than individual personality. Summarising social psychological knowledge based on empirical evidence about the processes that underlie prejudice, Abrams (2010) notes that while basic psychological processes of categorisation, stereotyping and identification with social groups set the frame for prejudice, it is status differences, differences in social values, and intergroup conflict that contribute to prejudice.

Othering, the process of perceiving and portraying something as fundamentally different and alien to oneself, enables people to differentiate in-group from out-group and Self from the Other in ways that affirm and protect the Self. From a depth psychology angle, it has been suggested that out-groups function as 'targets for externalization' (Volkan, 1990) becoming the container for disavowed and projected aspects of the in-group self. The 'indispensable' enemy, who We are certain is the despicable Other, is in fact littered with parts cast out from the self (Stein, 1990). Self-regard thus comes to depend on the denigration of the other group as described in Hindu–Muslim relations in India (Kakar, 1995).

Varying degrees of social exclusion accompany Othering, limiting access to information, resources, sociability, and identity and preventing participation in mainstream social, cultural, economic and political activities. Social exclusion also determines the boundary of our 'moral community', those whose suffering is recognised (Morris, 1997) and who fall within the scope of justice (Opotow et al., 2005). Moral inclusion is characterised by considerations of fairness for others, sharing resources with them and being able to make sacrifices to foster their well-being. Moral exclusion is characterised by lack of concern, responsibility or duty towards those outside, positioning them as undeserving and inferior. This sets the ground for dehumanisation. Race, caste, religion, gender, sexual identity, nationality and ethnicity have all served as markers differentiating those within from those outside the moral community.

The factor that seems central to the move from prejudiced attitudes to hate crimes and other acts of violence is that of perceived threat. The threat may be perceived to be realistic such as competition for jobs or scarce resources or territory, or they may be symbolic threats related to people's social identities such as the in-group's 'way of life', their culturally important values and norms (Walters & Brown, 2016). Perceived threat can upset the existing equilibrium of inclusion-exclusion between groups propelling them along a malignant course (Sonpar, 2015).

The present volume is not intended to offer a comprehensive account of theory and research on prejudice and violence. It offers a selection of essays that touch on the topic, sometimes directly and sometimes glancingly, in ways that deepen our understanding by making the subject a human one rather than an academic one. Therefore, the essays included are written not only by psychologists but also by others and include scholarly, academic writing along with experiential accounts and case studies. The themes are not exhaustive (the categories of caste, class and sexual identity are absent) and include the role of the family, and issues related to gender, disability, intergroup relations, trauma and intervention.

Those who suffer prejudice against them and are victims of discriminatory and devaluing practices find themselves 'on the edge of society' since they are excluded from participating fully and equally in the economic, social, cultural and political life of mainstream society. Their social and psychological existence may be fraught and precarious because of the social, physical, material and psychological harms they suffer. Everyday discriminations and slights and internalisations of devalued status contribute to psychosocial ill-being, and acts of violence lead to traumatisation.

Survivors of trauma living on the edge are in continuous apprehension of 'toppling over'. While some may suffer classic psychiatric symptoms of post-traumatic stress disorder, that is, hyper vigilance, intrusive experiences and numbness and avoidance, most will experience some degree of disconnection due to a breakdown of trust in people and in the world as having a social-moral order. Instead the world feels a hostile and lonely place, and there is a frightening sense of vulnerability in the face of unpredictable and uncontrollable events. Hyper-alertness to potential danger and behaviours geared to avoid threat become survival tools. The loss of mentalisation (the ability to reflect upon and understand the behaviour of oneself and others in terms of mental states) that occurs with the overwhelming emotions of trauma lead to the stereotyped and polarised thinking characteristic of Othering and thus a perpetuation of prejudiced beliefs and potential action. The cycle of trauma may thus go on.

On the other hand, being 'on the edge' offers a unique vantage point from which it is more clearly seen that normative assumptions are not necessarily 'normal' or 'natural', and to observe the operation of dynamics of power to which those who enjoy privilege are often blind. Further, those who are 'on the edge' are survivors rather than victims and their stories are not only about tragedy and trauma but also about resilience, courage, resistance and triumph.

In some ways psychologists and others in clinical practice also find themselves on an edge, particularly in the way they reflect upon social issues. Their particular interest in the voices of individuals has often been taken to imply the belief that problems lie exclusively within persons. But the stories of suffering heard in clinics are also a reflection of the oppression and violence of the world in which we live. The intrapsychic is also 'social' because people internalise social norms as a condition for their subjective becoming and such 'normative unconscious processes' pull for a repetition of the thoughts, feelings and behaviours that uphold social norms (Layton, 2006). Thus, the term 'psychosocial' explicitly recognises that all behaviour results from the interaction of factors lying within individuals, within their interpersonal and group relations and also within the larger social, political and cultural context.

The earliest site of socialisation is the family. In her essay 'Worrying about the Family', Johri points out that, 'Whether in the matter of

love, ethnicity or property, it is often the family that teaches us our
first lesson in dividing human beings into categories.' She interrogates
complacent assumptions of the 'universality' of family when social
anthropology shows us huge variety in the nature of 'family', and also
the notion of 'family love' which is so often mixed up with control,
coercion and violence. Families are inevitably contextually linked to
the social system and 'family love' is inevitably culturally scripted. This
raises questions about the potential of the therapy space for emancipation versus adaptation. Moving into the therapy room, Reenee Singh
in her essay 'Working Systemically with Family Violence' provides a
glimpse into the complexities of doing therapy: attunement to what is
going on beneath the surface presentation, considerations of theory
and technique, finding ways to bring difficult things into conversation,
enabling growth where there is emotional stunting, ending harmful
behavioural patterns, and so on. Importantly she also shows how socio-
cultural issues of race and class can enter the therapy room and play
out power asymmetries.

Gender-related discrimination and violence is an area well-
researched and understood from feminist contributions that have
brought power and structural analysis of gender inequities to the fore.
But unidimensional views have limitations and Hutnik in her essay
'Women and Violence' suggests the need for a multidimensional
framework especially when confronted with the complexity of real life
as happens in clinical work. She describes one such model that takes
into account multiple layers of analysis to account for violence against
women: the personal history of exposure to violence as a child, the
power asymmetries and other aspects that describe the dyadic relationship of a couple, the factors at the level of the exosystem that put stress
such as unemployment, poverty, social isolation, etc., and the level of
the encompassing macrosystem where violence-supportive cultural
attitudes and beliefs about gender circulate.

From another angle, Mehrotra in her essay 'Beyond the Stereotypes
of "Masculine" Violence and "Feminine" Silence', questions monolithic views about gender oppression that cast women as perennial
victims and men as perpetrators. Using telling examples from literature,
she shows how socialisation processes shape children's gender practices

into the dominant mould. But this moulding is seldom sealed tight and instances of men's vulnerability and gentleness, and women's spirited even if silent resistance, abound.

Anthropological research has shown that cultural definitions of masculinity play an important role in the antecedents of violence. In her essay 'Youth Gangs and Violence: Subordinated Adolescents' Road to Alternative Masculinity', Dasgupta focuses on youth gang violence and sports hooliganism to show how acts of violence become a route to an alternative masculinity of 'subordinated' young men whose access to adult male roles is difficult or blocked. Violence here serves to reinforce solidarity among gang members, accentuate the boundary from non-members, achieve status within the sub-culture, and also express a masculinity that is hard and tough. Some of these identity-related concerns are echoed in similar issues related to the social identity of ethnic, racial, national and other groups touched upon in other chapters in this volume.

'Cultural identity, like its individual counterpart, is an unconscious human acquirement which becomes consciously salient only when there is a perceived threat to its integrity. Identity, both individual and cultural, lives itself for the most part, unfettered and unworried by obsessive and excessive scrutiny', writes Kakar (1995: 192). However, as the social identification theorists (Tajfel, 1978) have shown, when group salience becomes high due to the perceived threat to one's group, social identity dominates personal identity and individuals perceive members of the other community in terms of stereotypical categories.

The experiential accounts narrated in three chapters in this volume refer to some of this. Hutnik in her essay 'Threatened Indian Identities' recounts her brush with a racist attack in Britain, a dark reality for many in UK. Some, she notes, deny having faced this reality completely while others have become prickly and hyper-conscious. Closer home in India she draws attention to the blindness to classism which underwrites much of the interaction between the privileged class and their 'servants'. Maliha Raza, in her essay 'Intimate Terrors, Ultimate Hopes' narrates her journey following the destruction of the Babri Masjid by Hindu zealots, an emotional journey through outrage and humiliation to fear, and an identity journey from being a 'normal' Indian to a fearful

Muslim. The outcomes of malignant processes of Othering are vividly described. Hutnik finds hope in the possibility that people in multicultural societies may draw from the best that plurality offers, while Raza hopes that true knowledge about the culture of other communities will reduce prejudice.

Didi's evocative and nuanced narration in 'Western Selves Eastern Selves' spans her decades of marriage as a German-American into an Indian joint family. In it she recounts her journey of negotiating differences in Western and Indian sensibilities, observing, differentiating, filtering and absorbing aspects of her immersion into Indian culture, her struggle to be accepted while retaining self hood, her chagrin at remaining an 'oddity' despite her best efforts, encountering deeply conservative prejudices masked by deceptive cosmopolitanism, and her gradual turn towards fulfilment in more personal aspects of self hood.

Seeking solutions to combat prejudice, Kanwar turns to her research on the hypothesised ameliorative impact of a modern value orientation in her essay 'Religion, Prejudice and Attitudinal Change'. She finds that while a modern value orientation, comprising parameters such as rationality, individualism, humanism, change orientation, etc., is more common among persons who have higher and professional education, come from higher social classes and small families, her clinical work indicates that the psychological dynamics underlying prejudice are more complex and have more to do with the self. It is only as clients become more accepting and nurturing of themselves that they begin to be accepting and compassionate of others, including social groups that were Othered.

Psychologists are as susceptible to prejudice as anyone else when they do not practice self-reflexivity, Sonpar notes in 'Psychologists in Times of Nationalism'. She suggests that by focusing on the dynamic processes accompanying identity-construction and -reconstruction, and locating these in specific situational and temporal contexts, psychologists can throw light on social phenomena ranging from group identification, belonging and solidarity to prejudice, hostility and violence.

Negative social attitudes powerfully affect the social experience of people with disability creating significant barriers to personal development and well-being. People with mental illness are systematically excluded from participating in the social and occupational life of the community and face stigma, isolation and denial of basic rights (Raguram, 2015). The social exclusion of people with mental health problems is experientially different in that it occurs in the form of stigma. Originating in the Greek word stigmata which refers to a mark of shame or discredit, the person facing such stigmatisation may internalise these negative attitudes thus experiencing low self-worth and emotional distress.

Stigmatisation involves devaluation. To this we can add the dimension of fear or anxiety that may operate less consciously. In trying to make sense of the social exclusion of stigmatised groups such as those with mental or physical disabilities, the psychoanalytical ideas of the uncanny (Freud, 1919) and the abject (Kristeva,1982) have been invoked to suggest there is anxiety and even horror when there is physical proximity to reminders of the frightening things—death, terminal illness, disfigurement, loss of physical or mental ability and control—we have banished from awareness so that consciously these frightening things lie outside of oneself. The fear then is not just of people who appear alarmingly different, but rather that they may not be different enough (Wilton, 1988).

In his essay 'The Lessons from Mental Hospitals: Unlearning Neglectful and Discriminatory Practices', Mander indicts state custodial institutions for the mentally ill, juveniles, beggars, women's rescue homes and so on as functioning as the 'dumping spaces for the rejects of society'. Indeed, in the practices and attitudes that characterise the functioning of most such institutions we see the devaluation, rejection and exclusion inherent in the structural stigma that happens when stigma is legitimised and perpetuated by society's institutions and ideological systems. Mander outlines ideas for making the care of the mentally ill congruent with their physical and emotional needs, with healing and growth, with dignity and self-reliance to the extent possible. Illustrating what one component of such care might look like, and drawing from their experience of working therapeutically with mentally ill people in a day care centre, Marjara, Pillai, Prakash and Zurmuehlen in their essay 'Reducing Violence in People with Mental

Disorders' present case studies of intervention to reduce violent behaviour in mentally ill persons. From their understanding that such behaviour often stems from feelings of being helpless and out of control, they show how psycho education of family members and teaching them to respond in firm but caring ways restores a sense of control and efficacy to both the mentally ill person and the family. Given that stigmatising social attitudes towards the mentally ill are influenced by notions of unpredictable and violent crazy behaviour, such interventions help undo stigma.

Situating her paper 'Dis(ABLED): An Invisible Minority' within the social model of disability, Ghai emphasises that it is the oppression inherent in a disabling society that makes impairment a disability. It is important, as the disability movement asserts, that the disabled be understood from their own vantage point. Disability gives an epistemic location from where life is visualised completely differently. Doing so reveals the positive contributions that disability can make to personal growth, the determined disciplining of the self as for instance to master the fear of falling, the opportunity to go beyond the constraints of mainstream norms and roles, to recognise the existence of an ontological self, a mode of being and living in-the-body. She argues for a view of difference in diagonal rather than hierarchical terms, a view that neither valorises nor devalues but simply accepts what exists.

The second part of this volume is concerned with the impact of trauma and how recovery might happen. The dominant conceptualisation of suffering following extreme situations of violence, disaster and emergency has been in the idiom of psychopathology, especially post traumatic stress disorder (PTSD). This biomedical model has been criticised for pathologising complex human responses to extreme situations, for ignoring sociopolitical context, neglecting community-level repercussions, and being blind to cultural expressions of suffering and coping. The essays in this volume go beyond the biomedical model of trauma in many ways.

Psychoanalytic theory dwells on the impact of trauma on the psyche as a breach of the stimulus barrier which overwhelms normal ego functioning, engendering a state of helplessness and regression, and affecting the capacity to mentalise. In her essay 'Trauma and Psychoanalysis',

Sarin traces the way that trauma has been understood in psychoanalysis where overwhelming external events and internal breeches of the repression barrier are seen as traumatising. She discusses this in the context of the developing psyche and its relational field. She also describes contemporary attempts to apply psychoanalytic understanding to intergroup conflict and to understand phenomena such as terrorism.

Papadopoulos in his essay 'Terrorism and Psychological Trauma: Psychosocial Perspectives', shows how the 'overwhelmingness' of acts of terror leads to psychological states dominated by over-simplified and polarised thinking and to epistemic confusions leading to 'psychologising political dimensions, pathologising human suffering, medicalising social realities' and so on. His Trauma Grid shows that reactions to trauma are diverse and not inevitably negative. Indeed, many respond to traumatic events with resilience while some experience positive growth through 'adversity activated development'. Psychiatric diagnosis like PTSD describe only a small proportion of those affected.

Parappully takes forward the idea that trauma is potentially growth-inducing in his essay 'Transforming Trauma into Gift: Spirituality, Religion and the Search for Meaning'. Drawing partly on his own research on parents of murdered children, he homes in on spirituality and religious belief as valuable resources precisely because they help master the seeming meaninglessness of traumatic events and find new meaning.

Working within the criminal justice system and with victims of communal conflict in camps, Rajat Mitra in his essay 'Terror, Trauma and Transformation' reflects on the question of evil in human nature and its relation to childhood-based cycles of violence, the embodied nature of trauma, the re-traumatisation inherent in social responses to victims particularly those who have suffered sexual violence, and the ingredients that go into healing, of which restoring a sense of safety within a trustworthy therapeutic relationship is primary.

Humanitarian intervention in areas where mass trauma has occurred due to natural disaster or violent conflict has undergone huge change in the recent past. Psychosocial well-being has replaced the narrow constructs of mental health and trauma, and counselling and other clinical interventions have come to play a circumscribed role. These changes are described by Sonpar in her essay 'Psychosocial Intervention in Conflict Situations'. A plethora of interventions cluster under the term 'psychosocial' including interventions that are specifically directed towards mental health, as well as community-developmental interventions that aim to foster changes in the material and social environment of affected communities, and social justice/human rights interventions. A number of such initiatives in post-conflict Sri Lanka are described that also demonstrate the principles of doing work in such settings such as maximising local participation and local capacity, cultural competence, promotion of social justice and providing 'psychosocial accompaniment' to all interventions.

Exemplifying some of these principles, Navlakha and Sinha in their essay 'In Giving we Received: Working with Survivors of the Gujarat Carnage' describe their work in the aftermath of communal violence in Gujarat. They describe the work of community volunteers who were themselves victims of violence and displacement, fostering 'normal' routines, facilitating social support and collaboration, listening to people's stories of all that had happened to them, meeting whatever needs emerged: help in paperwork for compensation, medical assistance as threat of disease loomed, schooling for children having no school to go to, and developing livelihoods' support. The healing however remains incomplete with their future security still uncertain.

Working with children in the conflict zone of Jammu and Kashmir using theatre workshops, Sanjay Kumar addresses the vexed area of inter-community relations in his essay 'A Child's Act: Working with Kashmiri Pandit and Kashmiri Muslim Children'. In his account of the several workshops conducted, through the scripts generated by the children as well as their actual encounters with one another, one sees the precariousness of working in a conflict zone, the multiple and discordant narratives that have to be navigated, the narratives that are silenced, together with the robust appearance of normal adolescent concerns like romance.

Taken together, the essays in this volume offer a psychosocial perspective on prejudice and violence that is close to the complexity of lived experience and ground realities.

REFERENCES

Abrams, D. (2010). *Processes of prejudice: Theory, evidence and intervention.* Equality and Human Rights Commission. Retrieved from www.equalityhumanrights.com

Adorno, T.W., Frenkel-Brunswik E., Levinson, D.J. & Sanford, S.N. (1950). *The authoritarian personality.* New York: Harper.

Altemeyer, R.A. (1981). *Right-wing authoritarianism.* Winnipeg: University of Manitoba Press.

Freud, S. (1919, 2003). *The uncanny.* London: Penguin.

Kakar, S. (1995). *The colours of violence: Cultural identities, religion and conflict.* New Delhi: Viking.

Kristeva, J. (1982). *Powers of horror: An essay on abjection.* New York: Columbia University Press.

Layton, L. (2006). Racial identities, racial enactments, and normative unconscious processes. *Psychoanalytic Quarterly,* LXXV, 237–269.

Morris, D.B. (1998). About suffering: Voice, genre and moral community. In A. Kleinman, V. Das & M. Lock (Eds), *Social Suffering,* 25–45. New Delhi: Oxford University Press.

Opotow, S., Gerson, J. & Woodside, S. (2005). From moral exclusion to moral inclusion: Theory for teaching peace. *Theory into Practice,* 44(4), 303–318.

Pratto, F., Sidanius, J. & Levin, S. (2006). Social dominance theory and the dynamics of intergroup relations: Taking stock and looking forward. *European Journal of Social Psychology,* 17, 271–320.

Raguram, R. (2015). The ache of exile: Travails of stigma and social exclusion among the mentally ill in India. *Psychology and Developing Societies,* 27(2), 254–269.

Sonpar, S. (2015). Including, excluding...annihilating. *Psychology and Developing Societies,* 27(2), 174–188.

Stein, H.F. (1990). The indispensable enemy and American-Soviet relations. In V.D. Volkan, D.A. Julius & J.V. Montville (Eds), *The psychodynamics of international relationships: Concepts and theories,* 71–89. Lexington: Lexington Books.

Tajfel, H. (1978). *Differentiation between social groups: Studies in the social psychology of intergroup relations.* Oxford: Academic Press.

Volkan, V.D. (1990) An overview of psychological concepts pertinent to interethnic and/or international relationships. In V.D. Volkan, D.A. Julius & J.V. Montville (Eds), *The psychodynamics of international relationships: Concepts and theories,* 31–46. Lexington: Lexington Books.

Walters, M.A. & Brown, R. (2016). *Causes and motivation of hate crimes.* Equality and Human Rights Commission. Retrieved from www.equalityhumanrights.com

Wilton, R.D. (1998). The constitution of difference: Space and psyche in landscapes of exclusion. *Geoforum,* 29(2), 173–185.

Part I

Violence and Prejudices: Mapping the Landscape

Chapter 1

Beyond the Stereotypes of 'Masculine' Violence and 'Feminine' Silence*

Deepti Priya Mehrotra

Deepti Priya Mehrotra is an independent scholar. She has taught in Lady Shri Ram College and Ambedkar University, Delhi. As a PhD scholar in political science, she studied contemporary women's organisations in north India. Her postdoctoral thesis is on gender, power and knowledge. Her books include Gulab Bai: The Queen of Nautanki Theatre, Burning Bright: Irom Sharmila and the Struggle for Peace in Manipur *and* Home Truths: Stories of Single Mothers.

Stereotypes are convenient benchmarks, bur real-life people rarely ever fit them. Social complexity is irreducible to a simplistic men-as-violators and women-as-victims formulation. Men are vulnerable human beings, who feel pain, get hurt—just as do women. Boys and men too suffer the wounds of violence—not only of the direct, palpable physical violation, but also in the ways in which they are *dehumanised,* their finer sensibilities are crushed.

---

* This chapter was first published in *The Journal,* Vol. 3(1), June 2001, by the Psychological Foundations Trust, New Delhi.

Masculine violence certainly does exist—a tiresome reality across class, caste, culture and nation, and this violence is often wreaked upon women, at physical and emotional levels. But it is important to keep in mind that masculine aggression is the result of social conditioning and is not a biological given. I'm convinced that we need to treat 'violent' men as victims of their conditioning—not just as criminals.

Of course, at one level, there is no excuse for violent behaviour. But we must understand why it happens and be able to make meaningful interventions. What is socially conditioned can also be challenged and changed. What manifests as pathological behaviour in isolated individuals is actually an integral part of a vicious cycle. The conventional, status quoist understanding is that men are *by nature* prone to more violence than women, a notion that justifies their violent behaviour. Even among activists, researchers and other professionals in the field, this misunderstanding still lurks. Formulations such as 'all-males-are-incurably-obsessed-with-penetration' are still glibly presented, in a decontextualised and universalistic way. This is a dangerous stand, for it naturalises tendencies that are culturally conditioned. In doing so, the very possibility of change is blocked.

On the other side of the coin, women are often portrayed as passive recipients of male violence—people who accept being beaten and tormented, in virtual silence. Such a portrayal is also simply untrue. Women are seldom the weak creatures they are painted out to be. Caught in a complex web of relations, they strategise, cope and struggle in myriad ways. Even when women are violated and victimised—as they certainly are, only too frequently—their victimhood does not have to define them. Often women use their experience with violation to grow stronger, devise coping strategies and develop life-skills.

Women's ways of challenging male domination are not always very visible. Much of the work of resistance is inner work and takes place in silence: it involves building up one's strength, consolidating energies, channelising anger, laying plans, formulating tactics. *Everyday forms of resistance* are just that: subterfuge, foot-dragging, strategic lies, gossiping that spreads information and ideas and alliance-building at informal levels. Violence may take place silently, and silence on the other hand, may contain the seeds of opposition to violence.

Violence is linked to unequal power relations and occurs at many levels, in many spaces, coalescing around axes of gender, class, caste, nationality, face, etc. Social relations are rent by the tension of multiple hierarchies, which interact in complex ways. Society is rent into multiple untidy grids, which slide and overlap, reinforce or contradict each other. Looking at people and social relations in this way means that we understand human reality to be fluid and open, not congealed or frozen. If we accept flexibility and fluidity as facts of personal and social life, then we become open to perceiving some of the really interesting things that are going on. These occur often at the junctures of the place where a woman or man steps outside the stereotype—ending up as either a winner or a loser.

THE MAKING (UNMAKING) OF A MAN

Growing girls and boys suffer the burden of social expectations and get hurt or distorted by these to some extent or the other. We know as a generalisation and an everyday fact that boys are usually taught to be more aggressive and competitive than girls. The feminist play *Ahsaas* (performed many times in and around Delhi during the 1980s) begins with a scene in which girls and boys play together. When the bell rings they go into class, where the teacher asks them what they want to be when they grow up. As they name their dreams, the teacher edits these: she expands the boys' ambitions to be doctors, engineers or aircraft pilots, and crushes the girls' hopes, telling them to aim at being 'good daughters', 'good wives' and 'good mothers'. The boys are sent out to play cricket, while the girls bring out their needlework. A little boy who is hurt while playing comes in crying, only to have the teacher admonish him, because 'boys should not cry'. She asks the girls to sing a song she has taught them, which they chant like parrots:

Don't talk loudly
Don't look high
Don't laugh loudly…
Cast your eyes down
Speak in a soft voice
Sit beneath…

Wherever this play was performed in colleges, schools, domestic courtyards or colony parks the audience identified with its basic tenor. Girls in the audience came forward with examples of daily discrimination. We recognised just how powerful social conditioning is—and the fact that we ourselves have not escaped it.

If we look closely at how the socialisation of boys takes place, we can see the influences that mould them into aggressive personalities. I deconstruct here, a part of a novel, *Alma Kabootari* (by Hindi writer, Maitreyi Pushpa), that brings this out in stark relief—an attempt to train a boy born into a 'criminal tribe'. In this poverty-ridden tribe too, boys are taught not to cry. Instead they must learn to divert their energies into aggression, attack and murder.

Rana belongs to the 'criminal' *Kabootari* tribe. He lives with his mother in a settlement at the edge of a village. His community survives by brewing liquor (women's job) and theft (men's job). Kadambai teaches her son how to use slings, lathis and an axe. He learns to use these weapons with ease and efficiency. But, one day, she asks him to get a sharp stone and aim at a bird—a bulbul as it sits on a branch of a *kaith* tree. Rana uses his sling, aims at the bird and it falls, lying flat and still on the ground below the tree. Kadambai asks him to aim again and this time a parakeet falls, wounded....

Now Rana is disconsolate. His shoulders stoop as he stands by the bulbul's corpse. Tearfully, he watches the parakeet gasp for breath:

> The bulbul was still breathing. Its wings moved slightly. The beak lay open. The tiny corn-like eyes were turning stony. Sand filled the parakeet's red beak. Green feathers were soaked in mud. There was a blood-wound on the stomach.... Like the birds' beaks, Rana's mouth was open. Like their still eyes, his eyes had no movement in them. The bulbul and parakeet had stopped breathing. Rana took long gasping breaths.... Once he had pestered his mother because he wanted to have a pet parakeet. He'd said that if their settlement were raided, he would take the parakeet's cage and run out with it (Maitreyi, 2000, p. 39).

His mother worries:

> My Rana is weeping over birds, how will he ever kill a man? You unjust boy, go, see how the police and 'respectable' folks have beaten up

our men, plucking them like birds! Laid them in the dust with blows of lathis and metal rods. For what crime? Stealing four brinjals from a field!... Rana, now you are no longer young. Forget the dream of keeping a pet parakeet. Otherwise you will suffer imprisonment like a parakeet! (ibid.)

The die is cast. It is clear that if Rana is to survive in a world rent by multiple and brutal violence, there is no option but to adapt. Rana's mother is sensitive to his suffering even while she is terrified that he may prove incapable. She eggs him on, even though she wonders whether she really wants him to be brutalised:

What job Rana does not want to do, does she really want him to do that? This question rising in Rana's eyes pierces her, but she is not able to say that you will have to do all this, because the Mukhiya wants it, the people of our colony want it, 'respectable' folks also want it. If you keep doing what they all want, then they will forgive us! (ibid., p. 53)

One day the Mukhiya, Sarmun, says to Kadambai, 'Rana will go for a dacoity before Diwali.... Kadam, if a boy learns the work while his bones are still soft, he never forgets it.... Once his flexibility is lost, you will repent. This useless fellow will just live off your earning!'

Before leaving, Rana says, 'Amma, I'm feeling frightened. Suppose the men of that village capture me?' Kadambai assures him that this will not happen and says, 'Even if you are caught, don't get worried. This is our work after all' (ibid., pp. 56–57).

She wants to embrace her son, but restrains herself because 'this kind of affection would make him weak' (ibid., p. 57).

Rana fails to live up to expectations. He faints when his companions kill a villager during the raid and has to be carried back. For three days he burns with fever and screams incoherently (ibid., p. 60).

Kadambai realises she will not be able to mould her son the way the world wants. 'Then what will happen? This foolish boy will walk all alone! The others will crush and smash him to death.... It is not easy to walk alone!' (ibid., p. 62).

Later, because of his 'incompetence', Rana, as well as his mother, are disowned by the community. Rana struggles to study, and establish himself in 'respectable' ways. But the 'respectable' will not let him become one of them. Rana finds that he belongs nowhere. Alienated and terrified, he finally loses touch with sanity and spends his days moaning and blabbering in a dark corner of the hut.

Vulnerable Violators and Unvanquished Victims

Clearly, men may sometimes be at the receiving end of society's rod. Class and gender interact in complex ways, linked with specific personal circumstances and sensibilities. Rana's story is dramatically defined within the vulnerable status of his tribe as a whole.

Yet, there are some elements of *masculine* conditioning that extend across class lines.

In refusing to live up to an aggressive *masculine* role, a man (from the working class or upper class) may literally give up significant privileges. He may experience, increasingly, a sense of *not belonging:* having no foothold left in society, being stigmatised. Therefore, he may be driven close to despair or insanity. Of course, there are other, more positive, possibilities (which we are not exploring here).

When a woman steps out of her prescribed gender role, then too, there is likely to be a backlash and intensified attempts at control. Yet, sometimes when a woman breaks out of her *feminine* conditioning, she may win palpable rewards. Being hitherto exploited, she may be able to develop a more assertive personality and make tangible gains over time.

The short story, *Wrestling* (written originally in Tamil by Ambai in 1999) beautifully portrays the tensions and possibilities as one woman tries to break out of her role expectations. The servant knows the master better than the master ever gets to know the servant. Perhaps women often study their menfolk more than the men study them. They may not talk about their knowledge, but simply make use of it in order to negotiate a better position. The skill, intelligence and quiet tenacity with which a woman may maneuvre to break out of a torturous patriarchal bind, is brought out in this story.

Shenbagam, a girl from a poor family, is brought up in the household of her music teacher, Ayya. She is easily his best student and he teaches her to sing and play the veena. She is far better than Ayya's son, Shanmugam. Shanmugam loves Shenbagam, but he is jealous of her because she is the better musician. The two marry but Shanmugam stops her from performing in public: 'Why should she rush all over the place? She can sing as much as she wants to at home. If she gives performances, she will only tire herself out. I can do the running around. Let her take it easy' (Ambai, 1999, p. 40).

This strategm makes him look mild and considerate, while it is blatantly manipulative and self-serving. His father expresses anger, but as the husband, Shanmugam's word is law. Shenbagam is silent. On the surface, she has been vanquished. But her silence is merely a cover beneath which her anger and energy simmers.

Shanmugam sings in public, earning all the paraphernalia that comes with success. Shenbagam sits behind him on the stage to give him milk once the performance is over. However, after every performance he wants her to critique his singing and late at night she sings for him. This goes on for years. Now Somu, a young student of Shanmugam's, who has begun to accompany him has understood the dynamics between Shanmugam and Shenbagam, and he sympathises with her. One day, at a music concert, Shenbagam regains her space:

> Shanmugam began the first song and then paused at a point, as he always did, for Somu to join him. But Somu's attention was wandering. Shanmugam paused a second time, to allow Somu to join in, but the boy paid no attention. A second later, Shenbagam leaned towards the mike meant for Somu, and took up the line Shanmugam had just sung. When Shanmugam's head snapped round in astonishment, her eyes locked with his. Her face brightened and she smiled. The audience burst into loud applause. Shanmugam looked at her like one who had been trapped in an unexpectedly complicated hold and had been wrestled to the ground. Somu took the tambura from Shenbagam's hands and pushed the mike towards her. Shenbagam led the song on to the next line herself.

Perhaps Shanmugam was sweating, even in that air-conditioned hall. Taking the jarigai shawl off his shoulders, he put it down and began to sing, with Shenbagam (ibid., pp. 42–43).

Text and Context

Exploring the space of the stereotypical scenario of crushed women and power-crazy men pitted in hopeless battle is illuminating. Gender oppression, it turns out, is not a rock-like monolithic formation. If we access the multiple layers wherein meanings are created and negotiated, then we recognise and honour male vulnerabilities and women's strengths. We then understand in a different way the linkages between 'masculinity' and 'femininity', violence and silence.

REFERENCES

Ambai (1999). *Wrestling* (pp. 27–44). Gita Krishnankutty (Ed). English Tr. by Uma Narayanan and Prema Seetharam. Katha Perspectives.

Maitreyi, P. (2000). *Alma Kabootri,* Rajkamal Prakashan.

Chapter 2

Women and Violence*

Nimmi Hutnik

Nimmi Hutnik teaches at the Department of Mental Health and Learning Disabilities in the School of Health and Social Care, London South Bank University. She is also in private practice as a Cognitive Behaviour Therapist (CBT). She has a doctorate in Social and Developmental Psychology from Oxford University. Dr. Hutnik was one of the earliest therapists to use CBT in India.

Violence against women is increasingly recognised as a major factor in the destabilisation of ecological balance in the Indian subcontinent. Amartya Sen's now famous study (Sen, 1990) on sex ratios in countries where both sexes receive similar health care (Europe and North America) compared to sex ratios in countries where females are discriminated against (India and China), followed that there were more than one million missing women. Coale's demographic refinement of the Sen study (Coale, 1991) put the figure nearer to 60 million. Most of these 'missing women' are victims of feticide, (Coale and Bannister, 1992; Ramanamma, 1990), infanticide (George, Abel and Miller, 1992; Dasgupta, 1987; Chatterjee, 1990), selective discriminatory health care in favour of boys (Bhatia, 1985), female suicide due to marital conflict

---

* This chapter was first published in *The Journal*, Vol. 3(1), June 2001, by the Psychological Foundations Trust, New Delhi.

(Paltiel, 1987), bride-burning (Pawar, 1990; Kelkar, 1992; Karkal, 1985; AWAG, 1986) and other forms of gender violence.

PSYCHOLOGICAL VIOLENCE

That women are routinely subject to physical abuse and sexual assault is well-documented (Agnes, 1988; Rebello, 1982; Mahajan, 1990; Rao and Bloch, 1993; Rahi, 1998). This is partly due to the fact that measures of physical abuse and sexual assault are relatively unequivocal. Psychological violence against women is less amenable to scrutiny, because it leaves no objective evidence on the body. It remains, therefore, virtually undocumented on the Indian subcontinent, as elsewhere. Only two Indian studies (Rao et al., 1994; Jha, 1998) attempted to investigate non-physical violence like public humiliation, criticism, shouting, withholding affection and controlling money and mobility. Yet, studies at home and abroad indicate that women consider psychological violence more devastating than physical assault. They report that the mental torture, the living in fear and terror, the depression and loss of confidence is virtually unliveable (Casey, 1988; Jha, 1998). The quieter, less sensational, but often more intolerable forms of violence such as excessive control over an adult daughter's or wife's activities and mobility, verbal abuse, economic resource abuse and coercion towards arranged marriage are often not even recognised and labelled as violence. Yet, clinicians in professional practice regularly see survivors of psychological violence.

Savita, 26, is an example of a typical middle-class Indian woman. She is in love with Raju and wants to marry him. Her parents will have nothing of it. Raju is of a different caste and is certainly not rich enough to make a difference to the status of Savita's family of origin. For two years she met Raju surreptitiously, without telling her parents of Raju or her intentions to marry him. After she told them she received heavy verbal and emotional abuse from both parents. Now her every movement is monitored by her mother, who rings her up at work several times a day to check that she is at her seat and calls her just before she leaves to make sure that she takes only 20 minutes to come home.

Sonia, 17, is also subject to this kind of over-control. She is not allowed to meet her friends after school for a movie or a meal at the local restaurant just in case there might be boys going out with them. She is not even allowed to speak to friends over the phone unless she uses the speakerphone so that her mother can tell whether she is speaking to a girl or a boy.

While physical violence and sexual abuse have received relatively wide coverage, the inclusion of psychological harm or suffering in the definition of violence (Economic and Social Council, 1992) should not be ignored. Both Savita and Sonia came into therapy, the one because she was suicidal and imbibing alcohol at a rate that was frightening her, the other for a dramatic decrement in school grades. Savita is learning how to recognise and label abusive situations and to develop effective strategies to cope with them. She is also learning to consolidate a more secure sense of self. Savita's parents do not know, of course, that she is in therapy and in spite of their rigid monitoring, she manages to dodge their intrusions. Sonia was (violently) taken out of therapy as the mother was confronted with the violence of her over-control.

The Socialisation of Violence

The kind of violence this research is predicated on are the inequalities of power and status between men and women in patriarchal societies. The *feminist community* has been reluctant to credit factors other than patriarchy in the etiology of abuse. While this is understandable in the light of decades of academic blindness to this reality, it precludes the investigation of many important questions. There are, after all, oldest studies that indicate in certain cultures, violence against women is virtually absent (Levinson, 1989; Sanday, 1981). If this is so, it belies the theories which portray aggression as an innate biological mechanism for survival (Darwin) that has become instinctual in manifestation (Freud, Locenz). Instead, it might be argued that people are socialised into violent or non-violent cultures. The carriers of cultural socialisation are primarily parents, mothers in particular, and the extended family. Thereafter, of course, school and the larger social ideology present in a particular social milieu. The question is: How do women inadvertently perpetuate violence against themselves? Saheli, an organisation which works with battered women in New Delhi, suggests that women comply with violence by accepting physical violence as a normal way of being (Saheli, 1986). According to them, across all classes of women, an odd slap or a kick is not seen as something major; the connection between an odd slap or kick and regular *physical* abuse is not made, and many women are willing to continue suffering abuse as long as 'he' promises to change his other habits.

According to the report of this organisation, no woman in this study was willing to condemn physical abuse unequivocally. The unquestioning acceptance by women of the status quo that men are dominant and have a right to be violent also perpetuates violence in that aggression in sons is tolerated at a much higher level than aggression in daughters. According to Thapan (1995), women in the middle and upper classes in Delhi collude with their oppressors also by accepting definitions of femininity and the female body that are not an expression of their innermost selves but an internalisation of male stereotypes of sexual attractiveness. A *study* done at NIMHANS, Department of Psychiatric Social Work, Bangalore (Bhatti, undated) showed that while violence is prevalent in all classes, the pattern of violence is different, Members of low-income families are involved in complementary power struggles: i.e., attack and resist, while members of middle-income families are engaged in symmetrical power struggles, i.e., attack and counter-attack. Thus, the way middle-class women react to violence is very different from the way their sisters do in the less privileged classes. Do their different reactions produce different types of violence from men? Bhatti concludes that because family violence is a life-style perpetuated by culture, it can only be counteracted by making changes in national policies.

The theory that violence is learned rather than instinctual gains further credence from the observation that witnessing violence between parents or caregivers is consistently related with either becoming a victim of a male partner's violence or becoming an abuser of a female partner (Hotaling and Sugarman, 1986). Certainly, sexual victimisation in childhood likewise emerges as a significant factor for future sexual aggression against women (Friedrich, Beilke and Urguiza, 1988). In fact, one in five sexually abused boys goes on to molest children in adulthood (Watkins and Bentovim, 1992). Although a number of theories have been put forward, it remains unclear as to the mechanism whereby violence begets violence.

Where There Is No Violence: Cross-Cultural Research

Cross-cultural studies indicate that cultural definitions of masculinity play an important part in the antecedents of violence. In societies where manhood is equated with dominance, power and toughness, violence is regularly encountered (Sanday, 1981; Counts, Brown and Campbell, 1992). Violence is singularly absent in cultures where non-violence is valued and men are at least equally as nurturing as are women toward their offspring. Many more cross-cultural studies need to be conducted, particularly in cultures where violence is virtually non-existent, so that a more refined understanding of how violence is learned can be developed.

Theoretical Framework

These observations have been intricately woven into a model proposed by Lori Heise to account for violence against women (Heise, 1998). The ecological model posits four levels of analysis. The first level, the ontogenetic level, investigates the amount of violent socialisation experienced by the person in childhood: Did the individual witness violence as a child? The second level, the microsystem, looks at dyadic relationships within the marital sub-system: How much conflict is there within the couple? What kinds of power dynamics are operative? Does the man hold exclusive decision-making power? The third level, the exosystem, looks at whether the man is employed, whether his job is stressful, whether his family is poor or whether it is relatively isolated through migration. The fourth level, the macrosystem, studies attitudes and beliefs that are culturally imbided: Does the man think he has the right to chastise his wife? Does the man adhere to rigid masculine and feminine roles? Appraisal at all four levels, should fairly accurately predict the occurrence of violence. Heise, however, expresses disappointment that in spite of its ability to accommodate the feminist perspective, so little research has been done to validate the model.

Appreciation and Critique

Other models tend to posit a single factor for the explanation of violence against women. Social learning theory, for example, suggests that individuals learn violence through a process of vicarious reinforcement and limitation. The Marxist analysis has looked at violence as a class-based reaction to inequities of power and wealth. The feminist perspective sees violence as the means by which men exert their dominance in patriarchal societies. None of these single factor theories can explain why some men become violent and others do not.

Heise's model is exciting precisely because it deals with the complexity of real life. It looks at violence in the individual's past and present conditions, and in the way it is tolerated (or not tolerated) and perpetuated in the cultural belief systems that are the individual's heritage.

The problem with the model is that it does not capture the dynamic nature of the spiral of violence. What happens in the marital sub-system as violence escalates? Or in the father and daughter dyad? Who says what, to whom? What happens next? When the abuse is delivered, what is the emotional fall-out in the mentor and the victim? How is the conflict resolved and the relationship resumed? For us, as mental health professionals, who routinely deal with the effects of violence in marital relationships, it is of vital importance that this dynamic is captured.

My own theoretical perspective acknowledges that a serious power differential exists between men and women such that men, more often than not, hold supreme sway over decision-making and finance and contribute only in the *naam ke vaste* ways to household labour. Within such a patriarchal structure, male power may take the form of beating, kicking, slapping, pushing (physical violence) or controlling, dominating, criticising or shaming (psychological violence). The feminist movement takes men to task for perpetuating such a terrible system of torture and inequality. And rightly so. However, in propounding a model that looks only at men as arbiters of violence, we neglect the woman's role in the malignant spiral of violence. Women too are violent. This is amply borne out in the way some women treat their children. Less obvious is the verbal violence: the shaming and the nagging that women engage in against their partners or their parents. In the absence of physical prowess, verbal violence is often used as the woman's most effective means of attack and self-defence.

Not for a moment must this be taken to mean that women provoke the violence that they suffer. This again would be committing the error of linear thinking of the A causes B type. Systemic thinking, on the other hand, looks at circularity: A acts, B reacts, A's behaviour is then modified and changed by B's reaction. And this changed behaviour stimulates a changed reaction in B.

Spirals of interpersonal interaction may be benign or malignant (Humik, 1999, 1997, 1991; Bhola and Humik, 1994; Sachdev, Humik and Menon, 1996; Sherwood, 1980). Protagonist A makes an aggressive statement. This constitutes a stimulus for a spiral of violence to be set into motion. What response does it evoke? B might choose to ignore it, or let it pass, she might withdraw in hurt or sulk, she might choose to react to it with as much aggression in her voice, nagging and shaming her partner, she might set a bottom line and state that she will not take this kind of treatment, she might then remove herself from potential abuse. Or she might choose to re-interpret the underlying message coming from her partner from the vantage point of love and compassion so as to build a bridge between two warring parties, herself and her partner. Ignoring violence, withdrawing and sulking and reacting to violence with an equal measure of aggression are likely to produce malignant spirals of violence.

Setting a bottom line, withdrawing oneself without sulks or silence from a potentially abusive situation and responding with love and compassion are likely to produce benign spirals. This would be true not just of male-female violence but *any* violent interaction. Of course, the ability to exit from a potentially malignant spiral of interaction or to turn a malignant spiral into a benign one is a high spiritual achievement, both for men and for women. It is the choice to rise above victimhood.

REFERENCES

Agnes, F. (1984). *Violence in the Family: Wife Beating*. Bombay: Women's Centre.
AWAG. (1986). 'Family Violence and Women', AWAG Paper presented at the Third National Conference on Women's Studies, Ahmedabad.

Bhatia, S. (1985). *Status and Survival.* World Health, April.

Bhatti, R.S. (undated), *Sociocultural Dynamics of Family Violence.* Bangalore: NIMHANS (unpublished Mimeo).

Casey, M. (1988). *Domestic Violence against Women: The Women's Perspective.* Dublin, Ireland: Federation of Women Refugees.

Chatterjee, M. (1990). 'Indian Women: Their Health and Economic Productivity'. World Bank Discussion Paper 109. Washington, D.C.

Coale, A. (1991). 'Excess Female Mortality and the Balance of the Sexes in the Population: An Estimate of the Number of Missing Females'. *Population and Development Review*, 17(3): pp. 517–523.

Coale, A. & Bannister, J. (1992). 'High Ratios of Males to Females in the Population of China'. Paper presented at the International Seminar on China's 1990 Population Census, Beijing. 19–23 October.

Counts, D., Brown, J. & Campbell, J. (1992). *Sanctions and Sanctuary.* Boulder, Co: Westview Press.

Das Gupta, M. (1987). 'Selective Discrimination against Children in Rural Punjab, India'. *Population and Development Review*, 13(1): pp. 95–111.

Dutton, M.A. (1992). *Abusive Behaviour Observation Checklist in Empowering and Healing the Battered Woman: A Model for Assessment and Intervention.* New York: Springer Publishing Co.

Economic and Social Council. (1992). Report of the Working Group on Violence against Women. United Nations, Vienna. E/CN.6/WG.2/1992/L.3.

Friedrich, W.M., Beilke, R.L. & Urguiza, A.J. (1988). 'Behaviour Problems in Young Sexually Abused Boys'. *Journal of Interpersonal Violence*, 3(1): p. 12.

George, S., Abel, R. & Miller, B. (1992). 'Female Infanticide in Rural South India'. *Economic and Political Weekly,* 30 May.

Heise, L. (1998). 'Violence against Women: An Integrated Ecological Model'. Forthcoming in the journal *Violence against Women,* SAGE Periodicals Press.

Hotaling, G.T. & Sugarman, D.B. (1986). 'An Analysis of Risk Markers in Husband to Wife Violence: The Current State of Knowledge'. *Violence and Victims,* 1: pp. 101–124.

Hudson, W.E. & McIntosh, S.R. (1981). 'The Assessment of Spouse Abuse: Two Quantifiable Dimensions'. *Journal of Marriage and the Family,* 43: pp. 873–888.

Hutnik, N. (1997). 'Non-violence in the Microcosm of our Relationships'. Paper presented at the Faculty Seminar of the California School of Professional Psychology, Los Angeles. 9 June.

————. (1991). *Ethnic Minority Identity: A Social Psychological Perspective.* Oxford: Clarendon Press, New Delhi: OUP.

————. (1999). 'An Unusual Intervention: Disability and Abuse'. *Psychological Foundations: The Journal,* June, 1(1).

Hutnik, N. & Bhola, P. (1994). 'Self-categorisation and Responses to Threat'. Paper presented at the VIth International Conference on Language and Social Psychology, Brisbane, Australia. 6–9 July.

India SAFE workgroup. (1995). 'Dowry Experience and Attitudes Survey'. *Survey of Abuse in the Family Environment in India.*

Jha, S. (1997). 'The Premenstrual Syndrome Experience: Ego Resiliency and Spouse Abuse as Correlates and Predictors'. Unpublished BA Dissertation, University of Delhi.

Karkal, M. (1985). 'How the Other Half Dies in Bombay'. *Economic and Political Weekly*, 24 August.

Kelgar, G. (1992). 'Stopping the Violence against Women Issues and Perspectives from India'. In M. Schuler [Ed.] *Freedom from Violence: Strategies from Around the World.* Washington D.C.: OEF International.

Levinson, D. (1989). *Violence in Cross-Cultural Perspective.* Newbury Park: SAGE.

Mahajan, A. (1980). 'Instigators of Wife Battering'. In S. Sood [Ed.] *Violence against Women.* India: Arihant Publishers.

Paltiel, F. (1987). 'Women and Mental Health: A Post Nairobi Perspective'. *World Health Statistics Quarterly*, 40: pp. 233–266.

Pawar, M.S. (1990). 'Women and Family Violence: Policies and Programs'. In S. Sood, [Ed.] *Violence against Women.* India: Arihant Publishers.

RAHI. (1998). *Voices from the Silent Zone: Women's Experiences of Incest and Childhood Sexual Abuse.* Published by RAHI.

Ramanamma, H. (1990). 'Female Feticide and Infanticide: A Silent Violence'. In S. Sood [Ed.] *Violence against Women*, India: Arihant Publishers.

Rao, S., Rao, V. et al. (1994). 'A Study of Domestic Violence in Urban Middle Class Families'. IMA Workshop report. New Delhi. India Medical Association as mentioned in A. Jesani *Violence Against Women: A Review of Health Issues in India.*

Rao, V. and Bloch, F. (1993). 'Wife-beating, Its Causes and Its Implementations for Nutrition Allocations to Children: An Economics and Anthropological Case Study of a Rural South Indian Community'. World Bank, Policy Research Department, Poverty & Human Resources Division, Washington D.C. Draft.

Rebello, S. (1982). 'A Survey of Wife Beating in South Kanara'. Bombay: Institute of Social Research and Education.

Sachdev, I., Hutnik, N. & Menon, A. (1996). 'Identity in Exile: Tibetan Buddhists in India'. Paper presented at the International Congress of Psychology. Montreal, Canada. 16–21 August.

Sanday, P.R. (1981). 'The Socio-cultural Context of Rape: A Cross-cultural Study'. *Journal of Social Issues*, 37 (4): pp. 5–27.

SAHELI (1986). 'Wife-battering: Issues Facing the Women's Movement'. Paper Presented at the Third National Conference on Women's Studies, Chandigarh.

Sen, A. (1990). 'More Than One Million Women Are Missing'. New York Review of Books, 20 December.

Sherwood, R. (1980). The Psychodynamics of Race. Sussex: Harvester Press.

Straus M.A. (1979). 'Measuring Intra Family Conflict and Violence: The Conflict Tactics Scale'. Journal of Marriage and Family, 41: pp. 75–88.

Thapan, M. (1995). 'Images of the Body and Sexuality in Women's Narratives on Oppression in the Home'. Economic and Political Weekly, 28 October, pp. 72–80.

Watkins, B & Bentovim, A. (1992). 'Sexual Abuse of Male Children and Adolescents: A Review of Current Research'. Journal of Child Psychology and Psychiatry, 33: pp. 197–248.

Chapter 3

Youth Gangs and Violence*
Subordinated Adolescents' Road to Alternative Masculinity

Chaitali Dasgupta

Chaitali Dasgupta is an independent consultant. Previously she worked at NAZ Foundation India. She has an MPhil Degree in Sociology from Delhi School of Economics. This piece was a part of her MPhil dissertation 'Between Child and Man: A Gendered Reading of the Male Life Cycle'.

Over the past few years, Men's Studies, which arose from Feminist and Gay Liberation movements, has stressed that hegemonic masculinity not only oppresses women but also cripples relationships between men. In order to demarcate from hegemonic masculinity, workers in the field no longer apply the singular term, *masculinity,* but use the plural, *masculinities,* in order to find spaces for different ways that males develop their identities. Masculinities can be based on heterosexual or homosexual masculinities, as well as on other differing relations of power. For example, age affects the formation of masculinities in that

---

*This chapter was first published in *The Journal*, Vol. 3(1), June 2001, by the Psychological Foundations Trust, New Delhi.

masculinity is accorded a different significance at differing moments during the male life cycle.

Adolescent males and their masculinities are differentiated and marginalised or subordinated vis-à-vis the agents of hegemonic masculinity, i.e., adult males and their masculinity (see notes at the end of the chapter). Adolescents in modern societies are highly problematised and constituted differently from men at other stages of the life cycle. They are not central to the economy and have become isolated as a dependent economic liability. Restricted from speaking in those spheres where public conversation shapes policy, and refused the power to make knowledge consequential with respect to their own individual and collective needs, adolescents are prohibited from speaking as moral and political agents. They are compared and evaluated in terms of the ideas and values held by the adult. The trinity of work, marriage and social order form the criterion against which adolescent masculinity is measured. However, the contradictory nature of adult masculinity limits the adolescents' access to these roles and hence keeps the latter in subordination. This situates adolescents in a state of anomie, which is characterised by the absence or limitations of the necessary means of acquiring the desired goals. They are placed in an inferior position vis-à-vis adult masculinity. Consequently, adolescents strive towards establishing their own achieved identities.

ACCORDING TO MARY DOUGLAS:

> *Culture provides in advance some basic categories, a pattern in which ideas and values are tidily ordered. It also has the authority to induce everyone to assent to its ideas and values. Yet they cannot neglect the challenge of aberrant forms.*
> (Douglas, 1966, p. 52)

Hegemonic masculinity too is contested and negotiated with by those it attempts to dominate. Marginalised adolescents thereby, produce their own means of achieving masculinity, i.e., an alternative masculinity, and one of the ways they do so is through violence.

As Merton (1994) has argued, societies where greater emphasis is laid on goals but little on means, push individuals facing such situations into adopting the technically most efficient means to the goals, even if these are illegitimate. To resolve the collectively experienced problems arising from contradictions in the social structure, adolescents form sub-cultures that generate a form of collective identity from which an individual identity can be achieved outside that ascribed by the society or culture. Being a member of a sub-culture gives the adolescents a feeling of security. Organisations such as the youth sub-cultures offer a culture from which certain cultural elements such as style, values, ideologies and lifestyle can be selected. These help the adolescents to demarcate the group and make an appeal to an identity outside the conventional; it allows the adolescents to experience an alternative form of social reality.

Gangs, a form of youth sub-culture, are social organisations through which adolescent males experience an alternative social reality. A constant feature of gang life, violence, forms one of the primary means through which gang members establish unity and collective identities, setting them apart from the others in the community. Violence and its threat play an important symbolic role in gang life, communicating a message to gang members and non-gang members alike. Gang members try to establish dominance or identity through violent acts and violence becomes a religious rite where the objective is to maintain the unity of the group *and* to protect it from that which is opposed to it, i.e., the *profane*. Expressly, violence serves to reinforce solidarity among gang members and accentuate the boundary from the non-members.

Violence in the gang can be directed towards the adult community, towards its own members or towards members of other gangs. The violence, which is directed towards the community, i.e., towards adults, arises directly out of the collective problem of marginalisation and powerlessness that the adolescents face vis-à-vis adult men. Combating the cause of their marginalisation, gangs, through violent acts, remind the members (of the gangs) of their common experience, serving to increase the solidarity of its members.

Violence directed towards members of the gang takes place in initiation rituals. Becoming a gang member requires prospective members to undergo some sort of an initiation process. The initiate has to prove whether he is tough enough to endure the rigours of violence. Initiation rituals involve shooting someone or harming someone or being challenged to a fight. Prospective gang members are often made to walk between a line of gang members or made to stand in the middle of a circle of gang members, who then beat the initiate with their fists. Being able to fight back ensures membership into the gang. Being able to shoot someone or harm someone gains the individual a high status in the gang. So, instead of the roles ascribed by adults, physical acts of violence become the means to achieve status; it becomes the marker of manhood or masculinity. The achievement of manhood through violence marks the masculinities of gang members as different and opposed to adult masculinities, Violence thus provides them with a collective identity vis-à-vis adults.

Violence in the initiation rituals also increases the solidarity among gang members by engaging them in a collective ritual. Taking place in the midst of an assembled group, the initiation reminds active members of their earlier status as a non-member and gives the new member something in common with individuals who have been with their gang for a longer period of time. Through collective violence, the adolescents are asserting their masculinities and a collective identity of their own.

Violence against other gangs and against members of the wider community also has the same ritual characteristics as in the above case. Violence against other gangs often increases cohesiveness among members, a process that occurs through fights or the threat of attack by rival gangs. Such threats recommit gang members to their own gang, uniting them against a common enemy. For instance, Jankowski (1991) in study of gangs, gives the example of a New York gang, which was facing organisation trouble. Its members were involved in fights with each other. In order to prevent the organisation's decline, the leadership of the gang made up a story stating that their gang was in threat of being attacked by another gang. They got a few of their members to hit some of the rival gang's members. This led to a full-fledged war between the two gangs. In order to protect their own gang, members of the New York gang united to fight the rival gang. This act of vio-lence towards rival gang members helped the organisation to regain its unity and solidarity, and hence its distinct collective identity.

Violence is not just a form of collective representation but it is also *expressive* of the manhood or masculinity, of the toughness and hardness of its male members. The physical acts of violence directed towards the community and gang members itself, become the means through which the adolescents establish masculinities on violence and aggression as opposed to the more controlled and disciplined adult masculinities. Violence thus becomes a rite through which the gangs mark the bodies of their members as different and opposed to that which the adult world tries to inscribe on them. Violence is also expressive of the efforts of the gang members to establish their dominance over the members of other gangs. By engaging its members in acts of violence, gangs try to prove the competence of its members and protect and meet the challenge to their status and reputation that come from rival gangs. Acts of violence conducted by the gang attempt to mark and reconstruct the body of its members as stable and powerful masculine bodies.

Before going on any further, it is important to reflect upon this notion of the body being the site of power and control. The rationalist bias in Western culture entails a radical separation of body and mind that accords primacy to the mind. The latter is the province of civilisation. In contrast, the body belongs to nature, the kingdom of desire, the source of threatening, irrational impulses and dangerous appetites, and it must be disciplined if civilisation is to survive. Since the beginning of the modern era, the image of the body as a machine which functions properly only under control of the rational faculty, has expressed such assumptions with profound effects. The body becomes the emblem of society. Bodily colour, texture, posture, movement, gesture, facial expression, adornment and so on, constitute a language structuring social action. Control over appearance, treatment and functions of the body then becomes a universally important aspect of social order. Control or power is incorporated or invested in the body through meticulous insistent work on people's bodies; on children in families and schools, on soldiers, prisoners and hospital patients, etc. In this way, social bodies are produced of the individual bodies. At this site individual identities and social relations are constructed together. The greater the conceptual distancing between social and physical bodies, the more threatening is the loss of control over the body and bodily processes to the social order. The body then, constitutes a major site of social struggles, and it is in the battle for control over the body, that types of social relations of particular significance for the way power is structured are constituted, whether it be class, gender, age and race.

Sports, for example, has been a very important form of control over the body both by adults, as well as by adolescents. For adult men, the objective of sports has been to constitute the modern 'normal' individual. The primary focus of attention in sport overall, is the body and its attributes—strength, skill, endurance, speed, grace, etc. Thus, through sports the body is disciplined. In the mid-nineteenth century, sports such as cricket and football were introduced in public schools. The strategy was to extend the horizons of authority beyond normal school work and to make the body of the adolescents uninterruptedly visible to the authority. The disciplinary nature of sports, accompanied by formal rules, was considered by the dominant groups as normalising their male progeny and transforming them into 'gentlemen'. Through the appropriated and rule-governed sports such as football, adult men attempted to 'improve' adolescents. The disciplinary codes that accompanied this type of sports were orderly behaviour, cleanliness, temperance, non-smoking, 'manliness', and 'self-control'. In this way adult men would be able to transform the bodies of adolescents into social or gendered persons.

On the other hand, due to this pressure in adopting the 'normalised' model of manliness, adolescents tend to re-deploy this power by resisting this control over their bodies and gaining control over their own bodies. *Football hooliganism* has been one of the methods in the field of sports through which adolescents have been able to resist the control over their bodies. They stamped sports such as association football and rugby league with their own character through disorder around the football ground. Football hooliganism involved physical violence with the police, with other rival fan groups and sometimes even with referees. Through fights and aggressive acts of violence adolescents exhibit unruly behaviour as compared to the disciplined and controlled behaviour that adults expect from them. The way they project their manliness, i.e., through violence, is antithetical to the controlled way that adults expect them to. In this way, adolescents succeed in inverting the 'civilising' pressures and controls that social institutions through the medium of sports try to inscribe on their bodies. Through physical acts of violence they are able to gain control over their bodies. In this way, they are also able to produce social bodies but bodies that differ from the type of social bodies that adult men try to produce.

The body therefore, is the surface on which power structures and masculine gendered bodies are developed; it is also the surface through which subjective identities are expressed. So it is an object of control, an object of thought and of special significance, and a way of resisting control or inscriptions.

Violence is not just related to control over the body but goes beyond that. A lot of the violence that members of gangs engage in, is fights with rival gangs over gang territory or 'turf' as it is commonly termed by gang members. The turf of the gang is the place where the members of the gang 'hang out'. Gang boys mark their turf and protect it from infringement from rival gangs attempting to 'move in'. A suggested explanation for this can be found in the religious character of gangs. The collective representation of the gang is similar to the religious phenomena, which Durkheim has defined as 'totem'. According to Durkheim, a totem is a species of things, which serves to designate collectivity to a group. The totem could be anything—animal, plant, and object. All those who share the same totem form a collective group separated from those who belong to different totems. The totem is like an emblem; it is the badge of a group. It is in connection with the emblem that things are classified as sacred or profane. Anything that bears this emblem is sacred and it keeps this character no matter where it may be represented. The object, which makes the gang similar to a totemic group, is the body of its members. All the members of the gang share one thing in common, which designates collectivity to the gang and that is the subordinated bodies of its male members. Like the totemic group, all those who belong to a particular gang form a collective group as opposed to others. This gives the gang its sacredness.

Following from Durkheim's definition of the sacred nature of the totem, the whole of nature, space and time are classified into sacred and profane by the inscription of the totemic symbol on it. In that case the 'turf' or the 'hanging out' space of the gang becomes sacred to its members because it is the place where either the gang started, or where its members lived. It is the space which belongs to the gang. The streets and other public places are spaces where the gangs enact alternative forms of masculinities. These spaces thus become representative of the gangs and the masculinities of their members and thus are sacred to them. It is in these sacred spaces that the members, through their activities, acquire status and reputation. Presence of outsiders, especially members of other gangs, threatens the security that the gang members attain from the ownership of territories. Ownership is a strong principle for most modern societies. The gang's 'ownership' of the territory in which it resides provides a symbolic participation in a value from which the members may otherwise be excluded. Like religious rites, which protect the sacred, the gang members, through fights, guard this sacred and powerful territory of the gang and consequently, their reputation and masculinities vis-à-vis other masculinities.

It is therefore through violence that adolescents are able to form a distinct and alternative collective identity by themselves and for themselves. Adolescent males try to break out of the status that adult masculinities inscribe on them through violent acts. Through collective acts of violence, adolescents recreate, reinforce and reanimate their masculinities vis-à-vis other masculinities. Violence then becomes not only the means of achieving alternative forms of masculinity, but also of making gendered/social bodies.

NOTES

1. Hegemonic masculinities define successful ways of 'being a man'. In so doing they define other masculine styles as inadequate or inferior.
2. Along with age some of the other relations of power that affect the formation of masculinities are class, skill, ethnicity, and race.
3. Adult masculinity is termed as hegemonic masculinity because in almost all cultures the standard human being, who holds the values and norms of that culture, is the 'normal' adult male. Being the 'normal' therefore, adult men term other masculinities as a set of differences from standard human beings and hence problematic.
4. An example of this is seen in the work place. For instance in the shop floor factories in South London the older men define themselves as doing 'real work' and the young apprentices are seen as their juniors (Back, 1994: 172). Back argues that where men are economically dependent on the sale of their labour, the expression of maleness provides a means to exert power; power is associated with maleness, its absence with feminisation. Apprenticeship in such a case is about becoming not merely a qualified worker but also a qualified man. Seniors compel apprentices to inhabit a feminist position. The commonest games played are called wind-ups, where the young apprentice is made angry and then his anger is shown as meaningless. They are junior/subordinate status with an under-developed masculinity, while the perpetrators, i.e., the older men, reinforce dominant masculine identities.

REFERENCES

Abercrombie, N., Hill, Stephen & Turner, Bryan S. (1994). *The Penguin Dictionary of Sociology, Third Edition.* Penguin Books. London. New York, Australia, Canada and New Zealand.

Almeida, Miguel Vale de. (1996). *The Hegemonic Male: Masculinity in a Portuguese Town.* Providence, Oxford: Berghahm Books.

Back, Les. 'The "White Negro" Revisited: Race and Masculinities in South London'. In Cornwall and Lindisfarne (Eds), 1994, *Dislocating Masculinity: Comparative Ethnographies.* London & New York: Routledge.

Brake, Mike. (1980). *The Sociology of Youth Culture and Youth Sub-culture, Sex and Drugs and Rock 'n' Roll.* London: Routledge and Kegan Paul.

Cloward, Richard A. & Ohlin, Lloyd E. (1961). *Delinquency and Opportunity.* London: Routledge and Kegan Paul.

Cornwall, A. & Lindisfarne, N. (Eds). (1994). *Dislocating Masculinity: Comparative Ethnographies.* London and New York: Routledge.

Decker, Scott H. & Winkle, Barrik Van. (1996). *Life in the Gang: Family and Violence.* Cambridge and New York: Cambridge University Press.

Douglas, Mary. (1966). *Purity and Danger: An Analysis of Concepts of Pollution and Taboo.* London: Routledge and Kegan Paul.

Dunning, Eric. (1986). 'Social Bonding and Violence in Sport'. In Elias, N. & Dunning E., *Quest for Excitement, Sport and Leisure in the Civilizing Process.* New York: Basil Blackwell.

Dunning, Eric. (1988). 'From the ted and skins to the ICF.' In Dunning, E., Murphy, P & Williams, J. (Eds), *The Roots of Football Hooliganism: An Historical and Sociological Study.* London and New York: Routledge and Kegan Paul.

Durkheim, Emile. (1893). 1947. *The Division of Labour in Society.* Glencoe. III: Free Press.

———. (1912). 1976. *Elementary Forms of Religious Life.* (Translated by Joseph Ward Swain). London: George Allen and Unwin Led.

Giroux, Henry A. (1988). 'Teenage Sexuality, Body Politics, and the Pedagogy of Display.' In Epstein, S.N. (Ed), *Youth Culture: Identity In A Postmodern World.* Massachusetts: Blackwell Publishers.

Hall, S. & Jefferson, T. (Eds). (1975). *Resistance Through Rituals: Youth Sub-cultures in Post-War Britain.* London: Hutchinson and Co. (Publishers) Ltd.

Hargreaves, John. (1986). *Sport, Power and Culture.* Cambridge: Polity Press.

———. (1987). 'The Body, Sport and Power Relations.' In, Horne, J. et al., *Sport, Leisure and Social Relations.* London and New York: Routledge and Kegan Paul.

Jankowsi, Martin Sanchez. (1991). *Islands in the Street: Gangs and American Urban Society.* Berkley, Los Angeles, London: University of California Press.

Keiser, Lincoln R. (1972). 'The Teen-Age Gang: An Introduction'. In Manning, Peter K. & Truzzi, Marcello (Eds) *Youth and Sociology.* Englewood Cliffs, New Jersey: Prentice-Hall Inc.

Manning, Peter K. & Truzzi, Marcello (Eds). (1972). *Youth and Sociology*. Englewood Cliffs, New Jersey: Prentice-Hall Inc.

Moore, J. et al. 'Residence and Territoriality in Chicano Gangs'. *Social Problems*, 31: pp. 182–194.

Segal, Lynne. (1990). *Slow Motion: Changing Masculinities, Changing Men*. New Brunswick, New Jersey: Rutgers University Press.

Short, James F. (Ed.). (1968). *Gang Delinquency and Delinquent Sub-Cultures*. New York, Evanston and London: Harper and Row Publishers.

Chapter 4

Psychologists in Times of Nationalism*

Shobna Sonpar

Shobna Sonpar is a clinical psychologist and psychotherapist in private practice, and was a Trustee of Psychological Foundations. Her research interests have been in gender, social justice and political violence. She has been associated with projects in Kashmir that build capacity for psychosocial support and with women's peacebuilding initiatives, and has researched militant lives and the role of psychosocial programming in Kashmir.

When I first heard that the theme of Indian identity was to be discussed for this essay, I was alarmed. In post-modern times when deconstruction of widely-held assumptions and pet theories has under-lined the contextualised and shifting nature of our constructs, is there not something essentialist about the idea of Indian identity? Is it not reifying phenomena that are dynamic, plural and fluid?

An article that I had recently read came to mind. In it, the author, Keemanovic (1999), describes how mental health professionals get caught up in fierce forms of ethnonationalism. He examined all the

---

*This chapter was first published in *The Journal*, Vol. 6(2), December 2004, by the Psychological Foundations Trust, New Delhi.

ethnopsychological writings of prominent Serbian and Croatian psychiatrists published between 1990–1998 (during the inter-ethnic strife that convulsed the Balkans) in professional journals, and found these writings to be clearly biased in favour of the psychiatrist's own ethnic group which was seen as superior in character to the rival ethnic group. In addition, these psychiatrists saw the source of the conflict to lie in a variety of negative complexes in the rival group (envious frustration, inferiority feelings, shame, castration complex, paranoid-schizoid developmental level and so on). To exemplify, a prominent Croatian psychiatrist, professor at Zagreb University, describes Serbs as cherishing the cult of war and military leadership, using destructive defences to overcome their inferiority complex due to their awareness of the inferior nature of their culture. He describes his Croatian co-nationals, on the other hand, as peaceful and freedom loving, a civilised people with culture and traditions that go back 1000 years. Prominent Serbian psychiatrists hold completely different views. They describe their co-nationals as non-militant, respectful of religious freedoms, clever, resourceful, spiritual, with a great capacity for empathy and authentic kindness. They see Croats as militant in religion, egoistic, superficial and materialistic. Both Croatian and Serbian psychiatrists use psychoanalytic language to explain these alleged differences in national character thus giving their writings the veneer of professional authority.

I also recalled the career of Hendrik Verwoerd, the prime minister of South Africa from 1958–1966 and the architect of the racist laws and segregation practices known as apartheid. He was in sympathy with the theory of eugenics and the ideology of master-race popular in Germany where he obtained a doctorate in psychology. Said to be a brilliant scholar, he went on to hold the chair of Applied Psychology at the University of Stellenbosch and later became Professor of Sociology and Social Work also. Later, as Minister for African affairs he put into practice his belief that Africans were meant to be 'hewers of wood and drawers of water' and therefore did not need education beyond basic literacy and numeracy skills. He propagated the oppressive segregation policy in the guise of humanism saying, 'This segregation policy, which also means the protection and care for the Native in the land of the Afrikaner, but decisively rejects any attempts at equality, gives the Native an opportunity to develop what is his own, so that he can have pride and self-respect as a Native, instead of being continually humiliated as a failed and imitation white' (Citizens Commission on Human Rights, www.cchr.org). Interestingly, Verwoerd's doctoral thesis was on 'The Blunting of the Emotions'.

Having chewed on these appalling facts for a while, I was ready to consider that psychology may indeed have something salutary to offer to the understanding of national identity. While the idea of a national identity, internally homogenous and different from others, is an important thread in the history of nationalism, the actual existence of something peculiarly Indian in essence is dubious. Yet the fact is that people do categorise themselves as Indian, claim an Indian identity and an Indian belongingness, and some feel passionately about this. They may (or may not) see their Indianness in essential terms (for instance, family-focused, spiritual, peace-loving, caring and respectful of the elderly, and so on), they may vary in the degree to which being Indian is a salient identity dimension, and they may vary in the extent to which they experience a consistency between their personal values and identity. Yet, they do identify themselves as Indian.

I believe it is in the study and analysis of the *processes* of identity construction and continuous reconstruction that psychology can throw light on social phenomena ranging from group identification, belonging, solidarity and esteem on one hand, to prejudice, hostility and conflict on the other. Process is the keyword. Taking a process view implies understanding these identity-related phenomena as located in particular situational and temporal contexts, and as multiple, fluid and shifting, with different identity dimensions coming to the fore at different times.

A process view also implies the exercise of self-reflexivity—that is, a keen awareness of one's (the social analyst's, the expert's) own location and rigorous scrutiny of the influence of this *'situatedness'* on the kinds of meanings drawn and constructions made. Loss of this self-reflexivity contributes to the kind of analysis of national character described in the articles mentioned above.

What then leads to the loss of this self-reflective capacity? As Sudhir Kakar (1995) reminds us, identity lives itself, for the most part, unfettered and unworried by obsessive and excessive scrutiny in a zone of indifference in everyday living. It is only when this zone of indifference is breached that dimensions of identity stand out sharply (painfully or exhilaratingly).

Conditions that constitute an identity threat are often those that threaten collective esteem or group distinctiveness. The need to maintain differentiation and self-esteem may be met by essentialising both the self and the other—We are like this but They are like that. Along with other factors, this process contributes heavily to the escalation of conflict as images of the Other become dehumanised and demonised in an 'enemy system' (Mack, 1990).

In a multicultural society identity-related concerns are inevitably significant, setting up tensions among constituent cultures as well as between these and an encompassing collective such as the nation. In her social identity theory of optimal distinctiveness, Brewer (1999) posits that group identification is the product of opposing needs for assimilation and differentiation. Individuals achieve equilibrium by identifying with distinctive social groups that meet both needs simultaneously. The need for inclusion is met by assimilating with the group while the need for differentiation is satisfied by intergroup distinctiveness. The clarity of in-group boundaries serves to secure both inclusion and exclusion. As long as in-group distinctiveness is maintained, the out-group may be viewed in a variety of ways—indifference, contempt, sympathy or admiration—without disturbing amity. It is perhaps this that Nandy (2001) describes when he writes about the cosmopolitanism of Cochin, a city whose easy communal amity includes communal distances and hostilities, but with a certain *optimality* of its loves and hates. However, social changes that give rise to the prospect of close contact, integration or influence could threaten the distinctiveness of group identity and kindle hostility.

These are issues that are very alive and urgent in India today as the following anecdote illustrates. Asha is a 19-year-old woman, a graduate, from a remote village in Kupwara district in the Kashmir valley. Her family is one of only eight Kashmiri Pandit families remaining in their village while others of their community fled to the migrant camps in Jammu to escape militant threat. Some months ago she was married into a family in Baramulla. A few days after the wedding, a puja was held in her new home. When her mother-in-law called her to join the puja, she said, 'I am just coming... as soon as I finish my *vazhu'* (the ritual ablutions performed by Muslims before namaaz). All hell broke loose—she was immediately made to return to her natal family, her marriage at an end. It came naturally for Asha to say what she did having lived in easy familiarity with the Muslim community of her village whose customs and rituals were neither alien nor abhorrent to her and with whom she shared a commonsense of belongingness as a fellow-villager. But saying what she did was seen as indicating a degree of assimilation with the Muslim community that jeopardised her claim to Kashmiri Pandit identity.

Indeed, for the approximately 6800 Pandits who remain in the Kashmir valley, identity-related concerns are of paramount concern. The struggle to maintain their distinctiveness, their *pehchan,* from the majority Muslim community is a source of great anguish. The threat they now feel comes from the fear of assimilation. On several occasions, elderly Pandits living isolated from their community in remoter villages died and the last rites would be performed, as best they could, by fellow villagers who were Muslim. This has been the impetus to the recent forming of an organisation to keep their identity and its associated practices alive. Their anguish is coloured by anger towards those members of their own community who fled Kashmir and who now taunt them as having compromised their Hindu identity by staying on in the valley. Their feelings towards the Muslim community are mixed. On the one hand, they warmly acknowledge the support, protection and affection they have received without which they would not have survived dangerous times. On the other, they feel insecure and resentful as a minority that experiences discrimination and has lost privilege, status and material well-being. But they are proud that they are Kashmiri, *asli* Kashmiri, having upheld their identity and culture in their own Kashmiri homeland for centuries. And this raises vexed questions about their position in relation to an encompassing Indian national identity.

The challenge for psychologists is to understand, analyse, intervene and ameliorate suffering in such contexts—and to do so while rigorously scrutinising the ways in which their own identity-related issues intersect and collide, and when endeavouring to sustain their peculiar stance of an empathic attitude.

REFERENCES

Brewer, M.B. (1999). The psychology of prejudice: Ingroup love or outgroup hate? *Journal of Social Issues,* Fall Issue. Available online at www.findarticles. com

Mack, J.E. (1990). The enemy system. In V.D. Volkan, D.A. Julius & J.V. Montville (Eds), *The Psychodynamics of International Relationships,* I, 57–70. Lexington, MA: Lexington Books.

Nandy, A. (2001).Time travel to a possible self: Searching for the alternative cosmopolitanism of Cochin. In *Timewarps: The Insistent Politics of Silent and Evasive Pasts,* pp. 157–209. Delhi: Permanent Black.

Kakar, S. (1995). *The colours of violence.* Delhi: Viking.

Keemanovic, D. (1999). Psychiatrists in times of ethnonationalism. *Australia and New Zealand Journal of Psychiatry,* 33: pp. 309–315.

Chapter 5

Western Selves Eastern Selves*

Didi Contractor

The author is an American expatriate who has spent over fifty years living in India after she married an Indian man. The following are excerpts, which she has selected from a personal record written for her family after the death of a close friend. Some of the names in the essay have been changed in order to protect identities.

My longest lasting friendships mirror different twists of myself. Sometimes, when life readjusts the angle, I lose sight of the objective external 'other' and am left dealing with a spectre projected by my own needs. Edith seemed to personify another 'other' of my own: my potential Western, alternative self. I wonder, now that she is no longer accessible as an external presence, a physical Edith in real time, is this Edith that memory projects in my mind, authentic? Death has shattered the mirror.

I needed a voice for a person I might have become if I had stayed in or had returned to the West, or had been more securely grounded by the pragmatic 'realistic' attitudes the West can be thought of as representing. I have, instead, lived out my life in India, guided by

---

* This chapter was first published in *The Journal*, Vol. 6(2), December 2004, by the Psychological Foundations Trust, New Delhi.

subjective intuitive values, searching among myriad mythic presences for overall underlying patterns, managing to submerge, and perhaps even isolate myself in what may well be only the dream world I think of as Eastern.

...

The Second World War raged while Edith and I were growing up in different parts of America. We were both shaped by many of the same ideals and received the same promises from mothers and mentors.

War raged. Victory, we were told, was to bring about the instant liberal blossoming of the humanistic values war was said to be being waged to defend. Meanwhile, safely elsewhere but forming an eroding emotional undertow, extremes of horror, rage and fear were driving people beyond the rational edges of despair. My Father, an anti-Nazi German artist who had won a medal for bravery in the First World War, was overwhelmed by empathy and sucked into the depths of an increasingly pathological depression.

War raged, Life seemed raw to me, distant, tentative and preliminary. Far exotic settings in my dreams held a greater inner reality than the mess in my room or the streets I rode through on my bicycle. Caught at the awkward ending of childhood, I stood in front of the mirror and stared, trying to find clues for an acceptable image of my future self.

.... By the time, several years after my arrival in India as a young wife in 1951, Edith reached Nasik where I was living within my husband's joint family. I was deeply enmeshed in elaborating the construction of my own graceful world in what, I had myself convinced, was my own predestined setting. My husband, Narayan, busy all week as the engineer in his own architectural office in Bombay, drove the three hours up to Nasik for intensely anticipated romantic weekends. Maya, my eldest, who was growing into a neat bustling little girl with her long hair tightly braided by her aunts, busied herself gathering flowers for her grandmother's pujas. Her baby brother, Rahoul, was already an endearing cuddly toddler with a curly wild mop of thick dark hair. My possessive mother, Alice had come and gone (found herself a Guru and, despite her intentions and best efforts, failed to budge me). My glamorous older friend Stella, a flamboyant surrealist painter, had made several visits bringing acquaintances from her exotic journeys but, mostly, for months on end, I was isolated during the whole working week, without a common language, terms of reference or values I could reach out through.

I tried to understand the culture around me and to adapt myself to the joint family but without actually, really and truly, letting go of my own values. I was ready to bow to the Hindu Deities, wear my sari in the desi Gujarati style, meekly braided my unruly hair, put lipstick aside and dresses away, but resolutely refused to alter anything really basic to my identity, and I smoked behind closed doors.

I was lonely and often exhausted myself attempting to meet my own ideals, but I usually kept some time and found some energy to entertain and sustain myself.

Narayan and his closest friend, Sudhir, who had also studied in America, used to tease me. 'Only foreigners walk for pleasure! Who bothers to look at the sunset? It happens everyday. In our culture we try to rise above the senses. You foreigners are incurable romantics!'

Despite their jibes, I walked. I watched sunsets. I watched the rattling bullock carts, and women with gleaming pots, loads of straw or bundles of firewood balanced on their heads sway along the road towards the bazaar.

I tried to meditate and studied the Upanishads. I read all of Proust and Virginia Woolf. I convinced Ba, my mother-in-law, that blue jeans were 'my native dress' and took welcome breaks from struggling with saris. Sometimes Narayan was amused; sometimes abashed; sometimes it seemed to me that he would also only really accept a truly Indian wife but then at other times I felt that he would actually prefer me to be more foreign. I planted lemon trees and grew lettuce on the North side of the Ramji Mistry Bungalow. I added decorative beds of colourful flowers to the formal front garden planted by my father-in-law, Sethji, to grow exclusively the scented flowers that could be gathered as daily offerings for the household puja.

Edith came introduced by seekers, Pat and Edward Grant, who drove through Nasik after meeting Alice at her Guru's ashram in the Punjab. Narayan leaned back in his special reclining chair, drew on his pipe and charmed them, as he had me, with his knowledgeable discourses on Indian philosophy and tradition. Pat and Edward, inspired by reading Huxley, Jung, and Zimmer on ancient oriental wisdom, had driven to India overland—glamorous pioneers ahead of the hordes who still surge in over that trail. I sensed that Edith was also travelling, as I had, in a search of an acceptable and advanced image of herself, a place and a way to feel at least sufficient and real, and perhaps also to escape her own mother's ambitions or to fulfil them in her own way.

Although Edith's luminously expressive eyes were a light brown, her soft hair slightly thin and very fine, and her skin pale, I now wonder if, as her calm carriage and the handsome strength of her facial structure could have implied, she had native American-Indian blood. Her high cheekbones and determined chin were softened by, seemed sort of blurred over or hidden by, a slightly plump mask; just as her firm contained manner, very American, downright and mid-western, was softened by a quiet dignity and reserved grace. Even her opinions, often strong, biting or ironic, were expressed in a calm, beautifully melodic mild purr, a bemused musical tone which quickly became tinged by surrounding lilts and accents.

Edith had met Pat at a prestigious East Coast women's college. 'At first', she confessed, 'I felt sort of awkward there. I was always good as a student, that was never the problem, but my background was so very different that I felt self-conscious. Hardly any other freshmen were from the mid-west. Almost no one else came from a regular public high school. The others were mostly from wealthy, private school, society-type East Coast backgrounds. I had read a lot so I knew something about their world, but reading doesn't always really prepare you on how to react in everyday situations. The others didn't know or care about my background. No one could believe that my father really was a plumber. Pat was more spontaneous; after all, her father owns a night club, not a bank. And I liked her. She was really passionate about serious ideas.'

Edith and I both saw ourselves as passionate about serious ideas. I looked to Edith to have brought news of any exciting new ideas I might be missing out on. We discussed books I had missed and argued about the concept of the raw and the cooked. 'A similar perception seems to underlay a distinction people keep making here,' I added, 'between *pukka* and *kutcha*'. We speculated if what was considered normal in one society was considered abnormal in another, what was normal after all?

When Edith arrived, I was recovering from a *severe* illness, probably typhoid. I was, painfully thin, the only time I have ever been thin. Edith had trouble resisting the big platters of white bread (there was still a French-run bakery in Nasik) with homemade butter, which the doctor had ordered for my recovery. She joined me in the long walks and yoga lessons that were a part of my plan for self-improvement. We talked and talked. The talk was as satisfying as the freedom to devour all that bread.

Rahoul had a boil on his bottom and Edith, cooing her sympathy, went along in a jingling *tonga* in to the ancient Nasik bazaar to buy medicines and dressings. We were jounced over the narrow cobbled streets. Weathered carved wood supported steep pottery tile roofs. I pointed out bits of old murals in black and white on dark red earthen ground. Jostling crowds of pilgrims, sadhus, peasants and tribal people still wore completely traditional costumes. There was no plastic, few readymade garments, less mill cloth, *very* few vehicles and everything that glittered was real. Gleaming gold and silver ornaments were being cast and soldered in shops. Bright brass and copper vessels were being rhythmically beaten into shape. Dust, smoke, and the smells of incense and decay floated through the lanes. We were both intoxicated by the complex sensations of that setting. Edith was seduced by Nasik and enjoyed the world I had constructed. Thrilled to have such an approving audience, I eagerly shared everything I could with her and felt confirmed by her interest and enthusiasm.

Edith set out to explore India armed with more addresses. These only included one of Narayan's friends: Sudhir, who was at that time, temporarily posted in the North. Most of Narayan's other friends were drinking brothers, a hunting pack that gathered to confirm each other's macho stances. Introducing any female friend, especially a Western one, to them would have been like throwing her, literally, to the wolves. Among Narayan's friends Sudhir was the only modest person with intellectual interests.

They met up in Delhi and Edith wrote me about their growing romance. Narayan and I were delighted.

Together they visited us in Nasik. I remember Edith, looking tall and regal in her sari, glowing with happiness as they displayed Sudhir's gift of a necklace made up from beads that were said to be from the excavations at Mohenjo Daro.

'See', said Sudhir proudly, 'how the beads match her eyes?'

She planned to spend the summer with her family in America, and then come back to marry in the fall. Before she left, we designed all sorts of plans for an intimately shared future and talked of raising families together. I was overjoyed. I had hopes that the symmetry of four, two of each, two foreigners, two Indians, might balance the friendship. I happily anticipated no longer being the sole scapegoat to carry resentments of the West.

Narayan and I were delighted. Sudhir's family were not.

Sudhir's mother was a beautiful proud woman. She was the only daughter of a formerly very wealthy family of indigo merchants. Her widowed mother, a tiny bundle in rumpled white, stubbornly used to impose severe restraints on her self during her frequent visits. I was puzzled to learn that in traditional India a daughter's parents, after gifting their daughter (and her dowry) to a husband's family, always avoided visiting at her new home. Convention prohibited their actually staying with or ever becoming dependent on a daughter's in-laws. Sudhir's impoverished grandmother had few other places to live. I think of that wry humorous old lady with paan stained lips as living for months on end in the hallway where she proudly made her own frugal meals on a roaring pump-up kerosene stove. Possibly this memory is exaggerated but it exemplifies my consternation and incomprehension faced with Sudhir's family's traditional conventions and pride.

Sudhir's mother, on hearing the news of Narayan's marriage to me in America, was reported to have declared that her own son would 'never do such a thing', being, 'after all, from a good family'. If Sudhir's father had been present he probably kept silent, as he usually did while in the domestic sphere. He was a large aloof man with a disdainful air who only seemed to relax in the company of male peers. Mouth full of paan, he would shake his knees and laugh at the ridiculousness of others' pretensions. I remember overhearing his comment on receiving a wedding invitation from a well-known doctor. The bride's unusual name was Medha, 'intelligence'. 'How can the good Doctor have assumed that she would grow up "intelligent"? Now Brothers, see her stupidity, she is getting married to a Swede!'

Years later Medha became another dear friend, another sort of mirror self.

During that summer, before Edith's return, Sudhir came back to live in Bombay. Narayan and Sudhir resumed their weekday evenings, laughing and drinking together.

During that summer, Sudhir's mother's hair went white. In retrospect it occurs to me that she may simply have stopped dyeing her hair. In any case, his family was not about to organise the wedding.

Sudhir insisted on having a proper Hindu ritual wedding. Their family's orthodox Pundits refused to conduct a ceremony to join a high caste Hindu to a barbarian, an 'untouchable' non-Hindu outsider. So Narayan and I took on the event in Nasik.

I baked a tall wedding cake in my flimsy tin oven over my own roaring kerosene stove. We rented one of the ostentatious Marwari bungalows nearby for the groom's party, where, on the day set for the ceremony, as a surprise for the bride and groom, I decorated a bedroom, like a set for the wedding night in a Hindi film, with the traditional scented garlands. Strings of jasmine ended with tassels of classic pink roses and yellow champa flowers from the trees that edged the walls of Sethji's garden.

The problem of Edith's conversion to Hinduism was solved by a ceremony conducted on the morning of the wedding. While I was busy decorating the bridal chamber the aged Sankaracharya of the Nasik *peeth* converted Edith in his dark decaying mansion. She was 'reborn' out of the sacred fire and even given a Hindu name, which no one ever did use.

After lunch I was amazed to hear Edith comment that she would 'really be stuck' if any change came about between her conversion and the wedding ceremony in the evening. She felt the conversion had isolated her in a savage no man's land, a heathen place of no return to her own social background, which she could now only be rescued from by the respectability conferred by marriage. Somewhat taken back by Sudhir's bristly reaction, Edith claimed to have been 'just joking'. Narayan, who usually treated just about everything as a joking matter, was also shocked. Whatever our other differences might be I also agreed with both Sudhir and Narayan that ritual and belief were sacred, never joking matters. How could she have participated in a serious ritual without genuine conviction! I was disturbed by the first faint foreboding of the uneasiness that would soon begin to grow and come between us all.

I helped dress the bride. I had recently received my copy of the New Yorker with the Salinger story, 'Raise High the Roof Beams'. Instead of 'fatal golden sandals' Edith's pale feet were decorated with henna. She was massaged with turmeric paste. A delicate pattern in white rice flour, hardly visible against her pale complexion, and red kum-kum, contrasting as sharply as beads of blood, decorated her forehead. The garlands of flowers kept slipping from her fine hair.

Sudhir came turbaned with a crown of flowers dangling before his face. I seem to remember Maya up behind the groom on the plump rump of a white mare but suspect the image is transposed from my later memory of Narayan's younger brother's huge wedding. For this small private wedding, the baraat consisted of only one brave sister and one genial conciliatory family friend.

Narayan and I sat in as Edith's family for the ceremonies. I do not remember if Narayan himself was translating for me or if perhaps he and Sudhir had rhapsodised over the texts in advance, or if by that time I could follow just enough of the Sanskrit to appreciate poetic symbolism. At the beginning of the ceremony a curtain was held between bride and groom while verses, extolling the greatness of the various forms of God and Goddess, were chanted. In old-fashioned traditional India, that curtain is lowered to reveal the very first glimpse of the mortal incarnation of God to Goddess and Goddess to God. I was moved to tears as we assumed our mythic roles as Parvati's parents and 'gifted' Edith, as Goddess, to Narayan's friend.

If the circle of friendship was now, as I felt, re-balanced and cemented by ritual, the cement began to show cracks in the cold light of the very next morning. At breakfast it seemed as though the many arguments that Sudhir's family had put forward in their attempts to change his intentions had now, after the fact, dawned on them all, even on Edith, as bitter realities. Blinded by my euphoric involvement during the wedding day, I had hardly noticed how pained Sudhir's sister, aware that her family now expected difficulty in arranging suitable marriages for herself and their older sister, was looking. Even the ever-jovial honorary family friend was withdrawn and almost rude. I can still hear the stiff stinging tone of Edith's reply when I timidly asked about the decorations I had intended to surprise and delight her with. 'That was hardly the appropriate time or place.'

Without thanking us for our preparations and participation, the Doli drove off in glum silence.

Over the next weeks and months Narayan's welcome at Sudhir's home cooled. Sudhir retreated into his work, somehow conveying that his concerns which, until now they had both always discussed and argued at length about, had become too technical or complex to share with Narayan. Rebuffed and excluded, Narayan was very hurt. Always quick to blame foreign (and feminine) attitudes, Narayan attributed Sudhir's rejections to Edith's influence. Their intense bond, which I had never really been able to penetrate, began to work loose.

Edith and I had planned to exchange many visits. Edith had brought back kits and instructions for various old fashioned American craft projects, like making rag rugs and patch work quilts, that we planned to collaborate on. But now she had taken up a job and was too busy to even come up to Nasik. I resolutely gathered my little family and went to stay with them in Bombay, desperate to rescue the friendship.

The visit was a disaster. Sudhir had always been a favourite Uncle, permissive and affectionate, especially with Maya. Now both Edith and Sudhir found Rahoul's continuous chatter too disruptive and Maya's food demands too finicky. Edith declared that I spoiled and indulged the children. To Narayan's amusement, Sudhir was called to deal with the cook, the vegetable vendor or the dhobi as Edith floundered in lingual misunderstandings. I could hear echoes of her mother-in-law when my suggestions were dismissed. 'That might be all right for you up in the country, but here,' Edith said in a firm tone 'I have to maintain different standards.'

She conformed to an even stricter and more traditional self-image as the Hindu wife than I did. Sudhir could wax eloquent on the poetic or sexual symbolism of each traditional attribute and lamented the intrusions of 'fashion'. 'The red color of the bindi is a symbolic substitute for the blood of the sacrifice. And now even my sisters and their friends have started wearing blue and green! Do they think that they now have green blood! Or maybe, they think they have "blue blood", huh?' Sudhir giggled.

'Red in the parting of the hair indicates activity in, uh ahem, the parting below. It is a sign of the consummation of marriage. And can you imagine they now part their hair on the side and apply blue to match their bindi. I ask you, what sort of perversion might that indicate?'

Edith always wore ankle bracelets and toe rings, and had her bundle of keys clipped on at her waist with the traditional jingling silver bauble. She collected and wore only handloom saris. She always only used real sindhoor for the bindi on her forehead and to daub in the central parting of her tightly knotted hair, which, as if in constant awareness of its erotic symbolism, she kept modestly, covered in the presence of her in -laws.

Instead of mirroring a Western self for me, Edith now outdid me, displaying an exaggerated version of my own attempts to conform. After the wedding and that disappointing visit, I uneasily re-examined my own behaviour trying to find flaws that might have caused their coolness and earned their disapproval. I tried to slip my dis-content back behind strands of abstract thought and distracted myself by concentrating on the everyday satisfactions of my life in Nasik. I took my delight in the children. Deven was born. I continued to read and to braid hope and myth into the strands of my life. Only now as I write do I understand how, both taking on similar identities, we also no longer needed each other as mirrors of potential selves.

Time passed. Memory scrambles sequence. Now I cannot even remember if Sudhir and Edith ever did return to the scene of their wedding. Around the time of Deven's birth I heard indirectly of Edith's pregnancy. I was hurt and amazed that she had not hastened to share such welcome news with me directly, but comforted myself that motherhood would soon soften her and children might bring us close again. But before, or fairly soon after Kanishka's birth, Sudhir was posted abroad.

...

The years of estrangement that passed during their absence brought change. I was restless. I would have liked to work but in those days, at least within the community of Narayan's family and sub-caste, working women were still frowned on. Narayan had already taken to retreating to the comfort of his bottle in shame whenever my presence drew attention, but what could I do? All my attempts to conform only added to my oddity. Whoever expected to see a 'memsahib' wearing a sari, much less in the old fashioned Gujarati style? For a few months we moved to Poona where Narayan had opened a branch of his office.

On a visit back to Nasik I found the lemon tress I had planted had been uprooted in my absence to make way for a vineyard my younger brother-in-law proposed to plant. I felt symbolically rejected. With the birth of each son I had become more and more accepted, but was still always made aware of being seen as an isolated stranger, and had never really felt included by Narayan's family. Now, with my flower beds and vegetable patch ploughed over, the security of my dream supported world threatened to begin to shatter. I felt crushed by feelings of failure.

During that same visit Sethji began to complain of an itching and burning on his neck; alarm grew as a welt, first as tiny as a mosquito bite, increased. Sethji was in his nineties and there was no treatment for the cancer.

We moved back to Nasik. Alice retired and sold the house in America. Under the shadow of Sethji's long illness Narayan suddenly managed to prosper. He took a vow and gave up drinking. To help him finance the development of one of the plots that Sethji owned in Bombay, I gladly invested the share Alice had sent me from the sale of the family home. The profits from this real estate effort made it possible for us to begin building a home of our own in the far suburbs of Bombay.

Narayan's youngest sister Manu was married off in splendid pomp, but during the celebrations one of his buddies coaxed Narayan to join in the drinking. Narayan was ashamed to have broken his vow. Shame only served to augment his need of solace during the following months until, on a full moon night in February, Sethji died, and Narayan took refuge from his guilt confused sorrow in even heavier bouts of drinking.

...

By the time we made the move to our new home near the city, Deven had grown into a leggy little boy. Alice arrived to live in India, bringing, in every sense of the word, all her baggage. Just as a detailed retelling of all of these events could expand each one into separate dramatic chapters and form a whole book, the events themselves continued to form me and to alter the attitudes and expectations I brought to the cautious but welcome renewal of the friendship with Edith, now back from America.

Alice's presence made a huge difference. Alice suffered from the ambiguity of maintaining an essentially puritan work ethic, driven by guilt; while also embracing liberating modern and romantic ideals. She believed in hard work, progress, individual freedom, the transformative magic of education and creativity, Eastern mysticism and Western socialism and she believed in me HER daughter, her only child. I was still in rebellion against Alice's values, annoyed by her basic (too often voiced) dissatisfaction with India, with Narayan, with his family and their social status, and her constant disapproval of our lifestyle, but I could not help but be grateful for her back up and support in so many other ways.

Edith's own mid-western, purely American background was very similar to Alice's. They shared many of the values and aspirations that my father's sophisticated mocking, reinforced over the years by Sudhir and Narayan's teasing, had weakened my own adherence to. Edith shared Alice's cultivated cultured stance, which often seemed snobbish to me. For example, while I was quite content to stumble around speaking the by-then-quite-fluent, though no doubted dreadfully ungrammatical Hindi that I continued to pick up by ear, Alice and Edith both made serious formal studies of Hindi grammar and cultivated high Hindi vocabularies. My own pronunciation was blithely foreign but their exaggerated attempts to be correct were as often even more incomprehensible.

'In my own society,' Alice had announced early on, 'I am a cultured well educated person and I am not ashamed to speak like one. I do not see why I should be any different here.'

I tended to chaff under Alice's authority. But Alice and Edith were in accord. Edith deferred to Alice, asked for and respected her advice. Edith and Alice formed a sort of coalition in support of one set of values, opposed to many that Sudhir and Narayan shared. I felt caught out of balance with either side, again the outsider.

...

Edith was the first person to arrive at the nursing home to visit me the morning after the birth of my daughter, Kirin. 'Do you think she is going to be right-handed? Isn't it amazing how our boys are all left-handed? Do you think it is something genetic with the mixed genes? Wouldn't it be wonderful to follow the old traditions and join our families,' Edith smiled tenderly down at the sleeping new-born, 'how fortunate that I have two boys to offer in marriage!'

With my older children now at school all day, Kirin still portable and Alice more than happy to babysit and to organise 'worthwhile' 'educational' activities for the children when they got home, I suddenly had more freedom; I made expeditions into town and began to expand my world.

In Nasik, during Edith's earliest days in India, I was the guide. I opened and shared my world and even my dreams with her. Now our roles were reversed. Edith took the lead. She had become an expert on the city and I enjoyed meeting the friends she had made and exploring the shops she had discovered while Alice happily supervised all of the children.

One very American belief Edith and I did share was in the responsibility of the individual to society and the importance of active involvement in community work for the public good. Edith pulled me into various activities. Alice encouraged me, perhaps also partly because she, very rightly, sensed that Narayan would most definitely not.

Still feeling deflated after the decade of always seeming to fail in my attempts to make myself acceptable to Narayan and his family, I was gratified and somewhat surprised to find myself valued within the peer group of foreign wives Edith introduced me into. The others had mostly married into more educated Anglicised English-speaking families which seemed, atleast on the surface, to be more open-minded. The unvarnished desi attitudes I had tried to adjust to in Narayan's home turned out, in practice, to have been easier to live with. I always knew what I was up against. The completely traditional attitudes held in the Nasik household, had forced me to try to understand desi India at a deep level; I had not been lulled, as most of these other foreign wives were, by the outward expression of advanced liberal values held by their Westernised, ostensibly broad-minded, families. In Sudhir's home, for example, everyone, even his mother, spoke fluent English, but I was aware of how prejudiced their actual stance could be. Illiterate Ba was, however, ready to accept the idea that everyone had, and what is more, had the right to have, different traditional ways of their own. 'Everyone has their own native customs,' Ba used to say. 'They have theirs and I have mine.' She had stopped objecting to my occasionally wearing blue jeans when I informed her that they were my own native dress. None of the other foreign wives were, so to say, native wearers of blue jeans and they were mostly completely at sea when their new Indian families faced by a crisis, turned out to actually hold and to be motivated by the, usually unspoken, prejudices, deeply ingrained by conservative traditional communal backgrounds.

I remember sitting at a meeting in Edith's living room during an argument over the uniforms in the school we had all been instrumental in organising.

Edith, despite her toe rings, was against the authoritarianism and the uniformity implied by uniforms. 'I am not going to be here,' she and Sudhir were soon to leave again for America, 'but this is a matter of principle.'

Doris Chattopadaya, daughter-in-law of the legendary Kamala Devi, at that time Head of the Handicraft Board, wore raw silk slacks, and was against anything that limited individualism and self-expression.

Gladys Kotawala, in a prim dress, worried about the practical difficulties parents and teachers experienced keeping track of their flock on school outings. 'It is just too hard to count the children and keep your eye on all of them when they do not in any way look the same.'

Laxmi Lal, herself half-Polish half-South Indian Brahmin, suggested a compromise, 'Why not just specify the fabric and leave everyone freedom in style?'

'We cannot,' said Gladys, 'allow miniskirts.'

Page Mehta, the daughter-in-law of a famous political family, who also wore toe rings, proposed setting some limiting standards.

I doodled an intricate lattice pattern and decided to resign.

I had found some creative work, pinned up my braids, stopped draping my sari in the old-fashioned manner, begun to earn and to wear make up again. Edith and I were both too busy to linger on our previous estrangement. Sudhir, more and more like his silent dignified father, withdrew more and more and then physically too and off they went to America. Alice's vociferous disapproval of Narayan, his other friends and his drinking, intense enough for two, forced me into a defensive stance. I found plenty to turn my attention to.

...

Edith next visited with her two sons on holiday in India during a brief war with Pakistan. We ignored the threat of air raids, and walked along the shore on the otherwise deserted beach at Juhu. It was low tide. The older boys rushed down the shining expanse of sand to examine the black rocks showing at the shoreline.

'Kanishka talks about coming here to swim. In America he goes to swimming classes and tells me how much more fun it would be to swim at Juhu. Somdutta,' Edith bent down to take his hand, 'do you remember Juhu?'

It was very difficult to feel apprehension on such a marvellously clear bright day. The older boys scrambled over the rocks, examined the sea creatures and plants captured in the exposed pools, collected shells, shared memories. They ran ahead over the hard wet sand. Every now and then they wheeled to a halt and examined the empty sky, hoping for the excitement of spotting enemy planes.

Edith and I had both achieved more self-confidence. I drew pride from my growing children, expanding concerns and the success of my work; Edith prided herself on Sudhir's professional success and on managing to remain uniquely Indian in America. Her boys had even been vested with the sacred thread.

I wondered aloud if it might not be hard for the boys. 'Won't it be difficult, say in swimming class, to be seen wearing a sacred thread in America?'

'America,' Edith informed me, 'is changing.' Having been unable to return after coming to India at the age of twenty one, I had no idea of changes in America. I had arrived in America as a small child and never really adapted enough to feel completely at home. My German father and I had both endured the hostility our accents evoked. Remembering how cruel people, especially children, even in India, could be to outsiders, I wondered how change could be deep enough to protect anyone, especially a child, who dared flaunt their oddness. Having been unable to return since arriving in India in 1951, I had no idea of changes in America. But I remembered how cruel people, especially children, could be to outsiders and wondered if children had also changed. The tide had changed. We called the boys back as the waves began to crash in over the rocks.

...

Several years later, we next met in America after Edith's world had fallen apart. She was bitter about the end of her relationship with Sudhir.

'He hurt me terribly; you know how sarcastic and withdrawn he can be! It was never easy with his family either,' Edith confided. 'But, you know, I wonder if you guess how, or how much, you made it all easier for me. You set a sort of standard. You could always be used as an example to represent whatever Sudhir and his family did not approve of. When they were trying to get at me to change, they could just criticise you and I could see how to win their approval. Sometimes I wonder how conscious that was on Sudhir and his mother's part. Anyway, by joining their critical attitudes toward you, I got a chance to establish my loyalty to them. They thought you and Narayan were pretty ridiculous and were all really relieved to draw Sudhir away from Narayan's bad influence.'

Did I tell her how hurt we had been? I could, however, feel some sympathy for her behaviour: anything to find acceptance! What a relief to know that the old rift had not been directly caused by flaws on my part.

We talked about Alice's death, 'To justify living with you, she had to feel that you needed her.' Edith pointed out. 'I think she felt that whatever she could approve of would somehow make you need her less.' Old anxieties and resentments dropped away. I admired Edith's independence and envied her success in taking financial responsibility.

Seeing Edith managing bravely on her own, helped me make painful changes in my own life after I returned to India, where, especially after that first return to what seemed to me to be an increasingly alien America, I felt even more at home.

...

Memories from subsequent increasingly frequent visits with Edith in America blur together. In America it was easy to be open with her; she was always generous. Warm and welcoming. We had long intimate talks, often while she worked on the intricate tapestry knitting she followed rigorous instructions for from a book. Together we re-examined elements of our shared past and sometimes even resolved more old issues.

I find myself repeatedly daunted on each visit by the ever-changing practicalities of daily life in America, which I find as awkward as my initial attempts to negotiate things in India had been; 'It seems as though there is always a technique to master, or instructions to be followed,' I complained. I was grateful for Edith's patience. She seemed amused and seemed gratified to be called upon to cue me in.

On each visit I found her apartment crowded with more and more Indian things; works of art, delightful toys and whimsical trinkets, all of the sort that one used to find in ordinary bazaars and traditional fairs all over India, but now, I was painfully aware these are easier to find in specialised craft shops for tourists or abroad.

Edith took me to the office where she worked, writing and editing educational textbooks. She was particularly proud of a section she had produced on India in an elaborately illustrated social studies text. 'I really enjoyed the research,' Edith confided. I was shocked by the romanticised description of a classical orderly upper caste India: an idealised contrast to the disorderly multiple realities of the complicated India I still live in.

The last time I was in America we were unable to meet and it was difficult to connect, even by phone. When she was in hospital, there was no answer. When she returned home she unplugged the phone while she rested up from chemotherapy.

'You understand what this means?' She asked when we were finally connected. 'You understand that I am going to die?'

'Oh Edith, that must be so hard.' What *can* one say? What *else* could I say? Somewhere in that conversation, including long pauses with the query, 'are you still there?' took on a sinister morbidity. I did try to talk about how much I think the Hindu view of death can help.

She did not, and felt she could not believe, 'I need proof.' She hung on for another year. A few weeks before her death, Edith did make arrangements for a Hindu funeral ceremony at her cremation. I remember the smoke drifting up at dusk from the havan at her wedding ceremony in the courtyard of the Nasik bungalow, which is now being demolished. Smoke arose though a crematorium chimney, returning her sight to the Sun and her breath to the Wind; dust billows up from walls as they crash down.

Chapter 6

Threatened Indian Identities*

Nimmi Hutnik

Nimmi Hutnik teaches at the Department of Mental Health and Learning Disabilities in the School of Health and Social Care, London South Bank University. She is also in private practice as a Cognitive Behaviour Therapist (CBT). She has a doctorate in Social and Developmental Psychology from Oxford University. Dr. Hutnik was one of the earliest therapists to use CBT in India.

A few years ago, I took my ten-year-old daughter Tanya and her friend Emma to the park to play. We were in Green Guildford, a white middle class area of England. As the two girls chased each other, one on a cycle and the other on a scooter, three ten-year-old white boys entered the park. When they failed to get the girls' attention, they sat at the swings, looked at me (reading a book quietly on a nearby bench) and talked among themselves. Soon they left and I settled more deeply into *Where Is God When It Hurts* (Yancey, 1998). The next thing I knew, a spinning tennis ball had hit my ankle. I quickly looked over my shoulder. The three boys grinned and waved at me acknowledging in that gesture that they had been responsible for the ball. Then one

---

* This chapter was first published in *The Journal*, Vol. 6(2), December 2004, by the Psychological Foundations Trust, New Delhi.

of them turned his back on me and pulled down his pants and before I knew it, I had had an eyeful of ten-year-old white bum!

The emotions began churning in my chest like a fan with enormous razors for blades. I went back home and reported this incident to my daughters. I was convinced this was racist and yes, I would learn to deal with this too. Anna, my 15-year-old was not so sure. Mum, she said, in that I-need-to-be-patient-with Mum kind of voice, if this is racist then I am dealing with racism every day. Perhaps you are, Anna, I replied.

I took this into supervision where I hoped to learn a bit about my own responses and secretly hoped for some sympathy, if not empathy for the pain that I felt. My supervisor, a 60-year-old Swedish woman who had lived in Britain for many years, married to an English man, tried *very* hard to convince me that this was not a racist incident: Had *she* been sitting in the park, the boys might have thrown the ball at her. Yes, she was white but was she not elderly and was she not a woman? I was not convinced and I went home further bruised and feeling unheard.

Prejudice in the contemporary Western world is much harder to define and identify than it used to be. Many people are reluctant to express prejudice in the blatant and uninformed way that they used to in say the 1970s and 1980s. This is because the ideology of multiculturalism has taken root in Britain and it is uncool, unless you belong to the BNP (British Nationalist Party) to be openly prejudiced. This means that prejudice has gone underground and has become subtle and therefore much more violent to the soul.

Why did I feel the pain that I did? It was not the physical pain of the tennis ball brushing my ankle. It was not the psychological pain of having been disrupted in the quiet reading of my book. The pain seemed larger, a spiritual pain almost. The taunting rudeness of that ten-year-old white bum went to the very roots of my Indian identity where I was being told that I am not them and that they were better. The essence of any violence, be it verbal or non-verbal is division and separation. The message is I am not you, I am separate from you, I do not value you, in fact my life would be better without you and I want you to know this.

How do I as an Indian living in Britain respond to this *everyday* experience of being told that at some fundamental level I am not valued? One response to violence is to react with violence. Many Indians here are up in arms about their identity as Indians, they socially construct violence where none was intended and precipitate microcosmic racial wars in routine drawing room conversations. Others deny that they experience prejudice at all and it is not uncommon to hear young British Asian students say that they have never experienced racism in their lives. And even when they find that they have to apply for twice the number of jobs that their friends do before they get one, they still hold that they have never experienced racism. This is just blindness. The employment statistics tell us differently. Still others find the stress of migration, the isolation, lack of community support and the endemic racism in the system so traumatic that they experience breakdown and present with all sorts of problems to the NHS mental health services.

What was to be my response?

Still seeking answers to my own pain, I listened to a presentation by Valerie Batts, a black American woman who looks closely at multiculturalism and anti-oppressive practice. Being an able statistician as well as an able therapist, she encouraged us to use an ANOVA model to understand contemporary racism. She suggested that I was asking the wrong question of my experience of violence by a ten-year-old. The question is not, Was this racist? Or sexist? Or ageist? It was probably a bit of all of these. The question needs to be: What percentage of the variance in this incident was racist? When posed in those terms, we are grappling with some form of prejudice all the time. And when sexism and ageism interact with racism, then we need triple the psychic energy to cope with being different in Britain.

I was at a workshop the other day, which was designed for Asian and black counsellors resident in Britain. We were asked to close our eyes and go back in our memories to the very first time we encountered someone of a different race or gender. There was pin drop silence in the room as each of us accessed our own private pain. I grew up in Canada at a time when coloured people were not allowed into white bars. My dad, who held diplomatic status, was so proud because as an Indian diplomat, he was awarded honorary white status and therefore permitted entry. And so I had internalised whiteness as rightness. I have spent many years undoing this aspect of my identity. Others at the workshop, talked about the three-year-old pain of discovering that they were differently dressed in salwar-kameez. Still others talked about anglicising their names to fit in, as they entered school. The personal journeys described told of pain and the pressure to conform. But they also told about how each person had learned to reclaim, or in some instances, to *claim* their personal power as people of colour.

Claiming one's own personal power in the face of the many messages in society, which indicate that we are a low status group and therefore somehow fundamentally inferior to white people, is no mean task. A long time ago, a number of social psychologists decided to study what people from disadvantaged groups do to create a positive social identity for themselves (Lemaine, Kastersztein & Personnaz, 1978). They divided a group of boys into two groups and gave them building materials to build the best possible house that they could. One group received a more than adequate supply of materials of good quality. The other group was significantly deficient in building materials (in other words, they were deliberately disadvantaged by the experimenters). What did the disadvantaged group do? Well, with the materials they were given they built the best possible house they could and then devoted the rest of their time and energy in building a beautiful fenced garden around the house. In this way, they more than equalled the advantaged group in the competition.

The statistics tell us that indeed Indians are a disadvantaged group in Britain. Compared to white people we experience a higher rate of unemployment. The rate for ethnic minorities (18%) is more than twice the rate for white people (8%) and Pakistani and Bangladeshi people experience particularly high unemployment levels (27% and 28% respectively). A formal investigation of 168 large companies in Britain found that although 88% of companies had racial equality policies, fewer than half of them had programmes to put them into practice. Black and minority ethnic people work mainly in the public sector in non-managerial positions. Or, our social exclusion from the mainstream means that we are pushed to create our own employment. Thus, we turn to what historically we know how best to do, as we migrated from Kenya and Uganda and the Indian subcontinent. We run the many grocery stores and post offices and restaurants and other small businesses in Britain. We have used our cultural disadvantage to the very best and are now a vibrant community whose presence is acknowledged and respected.

In terms of crime, racial violence and harassment in and around the home are a daily, frightening reality for many ethnic minority people. According to data provided by the Commission for Racial Equality in 1997–98 the police recorded 13,878 racial incidents in England and Wales, an increase in over 6% over the previous year. In Scotland the figure rose by 35% from 811 to 1,097 reported incidents. Twenty-one per cent of all reported racial incidents involved assaults and were serious crimes against the person. Minority ethnic people especially Pakistanis, Bangladeshis and Caribbeans who are young, poor, unemployed and live in high crime inner city areas are more likely to be *victims* of crime. Yet black and ethnic minority people make up a higher percentage of the prison population. Per 100,000 population in England and Wales, 1,246 black, 176 white and 150 Asians were imprisoned.

In terms of mental health, it is well known that black people and Asians are over-medicated, over-sectioned, over-diagnosed and over-represented on psychiatric wards (Hutnik, 2000). For example, black people are twice as likely as white people to be diagnosed with a mental health problem and are three-to-five times more likely than whites to be categorised as schizophrenic. This is because, from a white perspective black and Asian behaviour and thinking is more likely to be seen as bizarre and disordered simply because it is different from the norm (which is white, of course).

Thus, institutional racism and interpersonal racism is a daily reality for most of us here in Britain. This does not bode well for a general sense of well-being and empowerment. Racism is so woven into the fabric of society that many of us learn to tolerate it as a kind of background noise. But that is hardly the road to self and group empowerment. A more proactive approach would be to do what that group of boys in the social psychology experiment did: to find dimensions of comparison where we more than equal our more privileged compatriots and to make a creative synthesis within our identities of what is good in our culture *and* what is good in British culture.

In India too Muslims, and Muslim women, Christians and Christian women face prejudice and discrimination on a regular basis. I went to Sagar for a dosa with a friend and a young family—mother, father and little baby girl—walked into the restaurant. The baby girl was held in the arms of a young Christian servant (I use the term fully aware of its insensitivity and yet its accuracy in describing what is reality for many people) girl from Bihar or Odisha. The father and the mother proceeded to a table, the servant sat across the aisle at another table. The father and the mother ordered a sumptuous meal of dosas, idlis and utthappams. The servant girl was given only a glass of Coke. I looked at her face. It was dull, impassive and un-alive. I wondered to myself how much pain it covered, how much this pain was suffered in silence and is unseen and un-validated. In India, class prejudice is so deeply entwined within the fabric of society that it remains unchallenged to a very large degree.

I have had to struggle with my own class prejudice. I am working on shedding my pre-conscious, unverbalised assumptions about my own superiority. I am learning to see dignity where none is attributed. I am learning to transcend the separations that human beings make because these are false separations. J. Krishnamurti (2002) in his many works reminds us that the observer is the observed and that there is no distinction between them. This means that I am You and You are Me. Christ suggests that we need to love one another as we love ourselves, neither more nor less. We need to see with the eyes of love and then we will act from a position of truth and moral strength. Compassion is the filter through which all our awareness must pass.

So in my best moments, when I am hurt by racism or any other form of prejudice, I simply become aware of that hurt and look at it with love. I do not react to it with violent anger or even clever repartee (which is a great temptation). I treat that hurt with compassion for myself, but I also send compassion and thoughts of love to the one who has been violent towards me. This way, I see our essential oneness as human beings and the cycle of violence stops within me and goes no further. In my best moments....

REFERENCES

Hutnik, N. (2000). TA and minorities: Do we over-pathologize? *TA UK*, 61: pp. 15–18.

Krishnamurti, J. (2002). *The revolution from within*. Krishnamurti Foundation India.

Lemaine, G., Kastersztein, J. & Personnaz, B. (1978). Social differentiation. In H. Tajfel (Ed.), *Differentiation between social groups: Studies in the social psychology of intergroup relations*. London: Academic Press.

Yancy, P. (1998). *Where is god when it hurts?* London: Harper Collins.

Chapter 7

Intimate Terrors, Ultimate Hopes*

Maliha Raza

• *At the time this article was written, Maliha Raza had a Master's degree in Applied Psychology. She was a corporate trainer and an organisation development consultant for the United Nations. She had worked towards peace-building initiatives in Kashmir and post-riot Gujarat, and had set up Clear Light, a Centre for Peace and Awareness.*

On 6 December 1992, the fact that I am a Muslim was brought forcefully, shockingly to my attention.

It is not that I was not aware of my religion before this. I was born to educated, progressive Muslim parents. They were rooted in their tradition, yet not obsessive about religion or about religiosity. My mother used to be in purdah till she got married, and then she discarded it forever. There was never any question that my three sisters and I would ever do it in our lives. We did namaaz intermittently at best and Diwali and Holi were celebrated with twice as much gusto (and in the company of Hindu friends) as Eid. My father is known in Muslim circles as a scholar. He is well read about the history of Islam and its precepts, yet he cannot be characterised as a mullah type.

*This chapter was first published in *The Journal*, Vol. 6(1), June 2004, by the Psychological Foundations Trust, New Delhi.

Throughout my school years, I knew my religion was different from those of the majority of my classmates and yet I did not come across overt hostility towards me because of this fact. I believe I was a typical Indian schoolgirl. I wore the same dress that my classmates wore, spoke the same as them, ate similar food and was up to the same mischief as them. My differentness was brought to my notice only occasionally when I faced questions about why my name was so different or why Muslims ate only halal meat. However, because these questions were usually asked by my friends, and never with any intent other than satisfaction of childish curiosity, I do not recall feeling any discomfort in answering them.

My father was in government service—he dedicated 37 years to the service of the nation. As a Collector, my father was once designated as Head Priest of a Hindu temple. I also remember watching, as one of the chief guests at the local temple, the washing of the Sivalingam in milk. This would be considered shockingly radical to my more traditional co-religionists, but to my father it was all part of the job. I don't remember considering his behaviour as anything out of the ordinary, I sang Vande Mataram with great enthusiasm every day in school assembly and still recall all the words.

My Islam has always been an inner belief, as is my faith in Allah. Religion was for me a secure haven, which I retreated to when life became too tough to manage on my own. I read the Quran to find guidance when I faced moral dilemmas and not to gain brownie points with God. I found myself much more comfortable being a Muslim in the company of my Hindu friends than being a Muslim in a traditional Muslim environment, primarily because I never adhered to the rituals, mannerisms or the dress of my community. I always felt comfortable in my Islamiyat, as well as in my Indianness. I didn't need to prove anything to anybody.

I know a number of other Muslims of my own economic class— friends, family members, associates—who would have a similar experience. My younger cousins, for example, cannot be distinguished from their Hindu or Christian counterparts by the dress they wear, the language they use or their likes and dislikes. Being like the rest of society is the norm. Recently, in fact when my cousins decided to don the purdah—out of sheer need for experimentation—she was regarded with much amusement by the rest of the family, elders included. I am married to a Muslim man whose family boasts of a number of very well known freedom fighters. After partition, most of his family chose to stay in secular India rather than Islamic Pakistan. My husband and members of his family pray much more regularly than I do but there is never any pressure on me to do the same. To pray or not is considered a personal choice. I wear what I please and behave the way I want.

As a professional, I work thirteen hours a day, contribute to creating wealth for the country, pay my taxes, invest, donate to charitable organisations. In short, I like to call myself and innumerable others like me—urban, educated, open-minded Muslim Indians. I am not a terrorist, I am not affiliated to any militant organisation. The first time I heard of Osama bin Laden is the first time many of my Hindu and Christian friends heard of him. I know as much about *Islamic Terrorism* as anybody else does. I am hardly interested in the Babri Masjid or the Mathura Mosque, being too busy trying to earn my living and in lodging complaints about my overly sensitive electricity meter. I hardly care if Eid was declared a national holiday or not, being more bothered about how I can ensure professional excellence. My great challenge has always been being able to reach the high targets–professional and personal that I set for myself—until somebody decided that I didn't deserve to be Normal.

On 6 December 1992, I had just finished my postgraduate studies when the Babri Masjid came down. I remember watching on TV those hordes of screaming bedraggled youngsters carrying rods and hammers atop the dome, and finally the whole edifice come crumbling down in a shower of dust. Watching it, I was able to separate the thoughts that went through my mind from the emotion that assailed my senses. The thought was expected—I'm sure this is going to be followed by riots, how many people will die, what do those politicians gain by it—and indeed mundane from all counts. My emotion though was unexpected for me, because I never had thought till then that I could feel so strongly about an issue that could be considered at best a political tamasha and at worst a stunt gone terribly out of control. To my own horror and surprise I felt invaded, raped, humiliated and overriding it all was a sense of rage—escalating, engulfing, terrifying. I was swamped by feelings of helplessness and frustration.

I know for a fact that most of my educated Muslim friends and associates felt similarly, for they expressed as much in my presence. But as time went by (the riots and bomb blasts adding insult to injury), a different emotion came forth, emerging from the layers of anger and hurt. And it was fear. Certainly, we managed to coat it with rationalisations—we were strategising, not catastrophising, we were planning, not panicking—but to my trained eye, I could see it for what it was. One sentence to sum it all: It is not going to be safe for Muslims to live in this country any more. The classic fight or flight reaction took over. Some families made plans to emigrate and others decided to swallow their pride and move to Muslim ghettos for safety. Horrifyingly, people I knew collected bricks and stones and stored molotov cocktails on their rooftops. A young friend called up to say he had joined the neighbourhood watch of the colony he lived in, and he advised us to do the same. Family friends decided to move into our house for a few weeks, 'There's safety in numbers,' they said sheepishly, shame and fear writ large on their faces.

Perceptions are like filters, you put one on and events get coloured in the same tint. Perceptions may or may not be the truth, but it is the truth the perceiver lives in every day of his or her life. Perceptions affect the behaviour of the perceiver, and like the hunted animal who sees the predator move in every rustle of a leaf, I saw more and more incidents happen and found the opinion that Muslims are no longer safe in India, becoming more and more solidified. My friends had occasion to point to incidents and events and say 'See, this proves it!' When the Christian community decided to vote en bloc for the saffron brigade, several Christian friends tried to persuade me to do the same. 'The sooner the Muslims join the mainstream, the safer it will be for them,' they told me superciliously. 'Look at us—that's what we've always done and that's what we'll do this time. For them, you'll always be outsiders and therefore convenient for target practice.' Then Graham Staines and his children were burnt to smouldering cinder in a jeep, and in Gujarat churches were burnt down and Christian houses marked.

There was a great temptation to say, 'I told you so!' but the rising tide of bile formed a thin film of horror before the eyes.

Though the Gujarat pogrom was an eye-opener to those who decided to stand on the sidelines and watch, I saw lethargy in the response of the upper and middle class Muslim to the horrifying killings being reported every day. Many, it appeared, had already resigned themselves to the fate of their community in India. The only incident which made people sit up was the brutal burning alive of a prominent politician. This because for the urban Muslim it was too close to home. If it could happen to *someone like us* it could well happen to us. In urban Muslim households today, Ehsan Jaffrey is more a phenomenon to point to than somebody who once lived and went about his work like everyone else. The elections that followed exacerbated the feeling of being friend-less in a hostile land. 'All of them are saffron,' a friend exclaimed after reading a news item about yet another political party tying up with the rising star.

The feeling underneath all the justifications was what a hunted animal would feel in a forest full of predators. My own feeling is one of being marked, pointed out, different. I am not an Indian now, I am a *Muslim* Indian, I am not a professional, I am a *Muslim* professional, I am not a woman, I am a *Muslim* woman. My identity was stripped to the basics and paraded naked in front of me, much as women were stripped naked and paraded in Surat after the post-Babri Masjid riots. When I ask the waiter in a restaurant whether the meat is halal, I find myself lowering my voice instinctively. When somebody asks me what language my name originates from, I hesitate to say, Arabic. My friend Immi who works in a well known media company talked to me about how he feels as a Muslim Indian today:

> While watching the recent India-Pakistan match with some of my Hindu friends, I was rooting for India and they thought I was putting on an act. They feel that in my heart I support Pakistan. My patriotism is suspect. When India lost a match, I was so depressed and one of my colleagues walked up to me and said, 'Tum to bahut khush hongey na, tumhari team jeet gayi.' I felt like slapping him. I was so hurt. I feel I'm being doubted all the time. Hindus or Sikhs can voice their free and frank opinion about an issue like Iraq, or Palestine or

Pakistan. But I can't voice my opinion without people suspecting my credentials. Whatever I say is taken in the light of my being a Muslim. I have to think carefully of the impression I might make before opening my mouth.

This feeling is echoed by my friend Naima:

> Frankly, I am scared. Superficially, people may say a lot of things, but the undercurrent is that of hostility. As long as I'm part of the crowd, as a Muslim, I can make a strong statement against what happened in Gujarat. But the moment I stand out, I am sure I'm going to be under attack.

I know a lot of people don't feel safe in their countries either. The Spanish populace must be feeling very insecure indeed after the bomb blasts in their city. The Americans must feel very insecure when they board their domestic flights after 9/11. The Iraqis must live in perpetual fear of their lives everyday. Even Delhites fear for the safety of their family whilst returning from a late night movie. Their fear however is different from mine. Their fear is not personal. What might happen to them is a random event. The probability of a bomb ripping apart the home of a Christian in America is the same for a Muslim in America. A thief might rob and kill in a Hindu's house in Delhi, or that of a Sikh or of a Muslim. The danger is real but not personal. The thief has nothing to do with *me* personally, nor with who I am, what I believe in or whether my name has its roots in Arabic or Zulu. Their fear is impersonal.

But *my* fear is very intimate. It is too close to my name, my belief, my value. It is *I* who is targeted, marked, watched. Let me bare to you these intimate terrors of mine—I am hounded frequently in my dreams, by a raging mob intent on pouring petrol over me and setting me alight. The elections are a death knell an ominous bell tolling in my subconscious. Demons dance atop the dome of my house yelling, *ek dhakka aur do*. I fear for my safety, I fear for my loved ones. I fear for my life.

For such a large number of people, such a large fear, every day of their lives—is a hard burden to bear.

How *can* it be? When I look at myself, I consider the perceived security that I can rely on. I live in an educated urban neighbourhood and my neighbours are on friendly terms with me. I presume they would not suddenly turn into raging demons and decide to burn down my house. I have a live-in security guard who I dare to consider in this context far more trustworthy simply because he shares the same religion as I (though I have no way to determine whether he might not rob or murder me in the middle of the night not withstanding our common religion!). I am privileged enough to have a car parked in my driveway which I hope may provide me access to a quick getaway if required. I have friends who live in the so-called safe neighbourhoods (which under a more rational state of mind, I would call nothing but urban slums) who may accord me a haven if I need to scuttle away in fear of being dehoused by my erstwhile friends overcome by feelings of religious fervour and hatred. And finally, I have enough money saved to be able to buy a one-way ticket out of the city and set up operations wherever I may find political asylum. Despite all this perceived security, my fears won't leave me in peace. Then what would be the state of mind of those who live in real slums and are completely aware at all times that they—the poor, deprived and underprivileged—would be the first to be raped, murdered and slaughtered in the streets in the event of another pogrom the like of Gujarat? The burden of their fears must be vast. The demon, which lives just outside my window, must be residing right inside their private quarters. The terror that sometimes awakens me from sleep must be keeping them awake at night. So I wonder how we cope with these demons, they who sleep under the stars or clustered in ghettos and I, a member of the privileged upper and middle class of the community? I wonder whether their coping mechanisms are any different from mine.

When I was a child, afraid to walk into a dark room alone, my mother told me 'If you fear Allah, you don't need to fear anything else.' When I was studying for my tenth board exams, mortally afraid of flunking my mathematics paper, my father recited a verse from the Quran 'If Allah helps you, none can overcome you....' That verse often flits through my mind when confronted with the vexations of life and when I need resources of inner strength. Thinking back, I understand now that this simple philosophy was not unique to my parents. It wasn't a family technique for handling fear. In fact, my observations of how members of my community handle events that elicit sorrow or fear (bereavement, financial loss, divorce) brought me to the conclusion that this is the way most Muslims often cope with personal difficulties. It is a cultural legacy handed down from generation to generation. Stories of the prophets and leaders reinforce this belief. Muslim children are brought up on stories of how the young Yusuf (the prophet known to Christians as Joseph of the technicolour coat fame) braved being thrown into the well and all the difficulties thereafter heaped upon him, stoically, thus ultimately triumphing over his enemies; how Moosa (Moses) fearlessly took on the mighty Pharaoh and saved the chosen people; how Hussain the grandson of Prophet Muhammad refused to give in to the demands of the powerful and sacrificed his life for his people. The entire history of Prophet Muhammad as well as his companions is a saga of courage under adversity, a standing up to persecution, and the triumph of hope over despair in the direst of conditions. These stories are an essential part of the Muslim cultural diet. Specifically in relation to fear, Muslims as a community are taught not to let it overcome them. They are told in no uncertain words that to give in to zulm (oppression) is just as bad as to be zalim (oppressor). They are forever being told to follow the example of their religious leaders. Not giving in to fear is as much part of their cultural legacy as namaz or keeping the fasts of Ramadhan. This intolerance of oppression (real or perceived), this exceptional sensitivity to injustice (real or perceived), this allergy towards being singled out, taken to the extreme can turn into aggressive militancy or further still to terrorism especially if fuelled by immense fear and the need to cope with it by displaying valour. Coupled with this, is the phenomenon of the Islamic family—the concept that all Muslims are part of a single entity that the Islamic fellowship is a bond that goes beyond that of nationality, race or language. And in times of crisis, it is natural that the bonding and the banding together are intensified. So it would be sad but not a surprise for me to find that one of the first casualties of a communalised India would be the secular Muslim—a group in which I count myself.

In effect, I as a Muslim am being pushed by my fear to flock towards others of my community and away from the mainstream—a movement which can only lead to my own destruction. I am being forced by my sense of persecution to let go of all that is valuable and beautiful in my identity and uncover its baser side, which has nothing but hostility to offer. I am impelled by the danger to my life and not just my cultural identity to remove the polish of civilisation and return to my primal instincts—behaving like an animal—either fleeing from the perceived danger or turning around to attack. It makes me feel ashamed and sorry to see myself as well as other educated, forward-thinking Muslims come down to this level. Once we talked about how the Muslim Indian could contribute to society and the nation and now we talk about how the Muslim Indians can protect their life and property! When I ask him how he feels, Immi says with a quiet desperation,

> All this time I considered myself part of the huge community of India with its myriad cultures. I love to celebrate Eid as well as Diwali and Christmas. I want to live and work with the people here. But I'm being forced to realise that I am not a part of them.

The question then arises where did all this hate come from? Where did all the bonding go? It is tempting to put the entire blame on the shoulders of power-hungry politicians or the un-enlightened leaders who whipped up this mass hysteria for short term gains—but that's the convenient and much used answer. But the bitter fact is that we, the people, must share the blame. I must personally take responsibility as an educated, relatively well-to-do, knowledgeable member of my community—as an Indian as well as a Muslim—of not adequately disbursing my social responsibilities. As someone once said, 'If you're not adding value, you must be adding cost,' and I must question whether I have personally added value to resolving the issues faced by my religious community vis-à-vis the other communities of India. In fact, how many others of my ilk have done so? Why have I and other educated Muslims like me abandoned the future of the community to those who we ourselves admit are yoked to the shackles of the past, and who have not been able to help Muslims reconcile their Islamic lifestyle with the modern outlook? How did I use my education and my skill to plough back into society some of what I received from it for so long—tolerance, love, peace and togetherness? Unfortunately, the answer to this is pathetically inadequate. We as educated, liberal, forward-thinking, well-read, modern Muslims have not done enough for this community in terms of helping it counter the force of hatred that is being unleashed on it from all quarters.

Oh, there have been some who have tried, but those are few and far between. There has been no visible concerted effort to build bridges between Muslims and Hindus for example, or to stem the hatred by disbursing information, or to help the deprived sections make sense of what is happening and explore peaceful channels of response. At best we have written articles or made statements and at worst, we have washed off our hands and gone back to our lives.

But I still have hope. It is a hope for this nation, which I and others like me share. We can afford to have it because we have had the privilege of education. An education which tells me that exclusionist philosophies—philosophies which accord one individual's superiority over another by allowing them to heap on the latter unbearable indignities cannot exist for long in the world today. These philosophies have little to offer to women and men in terms of spiritual or social development. The world has in fact moved on after experimenting with a number of such philosophies—slavery, Nazism, apartheid. It is no longer acceptable to discriminate against people on the basis of personal values, beliefs, language or the colour of skin. All over the world, humanity is re-asserting its need for balance and harmony—consider the environmental movement, movement for free speech, anti-war demonstrations. Today's economy is the knowledge economy, and the only superiority is that of information not religion or caste. Today we have neither the time nor the inclination to waste precious resources on ideas, which cannot contribute to our advance as a *whole*. I believe (and hope) that it will not take long for the people of India—Muslims as well as Hindus—to realise this and throw out communalism, another failed idea, from India. The hope is bolstered by the activism of institutions, which retain their original regard for justice that was a trademark of this country long ago. Institutions like the Supreme Court, the Human Rights organisations, NGOs fighting for peace and justice, and the independent Press of India which have remained the standard bearers for social equality; individuals like Mallika Sarabhai and Teesta

Setalvad, who braved social ostracism and political persecution to speak out against oppression; the editors and writers of this journal who encouraged me to be frank in my opinions and allowed me to express them in print; and innumerable others who have fearlessly voiced their antipathy to violence and tyranny keep this hope alive. But is this hope enough?

What we need is not just hope, but a vision—a vision for the future of the nation and for my community. The Bible says without a vision, a nation and its people perish (Proverbs 29, 18). I believe that a community without a vision too must perish. The vision that we need must be one that will help Muslim Indians to become a contributing, value-adding community of this nation rather than be a drain on resources, a potential terrorist threat or a vote bank. And that vision necessarily must be one of harmony and balance—without which we cannot survive. That vision must rekindle the community's *spirit of enterprise*—which is an essential part of the Islamic identity. A spirit which constitutes boldness, courage, innovation and initiative—vehicles used on the information highway. A spirit which helps it to overcome poverty, illiteracy and the spectre of fundamentalism and narrow-mindedness and to move beyond these to secure for itself economic growth and political freedom. Immi, only 24 years old, speaks of this hope when he says,

> We must convince our children that there is a life beyond all this. Rituals, rites, religion is the domain of your personal system—keep it confined to your home and mosque. Be open minded, concentrate on work, focus on the potential you have, you are capable of great contributions, as proved already in various fields, move. Beyond these petty squabbles and get on with life.

This morass of despair, this all-pervading sense of persecution, this *fear* that the community finds itself in today, can only hinder the development of this spirit of enterprise. Fear is the breeding ground for violence—on both sides of the communal divide—but information is the archenemy of fear. It is only education that can remove this fear from the hearts of the Muslim Indian community as well as the Hindu Indian community. Once we have information, we have the weapon we need to battle against the ghoul of exclusivism—a ghoul which would have no place in the tolerant pluralistic culture of the true Indian society. Once we have knowledge, we have the power to create a space for the entrepreneurial spirit to arise within the nation and not just outside it, as we have demonstrated time and again to the world. Once we have education, we have the freedom to run in the global arena and achieve the potential we have as Indians, Hindus, Muslims, whatever.

Nietzsche (1989) wrote, 'He who fights with monsters should look to it that he himself does not become a monster. And when you gaze long into an abyss the abyss also gazes into you,' and my fervent prayer is that in dealing with the demons that assail this wonderful community called Indians we do not become monsters ourselves. And I as an Indian, a Muslim and a responsible member of the society must be the first to jump into the arena to unfurl the flag of peace and harmony with whatever skill or resource I have at my disposal. I think I can and my effort is with 'Clear Light'—a centre I am setting up which has as its main objective disbursing information about Islam and Muslims and dispelling myths and misunderstandings. However small it may be, this is my effort to make up for my own idleness so far.

REFERENCE

Nietzsche, F.W. (1989). (W. Kaufmann, Trans.). *Beyond good and evil: Prelude to a philosophy of the future.* (Apophthegms and Interludes, section 146). Retrieved from http: / /www. Antispecies.com/nietzsche/beyond_good_evil.php

Chapter 8

Religion, Prejudice and Attitudinal Change*

Neeru Kanwar

Neeru Kanwar is a practising psychotherapist and counsellor based in New Delhi. Her area of interest is social psychology. While her work has been primarily with persons suffering from anxiety and depression, she has held a particular interest in areas of childhood trauma, sexual abuse, communal conflict and couples' conflict. The overall guiding focus has been development of resilience and compassion in persons attending to social distress. Dr Kanwar is one of the founding members of the Indian Association of Family Therapy.

I hold my religious faith in a positive light, but am highly concerned by aspects of religion which can easily become excluding and discriminatory of others. I have seen this emerge insidiously, especially in the past years amongst the so-called sane, thinking and educated people around me. My memory of the expression of desperation on the face of the one Muslim girl in my class at school (in the 1960s) as she often struggled against articulated or unarticulated negative

---

* This chapter was first published in *The Journal*, Vol. 6(1), June 2004, by the Psychological Foundations Trust, New Delhi.

presumptions about her personal hygiene, her family's moral status, and her intelligence based on her religious identity, becomes now even more deeply etched. How can we subject people to such pain and trauma? Is this an aspect of religiosity or does it result from a negative attitude towards people of different religions? As any other student of psychology, I too have read Allport's classic explanation of why we think negatively of other people. He had defined prejudice as that actively angry attitude towards people only because they belong to a group that is presumed to have certain negative characteristics (Allport, in Mann, 1985). In my college days I had wondered if the answer lay in developing a modern way of looking at the world and the people around us.

In the late 1980s, working towards my PhD, I had studied different groups of young people in order to examine the impact of education upon a modern value-orientation. The Kothari Education Commission of 1966 had outlined attitude and value changes as one of the goals of education in our society. Drawing upon the work of social scientists as well as the ideological development during the growth of liberalism and the Renaissance Movement, I delineated a modern value-orientation as consisting of:

- *Rationality*, the pursuit of reason and challenge of constricting rituals, dogma and prejudices.
- *Individualism*, referring to the liberation of individual thought, adoption and affirmation of an independent stand.
- *Humanism*, as reflected in a concern for egalitarianism and universal justice.
- *Selective discrimination*, which is not a blanket negation of tradition.
- *Change-orientation*, manifested in a positive outlook, willingness and expectation of change.
- *Exposure* to a wide range of alternatives and options.

For the study I had constructed a Likert-type scale, following the various steps of collection of items: framing items; editing and validation through a scrutiny done by a panel of judges; try-out on 84 students; item analysis and selection of items with a t-value ranging from 2.34 to 11.8 and item-test correlation values ranging from 0.25 to 0.6. I carried out reliability studies through the test-retest method (correction value = 0.88) and the split-halves method (correction value = 0.90). The Hindi and English versions of the scale were also correlated in a study (correction value = 0.93).

I conducted a survey using this attitude scale with 590 male and female students at various stages of higher education ranging from zero years of After School Education to six and more years of Higher Education, from both professional and general streams.

Later, I also conducted an in-depth interview with 30 of the respondents. While the main consequent variables pertained to scores on the attitudinal modernity scale, the antecedent variables that I examined related to the educational and familial background. The data was statistically analysed through the use of:

1. Means and Standard Deviations of groups on the attitudinal modernity scores.
2. T-test to test the significance of the difference in means.
3. Correlation of antecedent and consequent variables.

Gender (female), family size (below five), father's and mother's educational status (greater number of years of higher education), own educational status and age, appeared to be the most commonly significant contributors of attitudinal modern orientation. In the area of 'Religion and Communal Life' the mean scores of the following were significantly higher on attitudinal modern orientation:

• Females
• Older respondents
• Youth from small-sized (1 to 5 person) families
• Those with higher educational status
• Those whose mothers had high educational status.
• Those who belonged to families with high incomes.
• Those who were undergoing professional education.

Results of my study reflected upon the value of education as an agent for socio-psychological change. However, other variables were also found to have contributed. For qualitative analysis, I also interviewed a small category of the respondents, asking them the following:

1. Did they believe that faith in God can help solve the most difficult problems?
2. Did they follow rites and rituals and why?
3. Would they be able to maintain good relationships with people from a different religion? I addressed three kinds of relationships: the professional, the social, and the marital.

I found that respondents who expressed modern value orientations were studying well, were more independent and had chosen unconventional study subjects. I found that female respondents were more inclined towards religious, ritual behaviour, yet they displayed a greater human connection with people from other religions. Relating to the marital sphere, I found that the respondents generally envisaged difficulties in adjustment because of differences in social customs, habits and practices. In this area, respondents verbalised stereotype positions and tended to believe that marriage was a relationship not only between individuals but also between families. Clearly they perceived that marrying people from a different religious group would lead to severe difficulties. The respondents who did think of marrying someone from a different religion tended to already be in a cross-religion romantic relationship. Here, conversion issues elicited some insecurity and anxiety.

I found it intriguing that my female respondents scored higher in all aspects of modern orientation. This was despite the fact that women were found to be more religious and reported a strong faith. Perhaps this indicates that it is possible that devotion to a faith can be associated with a capacity for openness and an understanding of others. I wonder if older subjects' modern value-orientation came because of a greater maturity, which may also relate to more years of education after school. Or, just to greater exposure to varying ideas. Possibilities of friendships with a wider range of peers from differing religion groups increase with age.

I found that a smaller family size of a respondent was also an important indicator here, as was a higher socio-economic status and a professional education background. These respondents appeared to have greater self-confidence and self-esteem, perhaps also by virtue of their status in society. In their interactions with others, religious identity aspects were not that important. My experience has also been that people who are passionate about a field of study, or art, or music, focus upon a common involvement rather than on the differences in the religious identity of fellow participants. Respondents from small families also displayed modernity in religious attitudes. This may relate to their generally higher socio-economic status or to their nuclear family situations that allow more scope for egalitarian, democratic relationship as well as a better sense of well-being because of greater attention given to each member.

My study had shown that an increase in level of education did contribute to modern orientation as reflected in attitudes towards religion but it did leave me wondering about the other variables that we must explore in order to develop a strategy to combat prejudice. This study is more than ten years old and most of the social problems in India today do seem to reflect a chaotic and haphazard mixture of the modern along with the non-modern.

Religious belief has been a source of deep faith, hope, support and succour for many. However, it is not just a personal, individual issue. It emerges in all forms of interaction. Inter-religious marriages are still rare and are sensitive and vulnerable to trouble. Prejudice and negative stereotypes about *the other's* religion may erupt into violent conflict as religious identity and ethnic grouping become forms of aggressive self-assertion. Perhaps all this has implications for self-development.

The importance of this self-development has been particularly underlined for me in my work with a client I will call Damini. Damini, a Hindu, and my client for four years had been feeling ravaged by an intense rage towards her husband, his Muslim identity and his drinking problem. She felt deeply hurt and wounded by his lack of moral principles and his neglect of her. She was bright enough to know that strange prejudices were coming into play in her rage towards him. In therapy she also began to understand the deep injuries that she herself had received on account of her dark skin colour, a matter of isolation in her brahmin, Hindi-speaking community. She had been born to a brahmin mother who had defied convention in order to marry a man from the Dalit community and the two had, I imagine, believed in creating a new world for themselves. However, the marriage had not been able to survive, given the pressures and strains of a negating, prejudiced world around them. One night, baby Damini's father left the family. Her mother, a shattered, broken woman, had returned with the baby to her maternal home and had eventually become inaccessible to her daughter, spending most of her life in an ashram. Damini's quest for warmth, love and her deep wish to be compensated for the deprivation of the past had drawn her into a marriage with an ideological stance similar to her mother's. However, the pain and grief of discovering that her wounds were not to be healed in this relationship had driven her to become bitter, anxious and also authoritarian.

There are obviously many theories on the existence of prejudice (Babad, 1983). Prejudice has been seen as the result of learning, identification and conformity to a group. This societal approach focuses upon conditions and events that contribute to intensifying prejudice and discrimination. These include conflicts between racial, ethnic, religious and ideological groups, political and economic competition between groups, tension due to insufficiency of the available resources, scapegoating, and the short-range consequences of planning and legislation.

Traditionally, one of the main issues related to prejudice and discrimination has been that of authoritarianism (Mann, 1985). One theoretical approach links the authoritarian personality to a dogmatic cognitive style, prejudicial attitudes and discriminatory behaviour. Men and women who are highly prejudiced are seen as characteristically authoritarian, directing their prejudice towards most groups that are different from them. Authoritarian men and women are seen to be generally intolerant, bigoted and righteous, perceiving and interpreting the world in extreme terms of good (ours) and bad (theirs). Many people are unaware of their prejudice, employing various defence mechanisms to prevent painful knowledge of their prejudice to reach their consciousness. Adorno et al. (in Babad, 1983) theorised that authoritarian women and men experience strong conflicts, yet lack adaptive (ego) tools for coping with the ambivalence. They have strong id impulses and an equally strong punitive superego. Over-defensiveness, rigidity, externalisation and projection of all unpleasant ideation upon others and at the same time glorifying self and family values are then ways of dealing with these conflicts. Prejudice helps those who are insecure about self-worth and have a weak ego, to project and ascribe undesirable traits and characteristics to various minority groups. It releases pent-up aggression, and hostility is displaced from a harsh parent on to a scapegoat.

The mode of thought, rather than a set of beliefs, a cognitive style characterised by rigidity and intolerance of ambiguity was studied differently, as dogmatism, by Rokeach (in Babad, 1983).This could exist as independent of ideological content. This means that those who profess to be liberal or modern could be equally dogmatic as those who are non-modern.

In my experience, prejudice has to be handled with great sensitivity to the social and psychological pressures. Highly prejudiced individuals easily react defensively, misinterpreting and distorting materials that challenge their belief with caricature or ridicule. As such, cognitive behaviour therapy may help in challenging dogmatic styles of thought but beyond that the selfhood of the person needs support and strength. I have found that attempts to directly reduce the anxiety-arousing threats may be successful. Self-awareness and social awareness, or sensitivity building groups that employ procedures to gain insight into defence mechanisms may also be useful. When dialogue is facilitated to develop an in-depth understanding of one's emotions and greater strength it also helps persons to bond with the fundamental experiences of emotions that move all human beings. In this sense, even severely authoritarian women and men have been known to be moved to compassion and understanding as they experience a greater sense of completeness of the self within. It was only after years of painful self-awareness that Damini and I could effect some movement in her stuck position towards the *other* religious group. As she began to accept and nurture herself, she also began to see the *other* as fallible, realistically limited and deserving of compassion. Now, after regular work in facing her pain, she appears to have become calm and also compassionate towards her husband who has also suffered emotional injuries in the past. She seems liberated from her rage and prejudice, but surprisingly has found a new quest towards spirituality, through Buddhism. Perhaps practice of religion per se is not directly associated with prejudice.

Inter-religious conflict seems to appear when an individual's personhood, sense of self and emotional needs are under threat. One of the findings of my study was that higher education does generate change in attitudes towards *the other* to the extent that rituals and blind faith come under question. However, higher education per se, does not seem to develop the confidence that helps men and women relate to people from different religions in deeply intimate ways, which is completely accepting of their religious identity.

My study indicated that age is also related to a lowering of prejudice. I had hypothesised that this may happen because of a greater maturity that ageing might bring. Perhaps ageing and higher education provide the personality evolution or maturing that lead us to become free from prejudice. In my understanding, we do need to develop our own sense of self, expand our awareness of our emotional needs, our pain experiences, better our knowledge of our fantasies and our emotional losses, before we can relate better with our own suffering and change our own attitude to ourselves. Then only can we join another in their suffering and be compassionate.

As we relate with others in a deeply intimate manner we relinquish stereotypes and prejudice filters and we do not then regard *the other* with dependency, fear or rage. Instead we are able to see them with deep regard for their struggles and the inner strength that they are able to bring forth.

REFERENCES

Babad E.Y., Biranbaum, M. & Bene, K.D. (1983). *The Social Self: Group Influences on Personal Identity*. New Delhi: SAGE.

Kanwar, N. (1993). *A Comparative Analysis of the Impact of Education upon Modern Orientation among Different Youth Population*. Unpublished doctoral dissertation, University of Delhi, Delhi.

Mann, L. (1969). *Social Psychology*. New Delhi: Wiley Eastern Limited.

Chapter 9

The Lesson from Mental Hospitals*
Unlearning Neglectful and Discriminating Practices

Harsh Mander

Harsh Mander is a human rights activist and Director of the Centre for Equity Studies. He has been closely connected with the movements for the right to information, right to food, tribal and Dalit rights, and custodial justice. He has also worked with leprosy patients and those suffering from mental illness. His books include Looking Away: Inequality, Prejudice and Indifference in New India, Unheard Voices: Stories of Forgotten Lives, Ash in the Belly: India's Unfinished Battle against Hunger *and* Fatal Accidents of Birth: Stories of Suffering, Oppression and Resistance.

As human civilisation has evolved in recent centuries, one of its most puzzling and inhuman innovations has been that of custodial state institutions, the notion that various categories of very vulnerable people should be locked away. Mentally ill people, abandoned, destitute and disabled people, girls and women rescued from sex work, survivors of extreme violence, and homeless, orphaned and

---

* This chapter was first published in *The Journal*, Vol. 6(1), June 2004, by the Psychological Foundations Trust, New Delhi.

abandoned children are among those who are imprisoned behind high walls in jail-like state institutions, often for many years, sometimes even for a lifetime.

In fact, for many of these social groups, which require because of their extreme and profound biological, social and economic deprivations and denials, the most intensive state and social support, custodialising and in many cases criminalising them constitutes the principal state response. This approach often also has wide legal, professional and social sanction. Within these custodial institutions, conditions are typically as oppressive and brutalised as in most jails, if not worse, with similar restrictions on freedom; monotonous empty daily routines and food regimens; austere, even sub-human physical conditions; harsh custodial management; and no opportunities for normal work, social interaction, recreation and cultural expression.

These institutions, like mental hospitals, juvenile homes, women's rescue homes and beggar homes, are in effect designed and function as dumping spaces for the rejects of society, where they are supported, at best, at the minimum physical level. Their emotional and physical needs, their aspirations, healing and growth, are of no concern in the design and running of these institutions. They are places primarily where families, the larger community and the state can abandon and forget its most vulnerable people.

Custodial institutions typically are also conceived as the final destination of vulnerable people. Once the state, often through the arms of its criminal justice system, places these most vulnerable people—whether an abandoned mentally ill person, a homeless mentally challenged woman, an abandoned child, a destitute old person, or a girl rescued from sex work—in such a custodial institution, it is as though its responsibilities end with this incarceration. Most laws and state policies contain no obligation, or even provisions, for the state to investigate the best interests of the custodialised person, and for their rehabilitation, their protection and free, fulfilled emotional and physical growth in the larger community.

Many of us today will acknowledge that the walls of such custodial institutions should be broken down, and these institutions should recede into the long and gloomy history of the governance of disenfranchised and powerless people. However, we need always to be vigilant that such humane and progressive discourse should not become the excuse for the state to withdraw from any responsibility to these vulnerable groups. We are not admitting of less, but affirming greater but altered, state responsibility.

It is beyond the scope of this article to dwell on the strategies for non-custodial, non-stigmatised care of mentally ill people within their families and the community. Its much more limited ambit is to explore how we can transform the character of existing custodial institutions, and also help their inmates to access a new hope and chance to live life. It is my argument that no new custodial institutions for mental health care should be created. And where such institutions exist, they need to be transformed into humane, transparent half-way homes, healing and rehabilitation centres, for protection, for the eventual restoration to self-reliance, dignity, and protected living within families and the open community.

Some possible strategies that would enable such a movement out of state institutions for most vulnerable people incarcerated in mental hospitals are outlined in this article.

HUMANISING AND DE-INSTITUTIONALISING MENTAL HOSPITALS IN INDIA

It may be emphasised at the outset that the process of humanising and de-institutionalising custodial state institutions for people living with mental illness (PLWMI) should occur within a much larger process, that of integrating mental health care at all levels of public health care— primary, secondary and tertiary. It is only such a combination of interventions that can lead to humane and professional treatment, care, and the restoration of the human rights of a segment of people who suffer today from perhaps this most grave violation.

Human rights, humane care and rehabilitation of persons with mental illness is one of the darkest chapters of India's mixed record of enforcing human rights and ensuring health care for all. The matter has attracted some attention in recent years largely because of spurts of judicial activism, public interest litigation, the efforts of a few dedicated rights activists and the National Human Rights Commission (NHRC).

There have been highly significant efforts to integrate mental health care with primary health care, as well as to strengthen and integrate psychiatric care with other medical care at secondary and tertiary levels. However, within the walls of mental hospitals, not much has changed for PLWMI, especially those who are further disadvantaged because of gender, caste or poverty.

Human rights work with PLWMI has tended to focus disproportionately on institutions for the custodialisation—often for several years or even a lifetime—of patients. This focus has led to the neglect of issues related to the care of more than 99 per cent of PLWMI who never enter the gates of institutions.

However, for reasons outlined at the outset, this article will deal briefly with the concerns of persons living within these institutions. As a recent survey by the NHRC, as well as several other independent reports have established, PLWMI in mental hospitals mostly continue to be subjected to various forms of inhuman treatment, which are particularly unconscionable in the light of contemporary advances in medical knowledge about the pharmacological and psychosocial management of patients with mental illness. Some of the major problems faced by patients in many, if not, most mental hospitals in India include some possible strategies that would enable such a movement out of state institutions for most vulnerable people incarcerated in mental hospitals.

- Untrained medical, nursing and orderly staff.
- Brutal treatment, violence, abuse, or neglect at the hands of staff.
- Chaining or other barriers to free movement even within the campus of the institutions.
- Almost exclusive reliance on pharmacological remedies, with little or no psychotherapy, counselling, or alternative therapies, such as group counselling, vocational therapy, theatre, recreational therapy, etc. Denial of the most basic facilities such as clothes, beds, clean toilets, regular bathing, etc.
- Poor food, and corruption in the purchase and management of food and other consumables.

- Denial of medical facilities for non-psychological ailments, this, combined with abysmal living conditions, leads to high morbidity and mortality of patients from non-entirely preventable psychiatric causes.
- Brutal and indiscriminate application of ECT without anaesthesia.
- Prison-like atmosphere, with excessive regimentalisation, a regime of fear, and opacity.
- Denial of access to families.

To make matters worse, there is little done to prepare the patients to resume life after discharge from the hospital. Neither they nor their family members are counselled even about the imperative for regular medicines, even less are they prepared for the emotional stresses of re-integrating with their families, and interrupted professions or educational careers. It is not surprising therefore that the patients who are discharged frequently return to the mental hospitals, for longer and longer periods, with less and less hope.

However, the most tragic are patients who are abandoned in the mental institutions, often with the active complicity of hospital staff. The members of the families of patients give false addresses, or fail to respond when the hospital authorities write to them that they should take back home patients ready for discharge. As a result, in all mental hospital many patients, especially women, are abandoned for years, decades, even lifetimes.

Their neglect is compounded by not only state abdication, but that of medical professionals who allow conditions of such unconscionable dehumanisation in mental hospitals to persist unchecked. They also have persisted with labelling some patients as incurable, burnt-out and requiring lifelong custodialisation.

The long-term answer to all these problems is to break down the walls of institutions, to end medico-legal and social practices which sanction the custodialisation and brutal treatment, neglect or abandonment of PLWMI. Treatment of new patients of mental illness, and new episodes of mental illness must be integrated in primary health care, with referrals to secondary and tertiary levels in units or departments of district and medical college hospitals. Such destigmatised care must encourage the participation of families and other caregivers, build their capacities and those of patients themselves, provide them ongoing support, and give services that extend well beyond pharmacological care of PLWMI.

No new custodial institutions for PLWMI should be permitted to come up. Only Out Patient Departments (OPDs) and wards in mainstream hospitals and clinics should be available for largely voluntary admissions of patients of mental illness, through their family members or friends.

At the same time, existing mental hospitals should be gradually transformed into rehabilitation centres, half-way homes for patients to prepare them for independent living, family support and counselling and day-care centres.

As a first step, a team of social workers should be constituted to work intensively for the care and rehabilitation of patients and humanising of the institutions. These teams should comprise a core of one or two clinical psychologists or psychiatric social workers, the rest should comprise lay, whole-time volunteers and workers who are selected for suitability of temperament, motivation and commitment, and then are trained intensively. The team should also seek volunteers from among the staff of the mental hospital itself, who wish to participate in the processes of humanising and de-institutionalising mental hospitals.

The regular entry of this team of social workers itself would create an atmosphere of transparency which would reduce some of the worst excesses of the institution. The team would work directly with patients, providing non-pharmacological therapies, and preparing them for re-integration with families and work after discharge. They would also work closely with family members, ensuring them support and counselling, and encouraging them to take care and give fair life chances to PLWMI in their families. Both patients and family members would be trained about the importance of following regular medication and other precautions to prevent relapse, and trained to detect problems when they arise. This group would also try to retrain the rest of the staff, and organise vigilance and monitoring systems to prevent corruption, abuse and neglect of the various kinds listed earlier.

It would also be an important responsibility of the group to prepare patients for occupations after their discharge. The occupations have to be carefully chosen, so that they do not add to the stress of the patients, but instead help restore a sense of self-worth.

There are several advantages to this model of social worker groups working within mental hospitals, with hospital staff. This model does not absolve the state of its responsibilities. It is replicable, accessible to the poorest patients, and works to scale (unlike others—like many half-way homes—which are accessible only to small numbers of well-to-do patients, without state support or responsibility). The groups of social workers may initially demarcate areas within the campus of the institutions for alternative care of patients who are being prepared for discharge, and for active participation of family members. However, eventually the entire character of the institutions itself should be transformed into open, therapeutic, non-custodial, rehabilitative, humane centres for services and care of PLWMI, and their families.

The support of the social worker groups should be available to patients in a structured way even after discharge. Periodical OPD visits, both for counselling and for collecting medicines, may be organised in one section of the hospitals. Home visits should be organised for patients who drop out, or have trouble with their integration.

PROTECTED COMMUNITIES: A LAST RESORT ALTERNATIVE TO CUSTODIAL INSTITUTIONS

It can reasonably be expected that a large majority of patients would in fact be satisfactorily rehabilitated with their families and the community, through these methods. However, it is admitted that even with the most humane partnership of state authorities, professionals and community leaders, there will remain a residue of vulnerable people who cannot survive independently without protection, but who are abandoned by their families or lack functional, responsible families to whom they can be restored. This small residual core of patients would include those who are (a) wantonly abandoned by their family members; (b) homeless persons with mental illness whose families cannot be traced; and (c) PLWMI who have dysfunctional, abusive families which are not conducive to sustained recovery of the patient and their human rights.

At present, if they cannot be restored to families or independent living in the open community, there appears no option except for their retention, often life-long in custodial institutions. However, it is my conviction that for this small core of patients, a lifetime without love and care behind the high walls of institutions is not really an option. Instead, groups of social workers should actively work towards building alternative foster family situations, in which groups of around approximately eight such patients live as a family with a caregiver (a woman, man or couple) in homes in the open community. The caregiver should be given training, a salary and ongoing support. The residents of the foster family should be encouraged to work and participate in the outside community. It may take time for the state to accept this, but a social security stipend to these PLWMI who are without family care should be ensured, as it should be for all persons with disabilities who are deprived of the care and protection of their families. I believe strongly that these forgotten, utterly vulnerable human beings should not be condemned to the loveless incarceration of custodial institutions, not even if this is genuinely seen as a last resort, the only way that they can be physically sustained and protected from abuse. If we believe that every human being counts, we must find a third alternative to custodial institutions or living in the open community. To my mind, this third alternative is in a protected community.

A protected community is essentially a space which is structured as closely as possible to an ordinary community of people. People live in individual homes, with other people they choose to live with, as foster families. They have freedom to derive emotional sustenance from one another. They have opportunities for work, recreation, education and service, but they are not bound to earn their full livelihoods because they are supported by state pensions. They have creative opportunities for healing and growth, in activities like horticulture and theatre.

However, protected communities would differ from ordinary communities, in that all residents and workers are sensitive to the special needs of the various residents and professional therapeutic services are at hand, and free movement of people into and outside the settlement is supervised enough only to prevent abuse and exploitation.

In the end, we will be able to see the collapse of custodial institutions for vulnerable people if those of its residents who can at all live with protection and relative self-reliance in the larger society are assisted and supported in doing so. But for the small residue of abandoned, vulnerable people who cannot survive unprotected in the wider society, we need to creatively ensure that they are still assisted in building and living in protected, supporting caring settlements.

Chapter 10

Dis(ABLED)*
An Invisible Minority

Anita Ghai

Anita Ghai is Professor, School of Human Studies, Ambedkar University, Delhi. She has also taught at the Department of Psychology in Jesus and Mary College, University of Delhi. Her interest is in disability studies and issues of sexuality, psychology and gender. Anita is a former President of the Indian Association for Women's Studies. She has authored the books Re-thinking Disability in India *(2015) and* (Dis)Embodied Form: Issues of Disabled Women *(2003).*

When I was first approached for this essay, I did not visualise any major problems in conceptualising it as I thought that all I needed to share with the readers was how people who are marked by the label 'disability', resist the negative connotations associated with their existential reality. After having done a piece called 'Living in the shadow of my disability' (Ghai, 1998), I decided that this time my focus should not be on struggles that the disabled have to confront. Instead, in keeping with the spirit of the issue, I would trace the positive contributions that disability makes to personal growth. However, when it came to

* This chapter was first published in *The Journal*, Vol. 4(2), December 2002, by the Psychological Foundations Trust, New Delhi.

translating my thoughts into words, I found that to communicate the meaning of any marginal life condition such as disability in a balanced way which neither valorises the experience, nor is stuck on its tragic undertones, can be a daunting task.

Living in a culture largely governed by demands for a perfect body, disability is either rendered totally invisible or accepted as a deficient and lacking life-condition. Consequently, the 70 million disabled people living in India are not accorded the status of being full and contributing citizens of this country. The consistent message is that it is better to be dead than alive, as disabled lives are constructed to be meaningless and valueless. That this sentiment echoes universally is clear from Anne Finger's narrative recounted in *Past due: A story of disability, pregnancy and birth* (Finger, 1990). At a feminist conference, Anne shared her experience about the inhumane treatment she received as a child who had been hospitalised because of complications from Polio. After listening to her experience a colleague told Anne, 'If you had been my child, I would have killed you before I let that happen. I would have killed myself too.' Finger obviously taken aback, remembers her reaction, 'My heart stops. She is telling me I should not be alive. It is my old fear come true: That if you talk about the pain, people will say, "See it isn't worth it." You would be better off dead.' If disabled people are perceived as not having a right to exist, discriminatory attitudes are inadvertently encouraged towards those who live in our societies. As an activist, I have often come across parents, caretakers and professionals, who implicitly or explicitly reiterate that disability is a retribution for past sins and it would have been better had these children not survived. Notwithstanding the nature of the disability, this has been a constant response, Disability is a personal tragedy to be borne alone.

Historically such responses are very rational as a personal tragedy model is applied to disabled people without questioning society's role in constructing that 'tragedy'. Locating the cause and responsibility of disability within the disabled person as his/her 'problem' has been a result of a medical approach to disability, which offers both care and cure to an extent, but the focal point is always the individual. Negation of pain and overcoming the impairment become recurrent themes in a disabled person's life.

In such a scenario, it took years of struggle to assert that disability is not death and is not caused by impairment or dysfunction of the individual. Instead, it is the oppression inherent in a disabling society that changes an impairment into a disability. Is the problem not being able to walk, or is it living in an environment, where the only way architectural design can be aesthetic is by relying on steps or staircases? The assumption is that everyone, regardless of age or even a common problem such as arthritis, can negotiate this terrain. More and more barriers are erected when only one way of seeing, hearing or registering the information is acceptable.

The affirmation that disabled people can do just as much as the non-disabled, apart from obvious things such as not being able to climb or walk, not being able to see and hear in the 'normal' way was highlighted by the social model of disability (as opposed to the medical model of disability). This model propounded that inaccessible societal conditions were instrumental in turning impairment as a medical issue into disability, which is a social oppression. This brought in a definitional shift where, impairment was conceived as lacking part or all of a limb, or having a defective limb, organism or mechanism of the body. Disability, on the other hand was understood as the disadvantage or restriction of activity caused by a contemporary social organisation which takes little or no account of people who have physical impairments, and thus excludes them from the mainstream of social activities (UPIAS, 1976).

This shift undermined the dominant medicalisation of disability and developed more realistic images of strength that resist the dominant discourse. It produced a demand for a more inclusive society that recognises the right to be different, without any negative connotations attached to that 'difference'. This notion of inclusion did not imply that disabled people are seeking to be accepted into the mainstream definition of 'normal'—a definition that is bound to exclude. Rather, the desire to distance from the mainstream values and engage in some deeply creative thinking about values that are dear to disabling existence became more significant. An affirmation of the disabled identity as a socially recognised identity took some doing, as disabled people were not considered competent enough to speak for themselves. Moreover since they are not conceived as part of normal society, all their activities continued in segregated settings, and their lives were seen as projects for programming. Thus, music became music *therapy*, art became art *therapy* and an ordinary interest in drama rendered the disabled as possible candidates for drama *therapy*. The understanding that disabled people too can enjoy the simple pleasures of life was missing. Confronting the tragedy in disability makes many disabled people clarify their values, re-prioritise their lives and redefine their selves into a person they like better. The enrichment and empowerment lies in the role that the disabled person gets to play in re-evaluating society's priorities and in interrogating its tokenistic inclusion of values such as equality. The slogan, 'Nothing about us without us' depicts this resistance, necessitating the right to self-definition and identity.

Disability thus, gives a perspective, an epistemic location from where life can be visualised in entirely different light. A positivistic framework normally views location of author/speaker as a problem that can affect understanding of objective reality. The element of subjectivity is minimised by 'de-historising, de-culturalising and de-bodying the subject with the subsequent production of knowledge'(Michalko, 2001). Consequently, whereas no one is asked to give an account for why he/she is walking, the one who cannot walk is held accountable, but is not considered as providing epistemic advantage or standpoint. This is in contrast to the category 'woman' which as Harstock (1983) would say, offers a standpoint. The assumption is that there is something essential to be experienced and learned from the standpoint of being a woman. The essential purpose of the disability movement is to assert that we too have a standpoint.

As Helen Liggett puts it,

> To participate in their own management disabled people have had to participate as disabled. Even among the politically active, the price of being heard is understanding that it is the disabled who are speaking (Liggett, 1988, p. 271).

Speaking as disabled assumes importance as it assists in rewriting the past and present in a more positive and empowered way. Just as the black feminist writer Patricia Hill Collins affirms,

By insisting on self definition, black women question not only what has been said about African American women, but the credibility and intentions of those possessing the power to define. When Black women define ourselves, we clearly reject the assumption that those in positions granting them the authority to interpret our reality are entitled to do (Collins, 1990, pp. 106–7).

From the vantage point of my own understanding, human identity traverses though a series of locations. Looking back at my own life, I realise that my physical disability acquired at the age of two, though creating a need for constant existential struggle, never assumed predominance. The essential identity in fact was of a middle class girl and later a middle class woman. It was only in my thirties when I experienced an acute sense of discomfort at the exclusion of disabled people from the opportunity to own and express their sexuality that disability became a conscious part of my identity. Adrienne Asch argues that disability is not part of her self-definition or 'lived experience', but it is the basis of most other people's definition of her (Asch, 1976). As my own negotiation with various nuances of disability unfolded I realised that disability assists in the process of recognising the existence of an ontological self. To know a mode of being-in-the-body, of living-in-the-body is in direct contrast to the epistemological self, a sense of self derived from others, a disembodied self, and a self away from the body. Being impaired is a fact of life for most disabled people. Sexuality is severely constrained by disability. However, disability further wraps around class, caste, and the rural/urban divide. In the ultimate analysis it is at these intersections that a negotiation for identity takes place.

Very often doubts are expressed regarding the possibility of a disabled person living a quality life when to the outside observer the individual is seriously disabled. That this can be achieved when the disabled person manages to re-equilibrate their lives into a balance between body, mind and spirit and between themselves and their environments is difficult to accept. The nuances of this attitude can be complex and deep-seated and become evident with projects such as the Human Genome. While a slight shift in the stereotypical images started emerging, the re-medicalisation of disability calls for yet another confrontation. Such projects give consent to policies, which seek to solve the problem of disability by eliminating disabled people.

After asserting for more than three decades that disability is a structural problem, this re-medicalisation has to be resisted. If at all, the real message of genetics is that we are all impaired. Most of us carry four or five recessive conditions, which could generate impairments in our children. Cancer, diabetes, schizophrenia are all problems that can have a genetic basis. Consequently, all this screening is quite impossible. Genetics is not going to work as a solution to the differences and difficulties of human embodiment. In this context, 'disability' only serves to pejoratively label and categorise 'difference'.

Disabled people are often patronised, patted on the back and called brave for succeeding at tasks that they themselves would see as ordinary. To the outer world, success at these tasks seems wonderful because non-disabled people probably have not experienced this mode of living. These problems arise because difference has been represented as a lack or limitation, which has produced hierarchical levels that have not played a constructive role in enhancing an understanding of the 'difference'. Deleuze (1994) elaborates,

> Contradiction is not the weapon of the proletariat but, rather, the manner in which the bourgeoisie defends and preserves itself, the shadow behind which it maintains its claim to decide what the problems are (Deleuze 1994, p. 268).

By putting forward a dichotomy of ability/disability the able-bodied have been able to preserve the status quo because their normalised embodiment decides not only the boundaries of 'what the problem is', but also the possibilities of an open dialogue. It is only when disabled people transgress the boundaries, which within the 'normal' mind are impossible, that a change takes place.

Many of my friends, though sensitive to the limitations imposed on me, remind me of the fact that in a way disability has offered me alternatives in life. While to a psychoanalytically trained mind, it might appear rationalisation of the highest order, it is true that had I not been disabled, my sense of being would have been different. I say this in context of the conservative cultural milieu to which I belong; I would have had to settle for domesticity and then probably would have had to spend my entire life in wearisome relationships! While, this interpretation is certainly debatable, what is significant is that the most invalidating experience at one level can provide an opportunity to go beyond the constraints of mainstream norms, roles and identity. It is for these reasons that a 'diagonal' approach allows a disabled existence to be perceived as one way of being without its automatic negation, or without inversely giving it prominence over non-disabled way of being. If we were to look at difference as 'diagonal' rather than 'hierarchical' then disabled people's way of being would neither be unduly valorised nor devalued but only exist.

It is this recognition that enables me and my disabled friends and companions to live with our disabilities in a way which is neither heroic nor tragic. My experience of residual paralysis that affected my mobility taught me the significance of resisting the fear by sheer negotiation with the self. I have this truly remarkable propensity for falling, which used to cause embarrassment and shame, every time I fell. I often recall a scene in a crowded building in Manhattan, when I tried to get on to an escalator and ended up with one leg on the step and the other leg hanging in the air, my *chunni* (longish scarf) flying in different directions. I watched from the corner of my eye and could read expressions of pity, fear, anxiety, anger, amusement and revulsion, just to name a few. While one part of me remembered the doctor at the medical rehabilitation centre, who would insist on training me to fall in *safe* conditions, so that I learnt to protect myself in *unsafe* conditions, the other part of me tried hard not to register the shame inherent in the experience. Such experiences can never be accepted if one follows the normative culture of an able-bodied society. This is when the collectivity of disability culture comes to the rescue, for that is the space within which you observe other disabled people negotiating similar experiences.

For me, the voice of a fellow disabled person, Leonard Kriegel, reverberated in my mind. After persistent resistance to his therapist who insisted on teaching him how to fall, he finally caved in and did what the therapist wanted him to do. Kriegel recalls that experience,

> I was not seized by the usual paroxysm of fear. I didn't feel myself break
> out in terrified sweat. It was over. I don't mean that I suddenly felt

myself spring into courage.... The truth was that I had simply been worn into letting go, like a boxer in whose eyes one recognizes not the flicker of defeat—which issue never having been in doubt—but the acceptance of defeat. Letting go no longer held my imagination captive. I found myself quite suddenly faced with a necessary fall—a fall into life (Kriegel 1997, p. 44).

For the onlookers, perhaps it is difficult to understand the complexity of the situation, as falling is more than being metaphorical for us. It takes years before one realises that there is learning involved in it. Just as a baby learns to crawl, to stand and then to walk, we learn how to fall and then get up again. Despite the sense of acute discomfort, there is no other way of getting out of the situation except a direct confrontation with one's own realisation of limitations and finding a lighter side to it. Kriegel says,

I was a willing convert, one who now secretly enjoyed demonstrating his ability to fall? I enjoyed the surprise that would greet me as I got to my feet unscathed however perverse it may seem.... I felt myself in control of my own capacity. For falling had become the way my body sought out its proper home (Kriegel 1997, p. 45).

Similarly most of us hope to generate laughter each and every time we fall or cannot read something, as there is no other way in which the incongruities of the situation can be dealt with. The ability to laugh in such situations can be truly emancipating. As Berger (1997), says that in some instances, laughing at one's self or with others redefines the experience. And redefinition is a must for it is only then that one can subvert the preconceived categories of identity that devalue both a disabled embodiment and sensibility. It is only then that understanding of experience not in the sense of either an essentialist identity of disability or ability, 'but as a continuous generative source' can be generated (Game 1991).

My submission is that though politically essential, actually a divide cannot be created on grounds of impairment. In fact many non-disabled people have impairments. Moreover, the contention that disabled people are oppressed and non-disabled people are not, is essentially incorrect.

Most classifications of disability do not take into account differences within the category itself. There are many disabled people who are not disadvantaged on other dimensions such as socio-economic status, gender, caste or religion. And there is no guarantee that the oppressed people will not become oppressors. The danger is of a movement which makes the disabled identity an essential identity and ignores the fact that not everyone with impairment identifies politically as disabled. The category as a real life condition might be used in order to get certain benefits, but it should not be a primary identification. The risk of over-investment in identity politics has to be recognised. A fixed disabled identity should not be posited because disabled people, too, are different from each other. Yet difference has to be balanced with solidarity, and that is what the disability movement is all about. To say that it is a homogenous movement will mean overlooking the intrinsic differences, which are a part of any collective. Within India, the disability movement is passing through different stages of activism. The pace is slow. So much so, a discernible impact might not be evident. Undoubtedly, even the tip of the iceberg has not been touched. However, the disabled are feeling much more empowered to highlight the oppression of disabled people.

Perhaps Nietzsche was right in affirming that one needs to embrace illness through illness. Nietzsche hoped to create new meaning.... You must see and interpret the world in a different way. As Colin Cameron writes in Tyneside Disability arts,

> We are who we are as people with impairments, and might actually feel
> comfortable with our lives if it was not for all those interfering busy-
> bodies who feel that it is their responsibility to feel sorry for us or to
> find cures for us, or to manage our lives for us, or to harry us in order
> to make us something we are not, i.e. normal (Cameron, 1999, p. 3).

Thus neither the assertion to claim a 'quality' life will be haunting, nor the need to be always normalising the disability. This also has the potential of subverting the attempts that denigrate or pity us because we are representations of what can go wrong with humanity's fragile existence. The experience of disability can become instrumental in the creation of a new meaning of life.

On innumerable occasions, I have asked this question to myself, 'Would I, if given an opportunity, become non-disabled again? (which in my case means that I would be able to walk again)' The answer according to a simple common conjecture should be a simple yes. After years of asserting that I am writing from the vantage point of a woman with visible physical impairment, I am suddenly very sceptical about this assertion. While it is true that disabling experiences are critical to identity formation and a fight for rights is imperative, however, what also needs to be communicated is that disability cannot be the sole index of an individual's identity. While as a collective the disabled definitely wish to celebrate their strength and resistance, the need to be accepted as individual human beings and not as full-time disabled people cannot be overemphasised.

I think this assertion is quite significant as it epitomises the fact that resistance is a precondition for advocacy of the cause. The attention of mainstream society can be drawn only when those who find it difficult to work in the conventional norms and boundaries raise their voices. Their success comes from the values that inform their work, the forthrightness of their stories and the resonance of their work with what others experience in their lives.

I am not denying that we need civil rights legislations and changed policies, and the removal of barriers. There is a need to relocate the problem of disability from 'them' to the environment and the constructions of culture. People are disabled not by their bodies, but by society. However all this can be accomplished only when there is a shift in individual consciousness. Disabled people need to feel the sense of empowerment, so that they can be liberated from the stigma of inadequacy and are encouraged to express the anger of oppression.

REFERENCES

Asch, A. (1976). Adrienne Asch: Civil Rights Investigator. In H. Rousso, S. Gunshee, O'Malley and M. Severance (Eds), *DISABLED Female and Proud*. Boston, MA: Exceptional Parent Press.

Berger, P.L. (1997). *Redeeming Laughter: The Comic Dimension of Human Experience*. New York: Walter de Gruyter.

Cameron, C. (1999). *Transgressions*. Wallsend, Tyneside Disability Arts Pg. 35.

Collins, P. (1990). *Black feminist thought: Knowledge, consciousness and the politics of empowerment*. Boston. MA: Unwin Hymen.

Deleuze, G. (1994). *Difference and Repetition*, trans. Paul Patton. New York: Columbia University Press.

Finger, A. (1990). *Past Due: A Story of Disability, Pregnancy and Birth*. Seattle: The Seal Press.

Game, A. (1991). *Undoing the Social: Towards a Deconstructive Sociology*. Toronto: University of Toronto Press.

Ghai, A. (1998). Living in the shadow of my disability. *The Journal* 2(1): 32–36.

Harstock, M.C.N. (1983). The feminist standpoint: Developing the ground for a specifically feminist historical materialism. In S. Harding and M.B. Hintikka (Eds), *Feminist thought discovering reality: Feminist perspectives on epistemology, methodology and philosophy of science*. Boston: D. Reidel.

Kriegel, L. (1997). Falling into life. In K. Fries (Ed.), *Staring Back: The Disability Experience from the Inside Out*. New York: Penguin Books Ltd.

Liggett, H. (1988). Stars are not born: An interpretive approach to the politics of disability. *Disability, Handicap and Society*, 3: pp. 263–276.

UPIAS. (1976). *The Fundamental Principles of Disability*. London: UPIAS.

Chapter 11

Worrying about the Family*

Rachana Johri

Rachana Johri is Professor at the School of Human Studies, Ambedkar University, Delhi. Prior to this she taught Psychology at Lady Shri Ram College for Women, University of Delhi. At Ambedkar University, she teaches Psychology, Psychosocial Studies and Gender Studies. Although her academic degrees are in the discipline of Psychology, her research interest and writing has consistently revolved around issues of gender.

For psychologists, the family is a central place from which all human life begins to take meaning and this is even more so for therapists. After all, where else do therapists turn to look for answers to questions regarding self-esteem, personhood and emotional well-being? I also have been trained to see the family as an institution designed to meet human needs—a universal natural outcome from universal needs.

Yet, two issues have always troubled me, and the two theoretical inputs of social anthropology and feminism buttress these concerns. The first concerns the ease with which we refer to *the family*. We refer to the family as if underlining everything we know to be different, there is that basic ever-present entity among all family units: *the*

*This chapter was first published in *The Journal*, Vol. 2(2), December 2000, by the Psychological Foundations Trust, New Delhi.

family—although we do know that there are many types of families and that each family is unique and that sociology and anthropology have provided a good vantage point through which to discover the sheer variety in families. The second issue relates to the fact that, as a feminist, I find that the family is the seat of some of the worst forms of oppression and that rigorous feminist theory has helped to unravel the power structures that operate in families.

When a friend gifted me a copy of a book called *Rethinking the Family* edited by Thorne and Yalom (1992), I was rather delighted. Always hooked to the idea of rethinking, and at that time involved in rethinking mother-daughter relations, I turned with some excitement to the book. The book was a new edition of a popular text on feminist questions about the family. Reading it helped me to deal with my own concerns in a more systematic manner. I learnt from this book that the social scientific understanding of the universal family goes back to the works of the renowned anthropologist, Malinowski, who first proposed that *the family* existed in all societies including the most primitive.

Malinowski believed, as do most of us, that families had to exist in order to nurture children. As a consequence, all families had, according to him, three features:

1. The families had clear boundaries. This defined which adults were considered responsible for a particular set of children.
2. Families shared a physical space, the concept of a home and a hearth.
3. Family members experienced a particular set of emotions, namely, *family love.*

This seems to constitute our definition of a family, although as psychologists, we generally give priority to the last feature.

However, in their piece in *Rethinking...,* Collier, Rosaldo and Yanagisako point out that there are cultures which do not possess a word for the family. In other cultures, there is no definite home and hearth in which familial activities are performed. There may be gendered living arrangements: all the men living in one house and all the women in the other; and married couples may often sleep apart, meeting only for sexual intercourse. As for *family love,* even in Indian society (internecine battles between siblings or close relatives over property are common enough), wives and husbands often did not, and indeed, were not, supposed to share love for each other.

Because this essay is based on a series of unresolved questions about the nature of families, in our understanding of psychology and psychotherapy, as in other unresolved matters, there is a certain incoherence and mix up of ideas. I know today that we cannot speak of the *universal family*. I also understand that families are contextually linked to other aspects of the social system. I believe that the family has the potential to teach us to love and care, support and share, and provide us with that all-important sense of emotional bonding. Yet families also teach us to exclude and to draw boundaries between people. Whether in matters of *love,* ethnicity or property, it is often the family that teaches us our first lessons in dividing human beings into categories. This is the place where love begins but it is here that we see also the products of its failures.

Looking at my own development in conceptualising *the family,* for as long as I can remember, I *knew* that families are a universal social institution. The primary task of families was to bring up children. Societies did *vary* in the kinds of families they generated, but for me the typical family was the *nuclear family.* This was made up of a husband and wife and their two children. Husbands and wives loved (or tried to) each other and their children. Their primary task was to help the kids to grow up well, to provide them with a good education and self-confidence so that they get jobs, find partners, move on in the world and become independent. Once they became adults, the worlds of these children and their parents would be largely separated. The adult children would meet their parents occasionally and their relationship would be one of *love* and concern but their lives would be essentially separate.

Of course, I had heard of joint families and I had seen mothers-in-law on television. I do remember the all-pervading demonised figure of Lalita Pawar, terrorising *bahu* after bahu, in Hindi films. But then Hindi films were never a vital part of my life although I still remember the anger I felt when I saw Dharmendra throwing a sobbing, pleading Nutan out of the house (I think the film was *Dulhan Ek Raat Ki*), or as I watched a Meena Kumari crying her heart out over an uncaring husband. I would ask, 'Why don't they just walk out?' In my mind, joint families were an archaic phenomenon. Of course, there were still parts of India that were uneducated and irrational. Joint families belonged there, somewhere. The same applied to arranged marriages. I had it all well worked out! By the time you were 16 years old, you came across a boy you liked well enough to date. Around 25 years of age, you were sure of the person you wanted to marry and somewhere along the way you did. Then you had children and the story continued. As I grew up, however, it became increasingly clear that the family, even as I imagined it, is not always so perfect a place. I found that the family was not always a happy place, particularly for women. It was not so much because of the women themselves, many of whom were remarkably resilient, but the relationships in which they were embedded, that placed them in oppressed positions, very often relationships that were supposed to be of *love*.

Yet, for many years, I continued to feel that the problem had to do with the type of family we were dealing with. We, as modern educated women, were not going to find ourselves in such positions. My first surprise came when I saw the women in my class at college opting for arranged marriages. I was confused when I saw friends, who had worked much harder than me for their degrees, suddenly get engaged in their final year, easily joking: 'Guess I should administer the 16 PF to them before I decide which one to marry.' More confusing were the girls who had sworn they would marry their boyfriends, but suddenly changed their minds to marry the husbands their parents had found for them. Some years later, it dawned on me that joint families not only existed, they were the prevailing norm.

Indian family life has been closely linked to procreation. A woman was, and often is defined by her ability to produce a child, particularly a male child. I knew this and also that mothers routinely opt for foetal sex-determination tests. For me, this was a puzzle. Why would mothers, especially those who were educated and sometimes from the most liberal of backgrounds, accept such choices? I understood by and by that these were because of an internalisation of patriarchal processes. It was also apparent that women were under pressure to have male children. But this was still too generalised an understanding. How could mothers who had been through the best of liberal education decide to abort a child, because she was a daughter? Worse, could I assume that the decision to abort one daughter might mean that she could not love her other daughters? What did all this imply about *family love*?

It was in search of a framework through which to answer these questions that I first started reading up on culture. Nancy Scheper-Hughes' paper on mother love (1990) in a Brazilian community immediately captured my imagination. Here, Hughes describes a poor community with extremely high levels of infant mortality. A doctor, feminist and anthropologist herself, she speaks of the horror she experienced when she saw mothers of infants drinking up tonics and using lotions doctors had prescribed for their babies. These mothers did not show the usual signs of love for their babies. There was little eye contact, feeding was perfunctory, few efforts made to save their baby from imminent death, and little mourning after its death.

How does this fit into the narrative of the family, as a space for the maintenance of emotional ties? If we accept this as one cultural variation in the practice of mother love, we need to rework either our definition of love or of families. Letting children die does not fit easily into either. Are these mothers devoid of *normal* emotion? Are they incapable of love and grief? Scheper-Hughes responds to this by contrasting the scenario after a baby's death with that of grieving the death of a grown-up child. During the latter, the mother was heartbroken and this conforms to our understanding of maternal love.

I have found mothers who have mourned over their inability to have a son to be very caring towards their daughters. Conversely, mothers who have fought hard to give equal opportunities in all spheres to their daughters, might completely reject giving them any freedom in marriage. During my work on my PhD thesis ('Cultural Conceptualization of Maternal Attachment,' 1999), I spoke with a mother of three daughters. In my report, I called her *Archana*.

Archana had lost both her parents very early in life. The early years of her marriage had also not been easy. She spoke with tremendous pain of the moments when her first daughter was born. Her mother-in-law, refusing to celebrate the child's birth, had wondered aloud if it would not have been better for the child to die. Despite a profound sense of anger and despair, Archana fought back. Beginning with the insistence that she would celebrate, she went on to do the same for each of her three daughters. She was aware of sex-determination techniques; indeed her doctor suggested that she opt for this procedure at the time of the third pregnancy, but she did not. As a mother, believing that daughters must be equipped for economic independence, despite opposition from the family, she gave her daughters the best possible opportunities, sending them to co-educational schools and training them to handle most spheres of life independently.

I find it difficult to capture in this short space the many moments of loneliness that Archana encountered in providing these facilities to her daughters. Yet, Archana could not bring herself to support her daughter's desire to marry a man of her own choice, because he did not belong to their community. She was aware of the contradiction this created for her daughter. Archana had not been able to imagine that emancipation in some domains might result in the freeing up in all domains, here, that of desire, the opening out of sexuality. She herself had completely separated out the sexual domain and she assumed that the same would happen with her daughter.

Archana saw herself as a loving mother. However, she was also tied to her very conservative community. It had taken her years to be accepted by the community. Today, she occupies a position of respect. In the village to which she belongs, people have begun to value the role of education in daughters' lives. The mother-in-law, who once did nor eat food for days because Archana had given birth to the third daughter, now adores her granddaughters. However, marriage outside the community was an area of current taboo. Archana described herself as being in a *dharmsankat*. She understood her daughter's pain, but felt that the daughter could not understand hers. How could she, after spending her whole life resisting the community's pressures yet maintaining her ties with them, give in to her daughter's desire?

I never spoke to Archana's daughter. I do know that ultimately the daughter accepted her mother's wishes. Now I partly understood why my classmates had opted for arranged marriages. Even without speaking to the daughter, I could imagine her pain. Yet, I could also see clearly the terrible anguish Archana herself was going through. She too, wanted her daughter to understand.

For me Archana's story symbolises the problems in understanding *family love* in these changing times. I cannot say that Archana was not a loving mother. However, her mother's identity was embedded within the identity of wife, daughter-in-law, and upper caste woman. In fact, her story is even more complex. This same Archana has also supported a niece, encouraging her to opt out of an oppressive marriage. Despite my feminism, I could not condemn Archana.

Clearly love is culturally scripted. I'm not necessarily comfortable with those scripts. As a feminist psychologist, I do criticise a society in which the mother has no choice but to produce baby after baby, or worse still, only sons. I presume that all societies have ongoing debates and internal critiques of the practices they see as oppressive.

My question has to do with our understanding of families and *family love* as therapists. Given the variety within our cultural context, are we sufficiently attuned to it? Can we be equally sympathetic towards both the daughter, whose autonomy has been curbed, and the mother, who needs her daughter to remain a member of her community? As a feminist, can I afford to identify only with the daughter, creating unwittingly a narrative of mother-blame?

Does psychological knowledge constitute an area of expertise that must be imposed on cultural groups who disagree with its assumptions? Alternatively, can cultural practices be sanctioned simply because they are accepted by a large majority? How do we understand the mother who insists that her definition of mother love is to get her daughter married in a particular way? I know all good therapists listen carefully to the voice of their clients and respond to the specificity of their experience. As therapists, we need to help our clients to either move away from disturbed families or reconstruct a healthier set of relationships with them. In order to do so we often examine notions of love, family and loyalty. In India, I fear that our training makes us available and sensitive only to those who share our cultural space. Our frames of reference foster individuality. At the same time, we retain faith in the institution of the family. Could it be possible to define therapy as giving space to marginal voices? In this sense therapy and psychology can be quite radical.

Despite my concerns about appreciating cultural stances I would be the last to advocate that we reinforce oppressive voices within our culture. Yet, reworking requires appropriate frames of reference. We could begin by acknowledging vast differences in the ideology that governs family life. We could begin to appreciate that all dominant cultural positions are likely to be oppressive. Personally, I doubt if any form of the family can be genuinely non-oppressive. I have my doubts about whether any family system can be genuinely fair to all, the old and young, women and men, the disabled and the disturbed. I worry that we have no other systems to turn to. For the large part, the family is our only resource and our only scapegoat.

I seem to have come full circle. There was a time when I knew for sure what family and family life were. Today I am not so convinced. I'm neither sure about the universality of families or of their essential goodness. I do feel that we need to listen carefully for differences and then work out where there is oppression and what spaces exist within each of these forms of family.

REFERENCES

Johri, R. (1999). 'Cultural Conceptions of Maternal Attachment. The Case of the Girl Child'. Unpublished PhD. dissertation. University of Delhi.

Scheper-Hughes, N. (1990). 'Mother love and child death in north-east Brazil'. In J.W. Stigler, R. Shweder & G. Herdt. (Eds), *Cultural Psychology Essays in Comparative Human Development*. Cambridge University Press.

Thorne, B. & Yalom, M. (Eds), (1992). *Rethinking the Family: Some Feminist Questions*. North Eastern Press.

Part II

Impact and Intervention

Chapter 12

Working Systematically with Family Violence*

Reenee Singh

Dr Reenee Singh is a Consultant Family and Couples Systemic Psychotherapist, currently working at the Child and Family Practice in London. She is the CEO of the Association of Family Therapy and Systemic Practice in the UK and the co-director of the Tavistock Family Therapy and Systemic Research Centre. Reenee is the former editor of The Journal of Family Therapy, *one of the editors of* Psychological Foundations: The Journal, *and is currently editing* The Handbook of Systemic Family Therapy, *which will be published in 2019. Reenee has written and published two books and numerous articles and chapters in books, mostly on issues of 'race', culture, intercultural couples and qualitative research. She presents her work at national and international conferences and teaches all over the world. To find out more about her, please visit her website at www.reeneesingh.com.*

The family, hardly that haven in a heartless world is actually our most violent institution other than the military at war.

—Goldner, 1999, p. 325.

*This chapter was first published in *The Journal*, Vol. 3(1), June 2001, by the Psychological Foundations Trust, New Delhi.

In this case example, I shall describe a few aspects of my ongoing work with the C family. Names and identifying details have been disguised to protect confidentiality.

Mrs C, a 40-year-old upper class English woman, referred herself to the clinic for concerns regarding her five-year-old son, Joshua. He was distracted and difficult to control, both at home and at school. His teachers complained about his lack of concentration and the fact that he was frequently aggressive towards his peers.

The onset of his symptoms coincided with his father leaving home 18 months ago, around the same time that his sister, Samantha was born. According to Mrs C, Joshua had witnessed his father being violent towards her. After he left the marital home, Joshua's father had sporadic contact with him at first, during which he had been violent towards Joshua once. Subsequently, contact had ceased and when I first met Joshua, he had not seen or heard from his father for the last one year.

To date, I have had 17 sessions with the C family, over a period of a year and a half. I am currently working towards termination.

ALLOWING SPACE FOR MESS

The first thing that struck me about this family was the *messiness* of our sessions. The quality of family interaction was chaotic and frag-mented—the children would run around the room, spilling drinks, opening cupboards and flinging out toys that were soon discarded. Mrs C would shout and threaten but was ineffectual in restoring semblance of order. Just as the children competed for their mother's attention, Mrs C seemed to be competing with them for my attention, so that it was impossible to engage anybody in a conversation. The messiness and levels of noise interfered with my thinking—this was not a family that I could *fit* into a clean, coherent framework, a theo-retical framework of understanding that would translate into a clear treatment plan and interventions that worked. My first instinct was to prise the mother and son apart, to send them to separate sanitised cells for individual treatment—surely there was nothing that I, working within a training context and within the constraints of a systemic model, could offer?

Instead I stayed with the mess and muddled along. In retrospect, I am convinced that working with the whole family was the best treatment option at the time, for although Mrs C would undoubtedly have benefited from long-term individual work, it is highly unlikely that she would have sought out such psychotherapeutic help for herself. She needed access to a clinic through the route of her son's problems.

Further, in working with the entire family, I promoted a sense of agency in her, instilling confidence in her own parenting capabilities. When they first came to see me, she was so overwhelmed by her responsibilities as a single parent and her history of being abused that she wanted to pass Joshua on to an *expert,* to a professional who would *fix* him and then hand him back to her repaired. Although I did see him alone for a couple of sessions, I deliberately resisted her attempts to hand him over to me. Over a period of time, partly because I continued to see the family together, I began to function less as a conduit, as a channel of communication between them, and she became increasingly able to relate to him on her own. In seeing the family together for the most part, I avoided the pitfall of becoming Joshua's champion, a role that would have been only too easy especially in the context of his good relationship with me and his mother's overly rigid ways of disciplining him. In allying myself with Joshua, I would have risked both alienating and disempowering Mrs C.

I now recognise that the messiness that first struck me about this case is a hallmark of many families where violence is prevalent. I understood it as related to issues of control and fear of loss of control that frequently emerge in the discourse of abuse. In this case, understandably, Mrs C was hyper-vigilant and terrified of losing control. As the subject of violence in her marriage, she must have experienced a shameful and frightening loss of control. With her children, she employed often unrealistic and rigid standards of behaviour and control. This seemed to set up a recursive pattern, a vicious cycle, where the more mess was not allowed or tolerated and the tighter it was clamped down up on, the more likely it was to erupt. Thus, in my work with the C family, my interventions have been to allow a space for mess while simultaneously setting firm boundaries about behaviour that is not acceptable in the therapy room. These seemingly simple interventions seemed to have provided a safe and *containing space* for the family.

OLD-FASHIONED KINDNESS AND NURTURE

There appears to be nothing in the recent systemic literature on family violence about kindness or nurture. Yet this comprised a large part of my early work with the C family. Perhaps the origins of this approach lie in the re-parenting model of child abuse (Dale, 1986) where the goal of therapy is to foster parents' emotional development to a point where they can parent more effectively. My intent, however, was not to re-parent Mrs C, or even to model *good* parenting for her. I introduced and conceptualised nurture for this family in the manner of the narrative approaches to family therapy (White and Epston, 1990). White and Epston argue that we have stories to tell about our lives and experiences, stories that we learn from our families and from the larger culture. Some of these stories lie within a dominant discourse of the ways in which we think and know about ourselves, in which others are marginalised. When Mrs C spoke about her family of origin and their upper class English values, it became clear that this was a place where children received little nurture. They were brought up by nannies and briskly told to *get up* and *get on with it* if they hurt themselves. Consistent with the norms of their social class, they were sent away to boarding school at a young age. Mrs C, then, had no template for nurturing parenting. She related to her children with a pronounced lack of comfort or empathy. During our third session, I remarked on the punishing standard she set for herself and for the children.

At the beginning of the fourth session, she reported that she had been upset with me and had understood my remark during the last session to mean that Joshua's problems were all 'her fault'. With the help of my supervisor, at the end of that session, I offered her an intervention about the stories that had been *served up to her*. I said that the stories seemed to have been about blame and criticism and that perhaps she had not been offered any stories about being kind and gentle to herself.

This intervention seemed to shift something for the family and marked the beginning of her being able to empathise with Joshua, as illustrated in the transcribed excerpt below:

An earlier conversation (before the fourth session):

Mrs C: He (Joshua) just doesn't listen.
T: What do you think he might be thinking about when he doesn't listen?
Mrs C: He knows I'm going to take away all his toys if he doesn't listen.

After the fourth session:

Mrs C: He doesn't come out of the bath when I tell him to.
T: What do you think that's about?
Mrs C: Maybe the bath's so warm and pleasant that he doesn't feel like coming out.

I understood the later conversation to mean that Mrs C was beginning to develop an ability to put herself in her son's shoes and I speculated that this developed from her receiving the idea of nurture in therapy.

Hypothesising that Joshua's symptoms of aggressiveness and lack of concentration had to do with the fact that he was continually distracted by processing the story of the violence that occurred in his family, the major thrust of my work has been to help him construct a story about the violence. My attempts in this direction have been embedded within the theme of helping him and Mrs C jointly piece together the story of why Joshua's father left.

My conceptual understanding of the clinical relevance of my interventions is based on Dowling and Barnes' (2000) work on the effects of separation and divorce on child-development and family relationships. Drawing on Attachment Theory, Bowlby (1988) and Dowling and Barnes (2000) use the concept of *internal working models* (Main, Caplan and Cassidy, 1985) to explain the way in which children represent and construct relationships. Internal working models are defined as 'affectively laden mental representations of the self, other

and of the relationship derived from interactional experience' (p. 107).
Dowling and Barnes (2000) posit that if a part of the working model
of a relationship includes violence, this then becomes a pattern that
children use, as a way of expressing themselves, playing both hitter
and hit in a number of different models (Main, et al., 1985) that do not
include violence.

Within a family session, Joshua was able to say, 'I want a new Daddy.
My Dad was mean. I saw him hit my mother and I was scared. Another
time, he banged my head against wall.' We were also able to talk about
the happy recollections. He drew a picture and talked about the time
when his father took him to the zoo. I helped to expand his internal
repertoire of family relationships, for example, his relationship with a
loving aunt and her family, which was characterised by an absence of
violence. I highlighted the importance of and also *the difficulty* in having
these conversations to Mrs C, who began to think about the possibility
of engaging Joshua in similar conversations at home.

GENDER ISSUES

Mrs C related to both her children differently. While she tended to be
negligent and harsh towards both of them, she singled Joshua out for
particularly punitive forms of discipline. A conversation in one of my
individual sessions with her about the meaning of gender in her own
family of origin did not go far. I understood her treatment of Joshua
to carry shades of her fear that, in his aggression, he would grow up
to be like his father. She thus began to counter his aggression with
more aggression. Dowling and Barnes (2000) write eloquently on
this issue:

> ... There are problems for boys when their violent fathers disappear
> from their lives. We have found that where husband has been violent,
> even very small pieces of bad behaviour by a son may carry a stigma of
> being "just like your father". Whether or not the father is still active in
> the life of the son, he is still active in the mind of the mother; and many
> attributions may be made towards the behaviour of sons which can
> contribute to confirming violent behaviour, rather than freeing them
> to develop other of relating to their mothers around of issues.

Mrs C is not yet in a place where she would be able to receive and make use of these insights about violence. Hence, I have been working more obliquely and behaviourally. I have been helping her to expand her ideas about Joshua's behaviour, so that she does not automatically relegate it to 'out of control' aggressive male behaviour. When she compares him unfavourably to Samantha, remarking that she hopes that Samantha doesn't grow up to be like him, I engage her in a discussion about the differences in the circumstances that might result in the differences that she observes; thus averting a dichotomy between 'good girl' and 'bad boy' behaviour. Working from a feminist perspective, I continue to question her assumptions behind the statement that Joshua can only relate to men, and to her sense of failure in not having a man in her life.

CREATING A REFLECTIVE CAPACITY WHILE WORKING WITH THE CONCRETE

The words *reflection* and *reflexive* have become increasingly popular in recent systemic thinking. It is beyond the scope of this article to enter into a discussion about the meanings and usefulness of these terms. Here, I use the term *reflective* loosely, to mean the capacity to step back and think about the multiple meanings of a situation, intrapersonal or interpersonal process. My work with the C family is geared towards creating a shift from reactivity to an ability to stay with and think about a concern.

As with others who have lived with the destructive effects of family violence, Mrs C's usual way of dealing with the world is characterised by fragmentation, dissociation and denial. An example of this is that she recently described to me a car accident that she had been in where she broke her nose. Without a pause, she went on to describe how Joshua had got an exceptionally good school report. I stopped her, pointedly, and explored the effects of the accident on her and the family, expressing my bewilderment at her glossing over something so important and reaffirming that she needed to take care of herself. Much of my later work has been just this: to facilitate an ability to pause, stop and explore, rather than deny or react immediately.

As a part of this process, I introduced a *reflecting team* (Andersen, 1987) into the fourteenth session, which comprised three members of my team who shared their ideas about their observations of family process. While Mrs C initially responded well to the team's interventions, in subsequent sessions, she found it difficult to recall and register the conversation. As a result, I have decided against using a reflecting team with this family although I may still invite one colleague into the room to have a reflecting conversation with me. The danger of working with a reflecting team in this case is that it could take over Mrs C's fledgling reflective capacity. It also seems to interfere with existing boundaries between the therapy room and the room behind the screen, with the children running between the two rooms during the session. This disrupts the session and dilutes the relationship between the therapist and the family.

From the beginning of my work with this family, I have been faced with the challenge of Mrs C's *concrete-ness,* her lack of verbal ability and insight. Fairly early on in the work, after we had established a relationship, I shared my dilemma with her and asked how she conceptualised the therapy we were engaged in. Was it only about finding strategies to deal with Joshua's behaviour, or was it also about developing an understanding of relationships? She responded by saying that she thought it was both, which gave me the mandate to help her with her reflective capacity. However, she still responds best to the concrete, so I now use this mode more often with her. For example, when I ask her a question about how much she thought that Joshua's behaviour had improved, I frame my question in terms of a scale from 0 to 10. In the absence of a shared way of working through language, I have examined my preferred style of working with beliefs and meanings and am evolving a far more *basic* style that revolves around play and that questions the therapist's implicit bias towards the verbal, articulate client.

TRANSFERENCE AND SELF REFLEXIVITY

Unfortunately, systemic therapy has not clearly articulated position on transference and on how to work with it. In this case, both Mrs C's and Joshua's emotional ties to me, to the team and even to the clinic and building, are apparent and have implications for termination and future work. In systemic terms, we have become an important part of the family system.

Mrs C negotiated her intimacy with me carefully, which I understood to be related to her wish to take some control of the process. She used the differences in our race, culture and class as part of the delicate tension between dependency and denying need, between inclusion and exclusion. In one instance from the fifteenth session, when Samantha was constructing a family from dolls in the therapy room, Joshua demanded that I be included in the family. Mrs C picked up a black doll, saying firmly, 'This is Reenee.'

Her stories about her family of origin included stories about their colonial times in India. The effect that such stories and the doll instance had on me was that I wondered whether she perceived me as an ayah who was playing a nurturing but subservient role to her family. When I first introduced the reflecting team, she welcomed them into our shared space, perhaps hoping that their similarity of race and culture would lead to magical solutions, solutions that I had not been able to produce.

With the luxury of a supervisor and team to consult with, I have worked with my reactions, and my perceptions of her reactions to the racial and cultural differences between us. I have thought too about the effect her abusive behaviour towards Joshua and the family's stories of violence have on me, especially when they brush up against my own insider knowledge of family violence. As a result, I have been able to remain firmly lodged within the therapist-family system, despite her occasional attempts to dismiss me, and occasional despair about whether I have achieved anything in the last year and a half with this family.

ETHICAL CONSIDERATIONS AND TERMINATION ISSUES

I would like to emphasise that I have worked with the C family in this way because it is a family where there is no current, ongoing abuse. Although Mrs C is often unduly harsh with Joshua, her behaviour does not fit into the category of *significant harm,* a category that, in this country and context, would necessarily entail Social Services involvement in the case. I would work differently if I were working with a family where there was ongoing violence, where my first ethical consideration would be to stop the abuse or the violence. I have chosen to write about my work with the C family rather than families where there is ongoing abuse, because I believe that this family exemplifies many others, where, as therapists, we are required to work with the long-lasting repercussions or effects of family violence.

I have mentioned earlier that I have worked with this family as a part of my clinical training, which will draw to a close in the next two months. Terminating my long-term work with the C family has become necessary. However, even without my training needs, my sense for a while has been that there is not much more that a systemic model can offer the family at this point in time. Given Joshua's age and from my observations of his rich play and the good use that he has made of his limited individual time with me, I believe that he would benefit enormously from individual child psychotherapy. I have thus referred him to a child psychotherapist in the building and will speak to her about the need to keep Mrs C involved and engaged in his treatment.

CONCLUDING COMMENTS

Goldner (1999) suggests that we need a multiplicity of perspectives to understand the multi-levelled complexity of family violence. In my description of work with the C family, I have touched on the levels that it encompassed: the intrapsychic, the interactional, the family of origin and the effects of the wider systems of race, culture, class and gender within a training context. My work with this family has often felt choppy and difficult. Perhaps this is inevitable when working with a family that has been through long-term, transgenerational emotional deprivation, neglect, violence and abuse. During the course of the treatment, I found that I had to think fast on my feet and work immediately in the here and the now, abandoning the certainty of theoretical understanding and favoured techniques in the interest of fostering a good relationship with the family. The conceptual frameworks that I have described in this article followed post-script from my interventions. I would like to invite the reader into a dialogue about alternate interventions and treatment models that they think may have been useful with the C family.

REFERENCES

Anderson, T. (1987). 'The reflecting term: dialogue and meta-dialogue in clinical work'. *Family Processes 26*: pp. 415–428.

Bowlby, J. (1998). 'Beyond rational control: anger, violence and mental illness'. In Dowling, E., & Barnes, G.G. (2000) *Working with Children and Parents through Separation and Divorce*. London: Macmillan.

Dale, P. (1986) *Dangerous Families*. London: Tavistock Publications.

Dowling, E. & Barnes, G.G. (2000). 'Beyond rational control: anger, violence and mental illness'. In Dowling, E. & Barnes, G.G. (2000) *Working with Children and Parents through Separation and Divorce*. London: Macmillan.

Goldner, V. (1999). 'Morality and multiplicity: perspectives on the treatment of violence in intimate life'. *Journal of Marital and Family Therapy 23(3)*: pp. 325–336.

Main, M., Kaplan, N. & Cassidy J. (1985). Cited in Dowling, E. & Barnes, G.G. (2000). 'Beyond rational control: anger, violence and mental illness'. In Dowling, E. & Barnes, G.G. (2000) *Working with Children and Parents through Separation and Divorce*. London: Macmillan.

White, M. & Epston, D. (1990). *Narrative Means to Therapeutic Ends*. New York: W.W. Norton.

Chapter 13

Reducing Violence in People with Mental Disorders*

Gayatri Marjara, Satya Pillai, Seema Prakash and Frank Zurmuehlen

Sanjivini is a registered non-profit organisation founded in 1976 in Delhi, working in the area of mental health and offering free and confidential services. The Sanjivini Day Centre provides day care for mentally ill persons. Sanjivini creates awareness about mental health issues through its community outreach programmes, referral services and support groups.

Gayatri Marjara, Satya Pillai, Seema Prakash and Frank Zurmuehlen were working at the Sanjivini Day Centre when this essay was written.

People with mental illness can often be violent. Sometimes this violence has a greater psychological than physical impact, when clients threaten, harass or verbally abuse their family members. Clients may also be physically abusive, pushing, biting, scratching, hitting out at others, and sometimes causing a great deal of injury. In this essay we

---

* This chapter was first published in *The Journal*, Vol. 3(1), June 2001, by the Psychological Foundations Trust, New Delhi.

describe the work we are doing at Sanjivini, Centre for Mental Health, Day Care Programme, in order to reduce such violence.

Most theories attempting to explain the phenomenon of violence and aggression converge on the correlation between helplessness and aggression. According to these theories, people behave aggressively when they feel that they cannot avoid a situation, and that they have no control over it. To have 'no control' means to perceive no relationship between the events in the environment and one's own inner experiences. This can be frightening. People with mental disorders, especially those with Schizophrenia, are often confronted with this experience, with the feeling that they cannot deal with a situation because of their hallucinations, delusions, or other thought disruptions. People with other mental disorders also experience this helplessness. People with severe Obsessive Compulsive Disorders, with repetitive thoughts and movements, can feel entirely unable to control their impulses to perform certain acts.

These potentially violent situations escalate when well-meaning family members, who have no idea of how to deal with the situation, try to deal with this behaviour. They may request, order or even threaten, in order to stop the behaviour, and the situation is therefore easily compounded when their ill relative does not comply. Aggressive behaviour is the human being's 'ancient emergency programme', the lowest level of problem-solving.

In this essay we present three case vignettes where violent behaviour occurred within the context of mental illness. We describe the impact that the aggressive behaviour had on the families of these clients. We then present our intervention approach, using two cases as examples. Our interventions focus on (re)establishing the feeling of control and reducing the sense of helplessness in clients and their family members, and are based on principles of Behaviour Therapy and Cognitive Behaviour Therapy.[1]

---

[1] All names have been changed in order to protect identity.

AMAN

Aman is a large, reticent, 30-year-old man who has been in the Sanjivini therapeutic programme for 15 months. He has a diagnosis of Organic Psychosis, complicated by OCD and Borderline Intellectual Functioning.

In the initial stages of our work with him, his family's expectations centred mainly on his attending the programme regularly and punctually, and on doing minor cognitive tasks to prevent deterioration. These included basic household chores like shopping for milk and taking his medication regularly.

Aman's preoccupation with cleaning and his refusal to do these tasks disrupted the family routine and thwarted their efforts to take care of him. The family would get frustrated because of Aman's slow pace in changing and because they were required to constantly repeat their directions in order to get him to carry out even the smallest task. When their patience was exhausted, they would resort to violence themselves. Unyielding and unable to see their efforts as helpful, Aman retaliated by becoming violent himself, or by provoking them into escalating the violence.

The situation remained locked in this pattern—the family viewed him as lazy, lying and resisting and Aman saw his family as unreasonable in their rules and demands and obstinately refused to comply with what he saw as their force. Over a period of time, communication between Aman and his mother and siblings broke down completely. Aman's father remained in distant contact with him and restricted himself to giving orders and directions. Aman, usually defensive and apologetic, always expecting rebuke, would go to great lengths to avoid any interaction with his father.

REENA

Reena is a 26-year-old woman who has been suffering for the past nine years. Her illness has taken a meandering course with several attacks of varying severity to times of partial to complete remission. However, the present episode has been continuing for over three years and has shown little response to medical or psychological intervention.

Reena is almost mute. She is extremely withdrawn and passive and stays preoccupied with her hands and fingers, which she moves in bizarre repetitive ways. At home, Reena is unable to complete even simple tasks like bathing and dressing. Her parents' pleas do not evoke any response other than the movements. Attempts to reason with her are brushed aside vehemently and she reports an unexplained 'difficulty'. Further attempts at persuasion lead Reena to react violently. She abuses, hits, claws and pushes her parents and sometimes will hurt herself. The family also reports that she will throw food, fling things around, and break furniture or appliances. There are times when the violence occurs spontaneously without any provocation or apparent trigger.

NEHA

Neha is a 22-year-old woman diagnosed with Schizophrenia and Mental Retardation. She has suffered from active psychotic symptoms and behavioural problems. Since her breakdown that took place four years ago, she has had difficulty in sustaining attention and found it difficult to carry out even simple tasks, such as bathing and brushing. She would spend a great deal of time preoccupied with collecting and hoarding, or reacting to her own thoughts and delusions. Childlike and confused most of the times, inexplicable events would provoke delusional thoughts and send her into spells where she became extremely angry or scared and did not have reasonable ways to express this. Some of her hallucinations had a sexual or violent content and were filled with visions of blood or people harming themselves.

Neha would shout at and abuse her mother or sister-in-law and sometimes become verbally assaultive at no one in particular. She frequently became angry when her demands for objects to fulfil her need for hoarding and collecting were not met. Starting with the demand for one object, she would move to another, raise her voice and start abusing until the object was promised to her. Her family would either indiscriminately give in to this insistence and constant demands, or her father or brother would hit her.

While in the therapeutic programme, Neha would begin to cry and laugh simultaneously, seemingly helplessly gripped with anger. The family saw her breakdown as a mysterious, unfortunate event and hoped that pharmacological and psychological intervention would lead to a reversal of symptoms. We began working on this violent behaviour from the time that Neha entered the Day Care Programme and we witnessed her resistance to being there. Neha's violence was targeted mostly at her mother who had brought her. She would stand threateningly over her mother and demand to be taken back home. When her mother refused to comply, she would begin with explicit abuses and then go on to hit, punch and scratch till she drew blood. Neha interspersed each attack with a pause followed by the same demand. This occurred many times and usually ended with the mother being pushed against a wall or corner, blood showing, hurt and scratched, completely at the mercy of deliberate blows, until someone intervened. Once the situation escalated to the point where Neha had to be sent to the hospital for psychiatric reappraisal.

In their patriarchal joint family system Neha's family members did not take a uniform stand in their dealings with her and with each other. The family dynamics revealed a pattern of helplessness and acting out. The mother accepted the beating helplessly just as the sister-in-law accepted the abuses. Neither did the mother protest for herself, nor did she make any attempts to protect her daughter-in-law. Whereas the father and brother would become angry and hit Neha in order to quieten her. The otherwise distant father was volubly angry with the mother, blaming her for not taking adequate care of Neha. None of the family members ever talked to Neha about how they did not like her behaviour, They never attempted to stop it assuming that it was part of her illness and that they had to simply put up with it.

IMPACT ON THE FAMILY

The families of such clients have a particularly difficult time, physically, financially, socially and psychologically.

The most obvious problem relates to the physical injuries that clients inflict on their relatives, directly or inadvertently. Neha's mother's scarred body bears testimony to the innumerable scratches, pinches, blows and bites she has suffered. Sometimes, injuries are severe enough to require hospitalisation. In our programme, S, a 40-year-old man, had learnt to deal with the provocation of his alcoholic brother by avoiding him. However, when he dropped out of the programme, S stopped medication and suffered a relapse. He then responded to his hallucinations and kicked his brother repeatedly in the face; for such injuries the brother required hospitalisation for a considerable length of time.

Hospital fees further deplete the already burdened family's resources, as does the money needed for repairing or restoring damaged household items.

M is a 27-year-old client in our programme. His family has to move house every six months because their house owner usually gets fed up with the loud arguments and frequent altercations with the neighbours which occur because of his behaviour. The family often loses their security deposit. M understands that he causes his ill mother a great deal of inconvenience, but finds it difficult not to react to his persecutory delusions.

In some cases, the violence has consequences with regard to the family members' jobs. Reena's parents are both respectable, dedicated professionals who often reach their offices late. They try and compensate for the lost time by working extra hours and volunteering to do extra things for their organisations.

The presence of a relative who is sick, who screams, shouts, hits and flings things around can be perceived as a matter of shame and sometimes families make all kinds of efforts to keep this a secret. They will actively avoid any social contact that may endanger this family secret and thus activities like attending social gatherings, meeting friends and relatives cease. Neha's sister-in-law is unable to call her brothers home because Neha becomes agitated and repetitively asks when they will leave. She has also abused her sister-in-law in front of them, which has led to further problems. The constant threat that their ill relative will act in a bizarre or inappropriate manner inhibits recreational and important socialising pursuits. Reena indiscriminately hits out at her parents in public. She once pushed her father so hard that he fell down.

The family thus gradually isolates itself, and the lives of the family members revolve around taking care of the violent relative, giving them little time for each other. Bonding activities are reduced and relations become strained, which places a heavy toll on the emotional health of the family. As each member unsuccessfully tries to handle the violent relative; shame, isolation, despair and danger are frequently experienced and because of the lack of adequate channels for supportive expression, these feelings accumulate and add to the distress. Even the young children in the family are adversely affected by the consequent chronic stress. Younger siblings feel frightened and insecure, learn hostility and other maladaptive ways of coping. Their personality growth is thereby affected. Neha's niece and nephew are frightened by her violence. Their mother frequently expresses concern that they will learn to throw tantrums to get what they want.

INTERVENTION

Psycho-education is the first part of our intervention. We provide information about the nature of the illness, the symptoms (delusions, hallucinations, etc.) to the family. This helps the family to understand the source of their relative's violent behaviour. With this knowledge, families are helped to identify trigger situations and the underlying patterns of communication that are liable to escalate the violence. Depending on the source of helplessness that leads to the violence, we provide the family information about the techniques of limit-setting and ways of encouraging reality-testing. Families are helped to reach a consensus on acceptable and unacceptable behaviours and set limits accordingly. Clients are also helped to see their own role in the situation and they are encouraged to set limits and boundaries. We help clients learn appropriate ways of communicating their concerns to others.

Once families learn that their relative's helplessness can be tackled, they are encouraged not to react physically, but instead communicate verbally. Families are taught to state their intent clearly and repeatedly, in simple language. They are told to give consistent information to the client, as far as possible. We emphasise that this consistency is maintained between words and actions.

Any indicators of change for the positive are encouraged and rein-forced, verbally and/or in the form of tokens. During family sessions, information about the client's pre-morbid strengths is recorded and combined with current observations of interest. This information is used to formulate alternative ways of channelling the energy towards positive activities. These activities become a point of positive contact for family members. Families are motivated to re-integrate the client in day-to-day activities.

It has been found that sometimes the violence or aggressive behaviour occurs because of raised expectations of families from the client. Therefore, another way of intervention is by lowering the family's expectations and then increasing them slowly so that clients can also tap their progress. This motivates clients and reinforces the positive behaviour, furthering the movement towards the positive.

Families are also encouraged to support each other and discuss matters related to the client. This increases emotional bonding and cohesiveness between family members.

In the Case of Aman

- Because we recognised that the rigid and locked patterns of communication were responsible for the violence, we worked with both Aman and his father separately in order to help them see this as well.
- We provided examples of alternative ways of communication that other father-son dyads were using in an attempt to expand their communication repertoire.
- We helped Aman learn to communicate with words instead of through mute resistance.
- We also worked with Aman so that he could see his own role in the continuing family violence instead of continuing to feel just victimised by it.
- We worked with the family to help them distinguish between 'lazy', 'stubborn' behaviour and Obsessive Compulsive Behaviours.
- We set clear limits upon the family by telling the father that he could react only verbally and not physically.
- We also helped the father see how some of his son's needs were normal for a young adult and thus helped him become less rigid in the limits he was setting.

- We encouraged Aman's father to enforce limits sensitively and to use incentives, not just sanctions.
- We worked with Aman so that he could learn to negotiate with his father.
- We encouraged Aman to recognise that he needed to make adjustments in order to get what he wanted as well. To do this, he had to learn how to deal with some of his compulsions.
- The father was then encouraged to create more space for taking care of Aman's needs within the family.
- As Aman learnt communication and negotiation skills, he saw himself as being more efficacious, and thus, became more willing to do what was expected from. This in turn led to increased self-esteem.
- We encouraged the father to recognise the positive changes and effort that Aman was making.
- We encouraged reinforcing the positive patterns of communication by positive time spent. Because the father saw cognitive tasks as valuable, we encouraged him to spend time with Aman doing crosswords together.

Progress Report: We have noticed a significant change for the positive in a year's time and Aman is now beginning to restore his relationship with his mother.

In the Case of Reena

We could not sustain the effects of our intervention with Reena because her attendance in the programme remained poor. We found that there were two main reasons for her inconsistent attendance:

- Her chaotic mental state did not allow her to attend the programme or even to verbalise her reasons for staying away and therefore these could not be addressed.
- The family is reluctant to take on the task of forcibly sending Reena to the Day Care Centre, as they fear that this will provoke further abuse and violence at home. The only way to tackle her refusal would be for them to take a firm, maybe a harsh, stand which is perhaps unacceptable within their value system relating to good parenting.

We have directed our interventions up to this point of time on mainly helping Reena's family identify the underlying continuing pathological patterns of dealing with the violence. It is important for them to understand that the only way they can get her to attend, is if they were to tackle the violence more proactively.

In the Case of Neha

- We first helped the family to distinguish between Neha's anger due to delusions, and the anger which occurred as part of a behavioural problem.
- We emphasised that they must deal with her violence proactively and not just bear it passively.
- We specifically encouraged the family to take a stand for themselves and for each other. In this way they were able to maintain a consistency in their message to Neha regarding her anger—that they would not accept it.
- We worked with Neha's mother especially, and taught her a series of sequential actions towards stopping the violence.
- We then taught this strategy to the family as well, and encouraged them to ensure that the mother followed the procedure without fail *every time the violence occurred.*
- We worked with Neha and taught her impulse control and delaying gratification.
- We also worked with the family so that they also learned the skills that would help Neha achieve impulse control.

Progress Report: Over a period of eight months Neha's violence was considerably reduced.

CONCLUSION

While recognising that violence is to a certain extent an inevitable part of mental illness, it is comforting to know that it can be tackled to some extent. We have found that interventions aimed at reinstating the patient's sense of control and reducing the helplessness of the family can be effective. By providing information about triggers and helping them understand communication patterns, clients and their families gradually gain more control in their everyday lives, thus enhancing their feelings of competence and self worth and reducing helplessness and the need for violence.

Chapter 14

Terrorism and Psychological Trauma*
Psychosocial Perspectives

Renos K. Papadopoulos

Renos K. Papadopoulos teaches at the University of Essex and is also a practising psychotherapist. He is Honorary Clinical Psychologist and Systemic Psychotherapist at the Tavistock Clinic, London. As consultant to the United Nations and other organisations (including the Rajiv Gandhi Foundation), he has worked with refugees and other survivors of political violence in many countries. He is a member of the Human Rights Centre and of the Transitional Justice Network at the University of Essex.

Although terrorism has existed for a very long time stretching back to the beginning of civilisation, it is only in recent years that it has received worldwide attention on an almost daily basis. Terrorist attacks in different countries have been receiving increasingly wider publicity, creating a climate of agitation. The perpetrators of acts of terrorism are committing them to achieve political gain of some kind, directly or

---

*This chapter was first published in *The Journal*, Vol. 7(2), December 2005, by the Psychological Foundations Trust, New Delhi.

indirectly, or to deliver a certain political message. Therefore, in order to develop a comprehensive understanding of terrorism, we need to locate it within its appropriate defining contexts which are historical as well as socio-political, religious, economic, ideological, etc. However, one of the characteristics of terrorism is its tendency to choose targets that include innocent civilians; inevitably, acts of terrorism affect even those who do not play an active part in these contexts. Mental health professionals form one group of the many groups of professionals that attend to the impact that terrorism has on the wider population. In addition, specialist psychologists are used to provide psychological perspectives to develop a deeper understanding of terrorism as a phenomenon and of terrorists as individuals.

TERRORISM AND PSYCHOLOGISTS

According to the Oxford English Dictionary, terror is 'the state of being terrified or greatly frightened; (it is) intense fear, fright or dread'. It is interesting that a personal feeling gives the name to a social phenomenon. It is as if we said 'sadness-ism' or 'happiness-ism' or 'anxiety-ism'. I am not aware of any other similar occurrence, apart from the 'Great Depression' (of the 1930s in the USA) and, of course, there, the word depression did not refer to personal feelings but mainly to the economic decline. The relationship between a personal feeling and a societal state, as in terrorism, creates an important connection between these two realms. It constructs a Janus-faced phenomenon with two sides—one personal/individual/intrapsychic and the other impersonal/transpersonal/ collective. Indeed, terrorism is a social phenomenon but it affects individuals who are not just nameless statistics but are human beings with real lives, families, hopes and fears and relationships.

It is of interest to reflect on the fact that the actual word terrorism was coined in the early 1790s to refer to the activities of the revolutionary government in France during the period which was called 'terror' when thousands of opponents of the regime were put to death. Yet, according to the current definition of the US Federal Bureau of Investigation (FBI), 'Terrorism is the unlawful use of force or violence against persons or property to intimidate or coerce a government, the civilian population, or any segment thereof, in furtherance of political or social objectives.' Whereas the original definition has the government as the perpetrator of terrorist acts, the FBI definition places the government as its victim. This illustrates another double face of terrorism—often, it is political considerations that define terrorism and not any objective criteria of external actions or emotional states. It is well known that a person or a group of people can be denounced by some as terrorist/s and glorified by others as self-sacrificing heroes and freedom fighter/s.

A more comprehensive definition of terrorism, from an academic perspective, suggests that it is an:

> anxiety-inspiring method of repeated violent action, employed by (semi-) clandestine individual, group or state actors, for idiosyncratic, criminal or political reasons, whereby—in contrast to assassination—the direct targets of violence are not the main targets. The immediate human victims of violence are generally chosen randomly (targets of opportunity) or selectively (representative or symbolic targets) from a target population, and serve as message generators. Threat- and violence-based communication processes between terrorist (organisations), (imperilled) victims, and main targets are used to manipulate the main target (audience(s)), turning it into a target of terror, a target of demands, or a target of attention, depending on whether intimidation, coercion, or propaganda is primarily used (Schmid, 1998, p. 28).

This detailed definition emphasises the delivering of a message (through methods of creating terror) as the main intent of terrorists; accordingly, their major aim is the generation of maximum possible terror rather than the maximum degree of actual destruction, although often the two are interrelated.

It is interesting to remember that, etymologically, the origin of terror is the Greek noun *tromos* (terror). Tromos means trembling, quaking, quivering, especially from fear. The root verb is tremo or treo and it means to tremble, to shiver (Papadopoulos, 2002a). It is an onomatopoeic word coming from the 'trrr' sound of a shivering person. This means that terror is a very basic word with a direct somatic base and of a universal nature. Hoffman connects the verb treo with the Lithuanian *tresti* which means 'possessed by orgasm with reference to a bitch' (Hoffman, 1950, p. 446). Therefore, in any form of tremor, shaking and trembling can be connected with this etymological root which means that the orgasmic connotation of terrorism should not be forgotten. This is an important point that is often forgotten: terrorism generates an excitement and fascination that can be comparable to orgasmic excitation. The current technology (especially satellite television) enables the instant coverage of terrorist phenomena and this creates a sense of immediacy and proximity that stimulate in people a type of interest and fascination that often escalates to a preoccupation that can be morbid, obsessive, thrilling, of almost orgasmic excitement. At times this kind of—what is referred to as—'hype' can reach mass hysteria proportions. These states that are fermented by the impact of terror are indivisible parts of the total phenomenon of terrorism. This facet of terrorism, on the one hand is very familiar and on the other hand, it is not easily available to us for reflection because it tends to be all engulfing. Terrorism whips up outbursts of emotion (positive and negative) that often are on the brink of becoming uncontrollable.

Consequently, the usual stance people assume in relation to terrorist phenomena is sharply divided into either outright condemnation or an unquestionable approval. It is almost impossible to maintain reflective thinking of these phenomena from a critical distance; instead, people tend to get sucked into their powerful and seductive vortex and without noticing it they inadvertently contribute to the further escalation of the resultant excitement, thus unwittingly, fuelling further destructiveness.

After the French revolution and its long aftermath, the word terrorism seems to have not been used much until it was revived again in the 19th century with the emergence of the anarchist and nationalist movements in Europe that carried out various terrorist attacks against authority figures of the establishment. From then onwards, until today, the term terrorism has been associated with actions that were first related to the anti-colonialist liberation movements and then (in the post cold-war era) with the resurgence of political and religious fundamentalism.

The governments of some countries find it threatening to even use the word 'terrorism' and prefer to use words such as 'militant' or 'separatist' 'subversive' actions; evidently, they fear that naming any act of political violence as 'terrorist' would give the whole phenomenon a different complexion that would not be advantageous to them.

Inevitably, psychologists, like all other human beings, are also vulnerable to being swept off their feet by the overwhelmingness of terrorism, and it will be useful to examine our own specific ways of vulnerability in this context.

Shortly after 11 September 2001, the website of the US news agency CNN carried headlines that American specialists had confirmed that the terrorist suicide hijackers responsible for the atrocities were not mentally disturbed, they were not suffering from psychopathological symptoms and, therefore, those specialists concluded that this was a new phenomenon. They emphasised that the culprits were well adjusted and mature individuals who were fully aware of their actions which were premeditated, in fact extremely well planned, and were not the outcome of a deranged mind. The statement implied that psychological explanations are useful only in throwing light on motives of people who commit acts of destructiveness whilst in various pathological states and, conversely, they are not useful and applicable in the case of healthy individuals. A further implication is that destructive acts can only be committed by psychologically unstable individuals; according to this view, psychologically healthy and 'normal' human beings are not capable of committing atrocities. Yet, as we know, 'normal' people have been responsible for virtually all the calculated and wilful destruction on our planet, including most of the wars.

This polarised perception seems to be another example of the overwhelmingness that terrorism creates. Views, feelings and perceptions tend to become sharply polarised. Indiscriminate polarisation with all its implications is one of the most important consequences of terrorism and psychologists are under strong pressure to succumb to this in the ways they address terrorism, terrorists and their victims.

Sharp polarisation is, indeed, along with all its many consequences, one of the main features of terrorism (Papadopoulos, 2003). One of the main consequences of polarisation is oversimplification; thus, the first victim of terrorism is complexity, our ability to tolerate complexity. Terrorism imposes polarised simplistic impulses devoid of reflective thinking of complex causes, effects and their interrelationships with their various intersecting contexts. Terrorism is based on, it generates and it perpetuates definitive and divisive distinctions that can be fateful. These divisive perceptions dissect the world into definitive categories and are imposed on individuals and groups of people, regardless of their own will or conscious perception. For example, when the Nazis targeted all Jews indiscriminately, not all Jews had a sense of Jewish identity—the Nazis imposed that identity on them. When terrorists attack a selected 'target group' (e.g., nationals of one country or members of one religion), the victims can include people who may not necessarily disagree with the terrorists' political sentiments; yet, their very belonging, according to certain criteria, to a certain group makes them potential targets by the terrorists in question.

A psychological approach to understanding terrorists that is based on a polarised 'diagnosis' about their healthy or unhealthy psychological state is also a victim of terrorist polarisation. Terrorists themselves have sharply polarised views as to what is good and what is evil and who is on their side and who is not; their unshakeable conviction leads them to spread terror and death to those they consider members of the 'target group'. Also, their acts have a polarising effect insofar as it divides those who were directly affected by them (the victims) from those who were not. Finally, the way others perceive their acts tend also to be polarised, dividing people into those who condemn these acts outright and those who condone them. In short, terrorism (like all violence) tends to engender sharp polarisation around self (Papadopoulos, 1998; 2005b). Psychologists, like all other human beings, are also engulfed by this polarisation but their own form of polarisation is of a specific kind. Being mental health professionals, we tend to view phenomena through our own lenses of the pathology/ normality dichotomy. Consequently, there is a tendency to seek psychopathological characteristics in terrorists and to focus on the equally pathological effects terrorist attacks have on people. This is understandable. Nobody can possibly condone indiscriminate acts of violence on innocent people, however, this is a political and ethical stance and not a psychological one, and here is the problem. It is understandable that psychologists *as citizens,* we condemn all acts of violence because they can be contrary to our views and values, they are opposite to our democratic beliefs, to our legal sense of responsibility, to our moral and ethical codes, to our humanitarian considerations, as well as possibly to our religious or other principles. However, all these considerations tend to get confused with our position *as psychologists* once we try to formulate our objections to terrorism using psychological theories.

Psychology helps us understand the uniqueness of each person's response to a given event. It does not allow us to make sweeping statements and condemnations. We can indulge in these as citizens but not as psychologists. However, the incredible pressure of human pain, outrage, anger, helplessness and all the other overbearing human emotions that are generated by terrorist acts tend to confuse us and to expose us to the naked polarisation that terrorism spreads. This state tends to lead to an epistemological confusion within which we are prone to commit many epistemological errors such as psychologising the political dimensions, pathologising human suffering, medicalising social realities, etc. (Papadopoulos, 1999, 2001, 2002c). The phenomena of terrorism, their implications and effects cover a very wide spectrum of discourses and by approaching them from a single, exclusive and simplistic psychological perspective, we are bound to commit many methodological and epistemological errors.

On 7 December 2005, Harold Pinter began his pre-recorded lecture on receiving the Nobel Prize for Literature with these words:

> In 1958 I wrote the following:
>
> There are no hard distinctions between what is real and what is unreal, nor between what is true and what is false. A thing is not necessarily either true or false; it can be both true and false.
>
> I believe that these assertions still make sense and do still apply to the exploration of reality through art. So as a writer I stand by them but as a citizen I cannot. As a citizen I must ask: What is true? What is false?

Pinter draws a distinction between reality in art and reality in politics. Reality in art is 'elusive... the real truth is that there never is any such thing as one truth there are many.... These truths challenge each other, reflect each other....' However, reality in politics is a reality that needs to be grasped firmly: 'I believe that despite the enormous odds which exist... as citizens, to define the real truth of our lives and our societies is a crucial obligation which devolves upon us all. It is in fact mandatory.' Pinter values both realities, considering both of them essential and complementary; however, he warns against a confusion that mixes and fuses the two. In a comparable way, psychologists need to delineate psychological reality from political reality, so that they will be able to attend to both in their different and appropriate ways; it is imperative that psychologists retain their critical distance and maintain their reflective thinking and do not succumb to the simplistic formulations that terrorist polarisation creates. It is important that as citizens, psychologists, like artists attribute to Caesar what belongs to Caesar and expect clarity about political issues, demanding that the culprits of atrocities face the consequences of their actions; psychologists should not attempt to use psychological theories to prevent legal justice but to assist it in following its own course. At the same time, psychologists should also pursue their search for psychological realities and the truth of each individual concerned. It is imperative that the two realms are not confused. Psychologists should indeed endeavour to be good citizens and accept our obligations seriously, but at the same time *as psychologists*, our duty is to attend to the psychological reality because other citizens cannot do that. We have been entrusted by society with the responsibility of attending to psychological realities and we need to discharge this duty to the best of our abilities and not to dilute it by confusing it with other preoccupations. Our specialist education and training equips us to examine meticulously the psychological realities and make interventions based on a thorough comprehension of them, without committing the epistemological errors that are endemic in these situations.

As a result of the ensuing polarisation and the specific professional epistemology, psychologists tend to focus on the negative effects of terrorism. From one perspective which is very logical, there can be no other possible effects but negative. What positive can ever come out of any acts of violence and destruction? This question is based on a perspective that focuses on the compelling logic of external realities of civic life as well as on ethical and other values. However, this logic is the predominant logic of narrow perspectives which entrenches itself in times of terror. This logic is the logic of polarity which, sharply divides phenomena and simplifies complexities. This simplification is most welcome at times and in states of distress, pain and confusion. People cannot afford to entertain complex formulations when they have just suffered an excruciating bereavement and are overwhelmed by grief and rage. They want to give in entirely to their bereavement, and to feel justified in being wrapped in their identity as victims which, in turn, allows them to be enraged at the acts of violence that caused their loss. These are most understandable human reactions. Our sense of compassion and sympathy with the victims makes us identify with their plight and we tend to share their polarisation and oversimplification. Any consideration of complexity that may shift us away from the simple fact that we are dealing with a loss, is felt not only as inappropriate and unhelpful to the victims but even as insulting. The human response of wishing to minimise pain in others and in oneself tends to sharpen the polarisation, and the simplification becomes even narrower. The division becomes sharper between perpetrators and victims, good and evil, health and injury, good and bad effects, therapists and patients, love and hatred, acts of violence and acts of peace, etc. Under the pressure of human pain, this logic of polarity and oversimplification becomes overwhelming and acquires a status of a seemingly crystal clear reality in an undeniable, forceful, convincing, gripping, persuasive and exclusive way (Papadopoulos, 2005a). However, this unshakeable logic with its glaring clarity can obscure a host of other considerations. This logic forms the dominant discourse which in turn subjugates many other discourses. Individual psychological realities are some of the many complexities that are obscured by this overpowering seeming clarity. Individual voices, discourses and realities are subjugated by this dominant reality. These individual realities can include a wide range of effects adversity has on people—some people collapse and are paralysed by the weight of their bereavement whereas others are strengthened by adversity, whilst others carry on without much deviation from their usual psychological state.

Nevertheless, our condemnation of terrorism on ethical, legal, political and other grounds should not confuse us and lead us into a blind perception of its psychological impact on people as being exclusively negative.

Conversely, it does not imply that we condone terrorism if we can discern certain growthful effects on some of its survivors. In addition to our stance of deploring terrorism, psychologists should also focus, despite the enormous pressures, on the psychological reality of each individual survivor without indiscriminately considering all survivors as victims. Not all people are psychologically damaged and traumatised by acts of terrorism and not everybody among those who have been traumatised, is going to be scarred for life. The polarised perspective on trauma predisposes us to ignore potential (or even actual) growthful gains in some individuals who have been exposed to adversities as a result of terrorism.

PSYCHOLOGICAL TRAUMA

Phenomena of terrorism (like those of becoming a refugee) do not fall within the usual realm of psychological theorising and treatment. Therefore, it is understandable that psychologists attempt to comprehend these phenomena by searching for some existing psychological theories that appear as applicable to these novel situations. Psychological trauma has emerged as the most suitable perspective as it is the only one that privileges the external realities. The psychiatric category of Post Traumatic Stress Disorder (PTSD) is the only such category that is based on the presence of an external event.

So what is trauma? Trauma is a medical term and it refers to injury or wound. In Greek, trauma means wound, injury and it comes from the verb *titrosko*—to pierce. Thus, the original meaning of trauma is the mark, the injury that is left as a result of the skin being pierced. Recent etymological investigations (Papadopoulos 2000; 2001; 2002b) revealed interesting new perspectives which show that *titrosko* comes from the verb *teiro* which means 'to rub' and in ancient Greek it had two connotations: to rub in and to rub off, to rub away. This means that, etymologically, it can be said that trauma is the mark left on persons as a result of something being rubbed onto them. Then, insofar as the rubbing is of two kinds, we could have two different outcomes: from 'rubbing in'—an injury, a wound, or from 'rubbing off' or 'rubbing away'—a clean surface where previous marks were erased (like when we use a rubber, an eraser to erase writing on a piece of paper). With reference to contexts of political violence, a person may be injured (psychologically) to varying degrees of severity as a result of being exposed to violent events ('rubbed in'): alternatively, a person may experience (in addition to the distress) a sense of renewal, rejuvenation and revitalisation when the powerful and potentially injurious experiences erase previous values, routines and lifestyles and introduce new meaning to their lives. This second outcome of rubbing is not a linguistic invention or a theoretical abstraction but it corresponds with the reality when people, following a painful ('traumatic') event, are shaken and gradually become aware that they now look at themselves and the world in a different way, e.g., appreciating life, friendship, warmth, etc., more than the pursuit of petty and meaningless quests.

With reference to the trauma approach to terrorism, these two meanings of trauma have important consequences. The first meaning of trauma (rubbing in and resulting in injury) is by far the most dominant one. We consider the persons on the receiving end of terrorism as being traumatised and in need of help. This, of course, is not untrue and such an approach should always be respected and followed. However, if we are not careful, this very reasonable approach can have some fairly negative consequences. The second meaning of trauma (rubbing off, rubbing away, resulting in the acquisition of new perspectives on life) is less noticeable although not less known. It is well known that following a difficult and intense experience, people may respond in ways that emphasise the renewing rather than the injurious effects of the experience. Despite (or even because of) the pain, disorientation, disruption, devastation and loss, people may still feel that the very same 'traumatic' experience also made them re-evaluate their priorities in life, change their lifestyles and acquire new values—all in all experiencing a substantial change and renewal in their lives. Having come so close to death or having experienced the unbearable anguish of substantial losses, people often emerge transformed, re-viewing life, themselves and their relationships in a new and revitalised way. This means that, paradoxically, despite their negative nature, devastating experiences (regardless of the degree of their harshness and destructive impact) may also help people reshuffle their lives and imbue new meaning in them.

Therefore, it is important to ponder on the fact that the usual way psychologists consider the effects of terrorism is in terms of trauma as injury and wound. Moreover, the meaning of trauma as re-evaluation and renewal is ignored despite the fact that it refers to an extremely common phenomenon.

Logically, the range of possible effects of trauma must fall into three categories: negative, positive and neutral. At the outset it must be emphasised that they do not need to be exclusive. This means that despite the fact that a person is traumatised, he or she may also gain from the experience. Psychologically speaking, based on the psychological rather than on social or ethical or other realities, reactions to adversity and the devastating consequences of terrorist acts can vary enormously from individual to individual depending on a variety of variables. These include the following:

- Personal: history, psychological characteristics, coping mechanisms, strengths/weaknesses, status, education
- Relational—supporting systems ('social capital'): family (nuclear and extended), community (local as well as wider, international)
- Gender
- Power position: degrees of helplessness and humiliation
- Circumstances of the actual devastating events: predictability, isolation, duration, lasting effects
- Meaning given to the events and the experience of these events: political, religious, ideological
- Hope

Each one of these factors can influence the way that a terrrorist act can affect each individual.

Overall, we can distinguish the following three broad categories of possible effects that trauma can have on a person.

1. Negative: The first is the actual psychological injury that can lead to a genuine pathological condition of shorter or longer duration. There is no doubt that certain people are indeed traumatised by the devastating effects of external events engendered by terrorism, according to the 'rubbing in' definition of trauma. However, within this category we can identify three degrees of severity:

a) Ordinary Human Suffering (OHS): this is the most common and human response to tragedies in life. Suffering is not always a pathological condition; suffering is part of life and it is not useful always to medicalise or pathologise it.

b) Distressful Psychological Reaction (DPR): this is an effect that does not always require specialist attention. Ordinary human resilience can deal with this type of effect.

c) Psychiatric Disorder (PD): the most common type of this effect is PTSD which definitely requires professional intervention.

2. Positive: The second category of possible responses to terrorism refers to phenomena that tend to be neglected by the mainstream professional theories and practices. Undoubtedly, there are people who not only survive, with a significant degree of intactness, the inhuman and cruel conditions they had endured, but, moreover, they become strengthened by their particular exposure to adversity. It is for this reason that this response has been termed 'Adversity-Activated Development' (AAD) (Papadopoulos, 2004); it refers to the positive developments that are a direct result of being exposed to adversity. There are endless accounts of individuals and groups who found meaning in their suffering and were able to transform their experiences in a positive way, finding new strength and experiencing transformative renewal. Such accounts are not just moving human testimonies but also challenge the societal discourse of trauma and the tendency to medicalise and pathologise human suffering. Such accounts also provide concrete evidence for the 'rubbing off' and 'rubbing away' definition of trauma, i.e., trauma as enabling the wiping off of previous life priorities and providing a clean slate to begin a new life. With reference to terrorism, this kind of response creates awkward moral dilemmas and complexities because one certainly does not wish to focus on the positive outcomes of despicable acts of political violence or terrorism. Nevertheless, at the same time, it would be equally inappropriate to ignore such responses. The way out of this conundrum is the development of sharp epistemological vigilance rather than throwing the baby out with the bath water and ignoring completely possible growthful outcomes.

Transforming adversity to positive development is a phenomenon that has always been known to humans. Philosophers and novelists addressed these phenomena long before psychologists became aware of their relevance. It is interesting to note that these ideas entered the specialist trauma literature relatively late, more or less about the same time when PTSD was introduced. However, psychologists such as Carl Gustav Jung, Victor Frankl and others identified these phenomena, using different terminologies much earlier than this specialist literature appeared. More specifically, Jung acknowledged the potentially positive function of the symptom and the teleological purpose of suffering, emphasising the meaning dimension (e.g., Jung 1931, 1943, 1945a, 1945b, 1951). Frankl (1959), using his personal experiences of being a concentration camp inmate during the Second World War, demonstrated how giving meaning to suffering can be transformative. In the last two decades, trauma literature experienced an influx of these ideas that use different terminologies to address the same positive use of adversity. These include such terms as stress-related growth, crisis-related growth or development, thriving in adversity, post-trauma growth, positive transformation following trauma, positive transformation of suffering, etc. (e.g., Affleck & Tennen, 1996; Folkman, 1997; Harvey, 1996; Janoff-Bulman, 1992; Lifton, 1993; McMillen, & Fisher, 1998; McMillen, 1999; Park, Cohen, & Murch, 1996; Saakvitne, Tennen, & Affleck, 1998; Tedeschi, & Calhoun, 1995; Tedeschi, & Calhoun, 1996; Tedeschi, Park, & Calhoun, 1998; Thompson, 1985).

The characteristics of AAD are:

- Adversity exposes limits: when adversity strikes, it pushes people to the end of their own plans. Usually people feel that their lives have come to an end and they do not know how to proceed. This reaching of limits which is experienced as an end can open up new horizons, beyond the previously planned or imagined.
- New perceptions emerge of oneself (of one's identity), of one's relationships, and ultimately, of the meaning and purpose of life.
- New epistemology emerges: the sum total of all new perceptions lead to the acquisition of a new way of understanding, speaking, relating which amounts to a new epistemology.

3. Neutral: The third possible response to political violence is that of resilience. It is important to emphasise that existing literature does not distinguish between AAD and Resilience. Anything that does not fall within the negative spectrum of effects is termed 'resilience'. Yet, it is important to differentiate between AAD and Resilience.

Resilience is a term that in physics refers to the ability of a body not to alter after being subjected to different severe conditions—that is why I term it here as neutral. By extension, we refer to objects (such as a car, for example) as resilient if they can endure adverse conditions. Then, metaphorically, we refer to a person, a family, or a community as resilient if they withstand pressures and do not alter their basic values or abilities. The key characteristic of resilience is that it retains characteristics that existed before, whereas AAD introduces new characteristics that did not exist before the adversity. Hence, resilient are those individuals, relationships, families, communities that manage to resist disruptive change and not lose their positive characteristics.

One of the important qualities of human resilience, as opposed to resilience in physics, is that it is mainly not a result of individual strength but, essentially, a relational process (Walsh 1993). This means that a person is more resilient if he or she secures collaborative and reciprocal support with others.

The main theme of resilience remains that despite the most devastating nature of events experienced by people, not all of them are crushed by them. In fact, the majority of individuals do not require professional attention because a great deal of their healthy functioning remains intact and unaffected by the devastation (i.e., it is resilient to change—either negatively or positively). It is indeed remarkable to see the dignity and resilience of the human spirit triumphing over the most appalling conditions of degradation, helplessness, humiliation, actual injury and loss. In the last couple of decades, professional attention to issues of resilience in this field (but also in the wider sphere of mental health care) has increased dramatically (e.g., Cicchetti, & Luthar, 2003; Clarke, & Clarke, 2003; Daniel, & Wassell, 2002; Glantz, & Johnson, 1999; Greene, 2002; Haggerty, Sherrod, Garmezy, Rutter, 1997; McCubbin, Thompson, Thompson, & Fromer, 1998a; McCubbin,

Thompson, Thompson, & Fromer, 1998b; McCubbin, Thompson, Thompson, & Fromer, 1998c; McCubbin, Thompson, Thompson, & Futrell, 1999; Stinnett, & DeFrain, 1985; Tec, 2003; Tizard, & Varma, 2000; Werner & Smith, 1992; Wolin & Wolin, 1993).

Finally, it should be remembered that these three responses to trauma and terrorism are not mutually exclusive. The same individuals may respond to adversity in different ways in different contexts. This variation may exist in terms of a progressive chronological order, i.e., at the beginning they react negatively and later neutrally and even later positively. However, this variation of response may exist at the same given time in relation to different contexts.

THE TRAUMA GRID

As psychologists, it is imperative that we keep in mind the totality of each individual's experiences in response to terrorism and also be mindful of how these relate to the wider network of their interrelationships, past and present, good and bad, positive, negative and neutral; in short, all the consequences of their exposure to the terror. It is for this reason that I devised the 'Trauma Grid' (Papadopoulos, 2004), in order to identify in a tangible and tabulated form the various consequences of a traumatic experience, both actual as well as potential.

THE TRAUMA GRID

Levels	Negative Effects			Neutral Effects	Positive Effects
		Injury, Wound		Resilience	Adversary-Activated Development (AAD)
	Ordinary Human Suffering	Distressful Psychological Reactions	Psychiatric Disorders, PTSD		
Individual					
Family					
Community					
Society/culture					

Essentially the 'Trauma Grid' helps to remind us that there are at least three major categories of responses to a traumatic experience and not just a pathological trauma in an isolated form. These are marked in the three main columns and horizontally there are the four different levels of individual, family, community and society/culture, so that we can see the total range of possible and actual consequences. The Grid helps us to be mindful of this totality in order to avoid compartmentalisation and polarisation. Moreover, the Grid is useful in reminding us that the box of individual pathology is only a tiny space in relation to the wider spectrum of other consequences that may also co-exist with the pathology. Yet, most work done in this field is limited to the one little box of individual psychiatric disorder; occasionally, this is extended to its neighbouring box of DPR. An additional useful function of the Grid is to help us appreciate that there can be different consequences simultaneously (as well as sequentially) at different levels. By being mindful of this totality, therapists have better chances to address more appropriately the effects of terrorism and to avoid the pitfalls of oversimplification, polarisation and approaches based on narrow perspectives.

PSYCHOSOCIAL PERSPECTIVES

Psychology helps us appreciate that every human reaction to any situation is unique to that individual. Yet this individual is located within several defining contexts such as family, community, culture/society, as the Grid indicates. These considerations are obvious and we think that we take them for granted; yet, these tend to be clouded by simplistic generalisations and oversimplifications when they are connected with phenomena associated with terrorism. The term psychosocial has emerged as one of the most apt characterisations of the approaches that attempt to address the complexity of these various realms (IOM, 2003; Losi, 2000).

The term psychosocial, with reference to terrorist phenomena, enables us to refer to the combination of intrapsychic and interpersonal dimensions within the context of wider socio-political realities. The psychological consequences of these devastating events affect individuals both in ways that are highly personal (based on each one's psychological make-up and personal history) as well as impersonal, transpersonal, collective and social, insofar as the individual experiences are inevitably coloured by a host of social dimensions, ranging from the political meanings that are given to these events to the social cohesion of those who are affected by them. Ultimately, the specific meaning that individuals and communities bestow on their suffering, as a result of political upheavals and terrorism, is dependent on a wide variety of factors that can be addressed most appropriately by perspectives that interrelate the individual with his or her wider socio-political and other dimensions within which individuals are defined.

The usual way that mental health professionals respond to the impact that political violence has on people is by means of the category of psychological trauma. This is not wrong as often people are indeed traumatised by these events. However, trauma is not the only outcome in these situations. There is a huge range of responses varying from the most pathological and disabling to the most positive, resilient and inspiring. This essay attempted to encompass the complexities involved in considering these wide variations at times when psychological pressures tend to constrict our perspectives.

As psychologists, we are impotent in preventing acts of terrorism. Yet we are not impotent in preventing some of the more invisible negative consequences that terrorism can have on us as professionals.

REFERENCES

Affleck, G. & Tennen, H. (1996). Construing benefits from adversity: Adaptational significance and dispositional underpinnings. *Journal of Personality, 64*(4): 899–922.

Cicchetti, D. & Luthar, S.S. (2003). *Resilience and Vulnerability: Adaptation in the Context of Childhood Adversities*. Cambridge: Cambridge University Press.

Clarke, A. & Clarke, A. (2003). *Human Resilience: A Fifty Year Quest*. London: Jessica Kingsley.

Daniel, B. & Wassell, S. (2002). *Assessing and Promoting Resilience in Vulnerable Children*. London: Jessica Kingsley.

Folkman, S. (1997). Positive psychological states and coping with severe stress. *Social Science and Medicine, 45*: 1207–1221.

Frankl, V. (1959). *Man's Search for Meaning*. New York: Washington Square Press.

Haggerty, R.J., Sherrod, L.R., Garmezy, N. & Rutter, M. (Eds). (1997). *Stress, Risk, and Resilience in Children and Adolescents: Processes, Mechanisms, and Interventions*. New York: Cambridge University Press.

Harvey. M, (1996). An ecological view of psychological trauma and trauma recovery. *Journal of Traumatic Stress, 9*: 3–23.

Hofmann, J.B. (1950). *Etymologisches wörterbuch des griechischen*. München: Oldenbourg Verlag.

IOM (International Organisation for Migration). (2003). Position paper on psychosocial and mental well-being of migrants. Geneva: Author.

Glantz, M.D. & Johnson, J.L. (1999). *Resilience and Development Positive Life Adaptations*. New York: Plenum.

Greene, R. (2002). *Resiliency: An Integrated Approach to Practice, Policy, and Research*. Washington, DC: NASW Press.

Janoff-Bulman, R. (1992). *Shattered Assumptions: Toward New Psychology of Trauma*. New York: Free Press.

Jung, C.G. (1931). The aims of psychotherapy. In *Collected Works, volume 16*. London: Routledge and Kegan Paul.

———. (1943). Psychotherapy and a philosophy of life. In *Collected Works, volume 16*. London: Routledge and Kegan Paul.

———. (1945a). Medicine and psychotherapy. In *Collected Works, volume 16*. London: Routledge and Kegan Paul.

———. (1945b). Psychotherapy today. In *Collected Works, volume 16*. London: Routledge and Kegan Paul.

———. (1951). Fundamental questions of psychotherapy. In *Collected Works, volume 16*. London: Routledge and Kegan Paul.

Lifton, R.J. (1993). *The Protean Self: Human Resilience in an Age of Fragmentation*. New York: Basic Books.

Losi, N. (Ed.). (2000). *Psychosocial and Trauma Response in War-torn Societies: The Case of Kosovo*. Geneva, IOM.

McCubbin, H.I., Thompson, E.A., Thompson, A.I. & Fromer, J.E. (1998a). *Resiliency in Africa-American families*. New York: SAGE.

———. (1998b). *A Sense of Coherence and Resiliency: Stress, Coping and Health in Families Resiliency in Africa-American Families*. New York: SAGE.

———. (1998c). *Resiliency in Native and Immigrant Families*. New York: SAGE.

McCubbin, H.I., Thompson, E.A., Thompson, A.I., & Futrell, J. A. (1999). *The Dynamics of Resilient Families: Qualitative Approaches*. New York: SAGE.

McMillen, J.C. & Fisher, R.H. (1998). The perceived benefit scales: Measuring perceived positive life changes after negative events. *Social Work Research, 22*(3): 173–86.

McMillen, J.C. (1999). Better for it: How people benefit from adversity. *Social Work, 44*(5): 455–468.

Papadopoulos, R.K. (1998). Destructiveness, atrocities and healing: Epistemological and clinical reflection *The Journal of Analytical Psychology, 43*(4): 455–477.

———. (1999). Working with families of Bosnian medical evacuees: Therapeutic dilemmas. *Clinical Child Psychology and Psychiatry, 4*(1): 107–112.

———. (2000). A Matter of shades: Trauma and psychosocial work in Kosovo, In N. Losi (Ed.), *Psychosocial and Trauma Response in War-torn Societies: The Case of Kosovo*. Geneva: IOM.

Papadopoulos, R.K. (2001). Refugees, therapists and trauma: Systemic reflections. [Special Issue on Refugees. G.G. Barnes & R.K. Papadopoulos (Eds)] *Context: The Magazine of the Association for Family Therapy, 54*(April): 5–8.

———. (2002a). Terrorism e panico. *Rivista di Psicologia Analitica* (thematic title: II Terrore Nell' Anima), *13*(65): 165–181.

———. (2002b). Refugees, home and trauma In R.K. Papadopoulos (Ed.), *Therapeutic Care for Refugees: No Place Like Home*. London: Karnac. Tavistock Clinic Series.

———. (2002c). Working with survivors of political violence. In J. Raphael-Leff (Ed.), *Between Sessions and Beyond the Couch*. Colchester: CPS Psychoanalytic Publications.

———. (2003). 'Terrorisme et panique'. *Cahiers Jungiens de Psychanalyse, Automne, 108:* 7–20.

———. (2004). Trauma in a systemic perspective: Theoretical, organisational and clinical dimensions. Paper presented at the XIV Congress of the International Family Therapy Association in Istanbul.

———. (2005a). Political violence, trauma and mental health interventions. In D. Kalmanowitz & B. Lloyd (Eds), *Art Therapy and Political Violence: Without Art. Without Illusion*. London: Brunner-Routledge.

———. (2005b). Mythical dimensions of storied communities in political conflict and war. In T. Dulic, R. Kostic, I. Macek, & J. Trtak, *Balkan currents: Essays in honour of Kjell Magnusson*. Uppsala Multiethnic Papers, 49. Uppsala: Centre for Multiethnic Research, Uppsala University.

Park, C., Cohen, L.H. & Murch, R. (1996). Assessment and prediction of stress-related growth. *Journal of Personality, 64:* 71–105.

Saakvitne, K.W., Tennen, H. & Affleck, G. (1998). Exploring thriving in the context of clinical trauma theory: Constructivist self development theory. *Journal of Social Issues, 54*(2): 279.

Schmid, A.P. (Ed.). (1998). *Violent crime and conflicts*. Proceedings of an International Conference held at Courmayeur, Mont Blanc, October 1997 by the International Scientific and Professional Advisory Council of the United Nations' Crime Prevention and Criminal Justice Programme. Milan, ISPAC.

Stinnett, N. & DeFrain, J. (1985). *Secrets of Strong Families*. Boston, MA: Little, Brown, & Co.

Tec, N. (2003). *Resilience and Courage: Women, and Men, and the Holocaust*. New Haven: Yale University Press.

Tedeschi, R.G. & Calhoun, L.G. (1995). *Trauma and Transformation: Growing in the Aftermath of Suffering*. New York: SAGE.

———. (1996). The post-traumatic growth inventory: Measuring the positive legacy of trauma. *Journal of Traumatic Stress, 9:* 455–471.

Tedeschi, R.G., Park, C. & Calhoun, L.G. (Eds.). (1998). *Post-traumatic Growth: Theory and Research in the Aftermath of Crisis*. Mahwah, NJ: Erlbaum.

Thompson, S. (1985). Finding positive meaning in a stressful event and coping. *Basic and Applied Social Psychology, 6*: 279–295.

Tizard, B. & Varma, V. (2000). *Vulnerability and Resilience*. London: Jessica Kingsley.

Walsh, F. (1993). *Normal Family Processes* (2nd. ed.). New York: Guilford.

Werner, E.E. & Smith, R.S. (1992). *Overcoming the Odds*. Ithaca, NY: Cornell University Press.

Wolin, S. & Wolin, S. (1993). *The Resilient Self*. New York: Villiard Books.

Chapter 15

Transforming Trauma into Gift*
Spirituality, Religious Belief and the Search for Meaning

Jose Parappully

Jose Parappully is a clinical psychologist. He has a master's degree from Loyola University, Chicago, and a PhD from California Institute of Integral Studies, San Francisco. He has headed Bosco Psychological Services, Delhi, since 1997. He has been a visiting lecturer at Montfort College, Bengaluru. Integration of psychology and spirituality at the service of personal healing and social transformation is one of his major interest areas.

Tragedy is part of the human condition. Pain and trauma mark so much of our individual and social lives. Day after day the printed and electronic media bring us heart-rending reports of human tragedy. Maybe we ourselves have been broken by suffering. Trauma is a 'horrendous experience' (van der Kolk, McFarlane and Weisaeth, 1996, p. xviii). Traumatic sequelae can sometimes be so severe as to debilitate and even fragment the person irreparably (Ulman and Brothers, 1988). However painful and fragmenting a traumatic event is, it can also become the initiatory gate and the pathway to growth and wholeness (Decker, 1993a, 1993b; Jaffe, 1985; Fahlberg, Wolfer and Fahlberg,

* This chapter was first published in *The Journal*, Vol. 4(2), December 2002, by the Psychological Foundations Trust, New Delhi.

1992; Higgins, 1994; Volkan and Zintl, 1993). As Shabad and Dietrich (1988) observe, 'Out of the ashes, at times literal ashes of loss and death ... a phoenix-like process of internal restructuring may be set in motion which can have a liberating, regenerative effect upon the survivor' (p. 467).

However, for a long time the health sciences focused mostly, if not exclusively, on the tragic dimension of trauma, particularly the long-term psychological difficulties that result from it (Blake, Albano, and Keane, 1992). It is only recently that researchers and practitioners have begun to pay attention to this regenerative dimension of traumatic experiences described as 'posttraumatic growth' (Tedeschi, Park and Calhoun, 1998) and 'thriving' (Carver, 1998; O' Leary, 1998; Ickovics and Park, 1998). Updegraff and Taylor (2000) show that victims of trauma can turn their vulnerability into a source of strength. Janoff-Bulman and her colleagues (Janoff-Bulman and Berg, 1998; Janoff-Bulman and Berger, 2000) point to 'the other side of trauma'—the existential gains—and to the need for developing a psychology of appreciation. Harvey and Weber (1998) observe that loss and growth form a remarkable dialectic and see the need for a psychology of loss.

Tedeschi and Calhoun (1995) reported that despite differences in assessment methods, an average of 50 per cent to 60 per cent of respondents across studies endorse some degree of growth in response to a variety of traumatic events. Posttraumatic growth has been experienced by women sexually abused as children (McMillen, Zuravin, and Ride out, 1995), recent female survivors of sexual assault (Frazer, Conlon, and Glaser, 2001), women with breast cancer (Cordova, Cunningham, Carlson, and Andrykowski, 2001) survivors of natural disasters (McMillen, Fisher, and Smith, 1997) and parents of homicidal victims (Parappully, Rosenbaum, van den Daele, and Nzewi, 2002). Life stories of highly generative individuals show that decidedly bad events are reworked to result in good outcomes (McAdams. Diamond, de St. Aubin, and Mansfield, 1997).

In confronting the challenges that follow traumatic experience, survivors often gain a new vitality, growth and maturation. Traumatic experience can precipitate marked changes in outlook or world view, and provide profound insights. It can lead to an increased capacity for love, to a deeper appreciation of people. It can bring about transformation of the spirit and self-actualising transcendence. The experience of trauma often leads to a re-consideration of life and its priorities. It strips life to its essentials to reveal what is truly worthwhile and leads the survivors to a new kind of wisdom. It becomes a turning point that moves them from the superficial to the profound.

Darlene, a mother whose son was brutally murdered, beautifully summarises these consequences (Parappully, et al., 2002). She said:

> It is incredible, the goodness that has come out of this. And you cannot deny that. You cannot deny it....Unfortunately, I have to say yes to that. If I say no, I am lying. I don't want to say yes. But I have to. My head would like to say no. And my heart says, Darlene, you have to be an honest person. So many wonderful things have happened to heal people, and deep inside themselves at a soul level, because of Mat's murder. I cannot deny it (p. 42).
>
> One way to kind of put it all under one heading...is that his death provided an opportunity to each of us that paid attention to his death, to grow suddenly and dramatically toward a positive direction as a human being, to become more spiritual, to become more love oriented (p. 44).

SPIRITUALITY AND POSTTRAUMATIC GROWTH

Recent research has shown that there are certain resources and processes that help promote these positive consequences that result from a traumatic experience. Among these are: certain personal qualities (Park, 1998: Tennen and Affleck, 1998), cognitive reframing (Bower, Kemeny, Taylor, and Fahey, 1998; Taylor, Kemeny, Reed, Bower, and Gruenewald, 2000), finding a positive benefit in the traumatic experience (Affleck and Tennen, 1996: Davis, Nolen-Hoeksema, and Larson, 1998), social status (Adler, Epel, Castellazzo, and Ickovics, 2000: Blankenship, 1998), social support (Schaefer and Moos, 1998; van der Kolk, 2002), reaching out to others in compassion (Parappully, et. al., 2002), social and political action (Bloom, 1998) and psychotherapy (Saakvitne, Tennen, and Affleck, 1998). This article focuses on a resource that is gaining more and more attention as an important factor in the transformation of trauma, namely, spirituality and religious belief.

Spirituality is openness to the transcendent. It is a subjective experience that exists both within and outside traditional religious systems. It arises from the awareness that there is an unfinishedness, an incompleteness to one's existence, that there are realities beyond oneself that give meaning, purpose and direction to one's existence. It has to do with a search for meaning, belonging, and connectedness beyond the self, and involves the core values that shape one's beliefs and behaviour. Faith in God or a Higher Power such as a Benevolent Universe is often part of spirituality. Religion is born of the experience of transcendence and finds conceptual and cultural expression in creed, cult and code (Parappully, 2002).

As with the concept of posttraumatic growth, it is only very recently that behavioural scientists and practising clinicians have begun to recognise the significant role that spirituality and religion play in human behaviour (Parappully, 2002). Currently there is a surge in the interest in religious and spiritual issues among behavioural scientists (Calhoun and Tedeschi, 1998).

There are several studies that suggest religion and spirituality can positively impact mental health and psychological well-being (Calhoun, Cann, Tedeschi, and McMill an, 2000; Gartner, 1996; Levin and Chatters, 1998; Worthington, Kurusu, McCullough, and Sandage, 1996). Religion and spirituality are particularly helpful in transforming negative life experiences (Elliot, Kilpatrick, and McCullough, 1999; McIntosh, Silver, and Wortman, 1993; Parappully, et al., 2002; Pargament, 1998; Pargament and Brant, 1998; Ramsey and Blieszner, 2000; Simoni, Martone and Kerwin, 2002; Thomson and Vardaman, 1997). Spirituality and religion make a 'unique contribution' to physical and emotional wellbeing (Thoresen, 2001). There is a 'robust positive correlation' between religious practice and health (McCullough, 2001).

In the study of the posttraumatic experience of parents of victims of homicide (Parappully et al., 2002) spirituality and religious beliefs and practices were found to be important resources that contributed significantly to posttraumatic growth. Faith in God, belief in life after death, being thankful and engaging in prayers and rituals were powerful resources that helped these parents to make sense of the tragedy, to accept it, to find strength and comfort, and to transform it. Andrea, one of the participants in the study, conveyed the power of religious faith to transform the pain and despair that followed the murder of her only daughter:

> I was absolutely devastated ....it was a horrible horrible night. And I can remember...I had gone to bed and all I did was to cry and cry and cry and cry and cry and then there weren't simply any more tears to cry. I had reached a depth of pain within me that there weren't any tears left. And I got out of bed, and it was in the middle of the night... and I was standing in front of my closet and on the closet was hanging a religious calendar, with a Bible quote for each day. And I looked up at the date for that day, and the Bible quote was: 'Those who sow with tears shall reap rejoicing.' And I just felt it was a word from God to say. You know if you hang on, I will get you through this and then we will bring a gift of life from this terrible, terrible death. And it was the beacon of hope that I needed to grab onto, which is not to say that all the pain was gone. It wasn't, But it was a point at which I knew I could live through this. And my life would go on (p. 51).

POSTTRAUMATIC GROWTH AND THE SEARCH FOR MEANING

Transformation of trauma appears to depend to a very large extent on mastering what Becker (1968) describes as 'the meaninglessness of accidental experience' (p. 42) by finding new meaning in the experience (Greening, 1997; Lantz, 1992; Park and Folkman, 1997; Thompson, 1985; Ulmer, Range, and Smith, 1991; Wheeler, 1993-1994). According to Wertz (1985) overcoming victimisation is 'an exact reversal of its meaning' (p. 209).

In his study of evil present in human cruelty and violence, Baumeister (1997) observes: 'As a general pattern, suffering stimulates a quest for meaningful explanation. The idea that suffering is random, inevitable, and meaningless has never been satisfactory to most people, and victims desire specific explanations' (p. 2).

In traditional psychoanalysis, healing of trauma comes through re-experiencing and re-working of painful memories. However, even psychoanalysis affirms the importance of the meaning question (Horowitz, 1992). In his innovative and challenging exploration of the psychoanalytic concept of psychopathology, Grotstein (1990) emphasises that it is 'the deficit in being able to achieve sufficient meaning and meaningfulness in one's self and object world to withstand the entropic pull towards nothingness and meaninglessness' (p. 286) that maintains the pathological condition.

There is abundant documentation in clinical literature that people who have experienced suffering and injustices search for explanations for their misfortunes (Davis, Nolen-Hoeksema, and Larson, 1998; Janfoff-Bulman, 1992; Park and Folkman, 1997; Wortman, Silver and Kessler, 1993). After reviewing research literature on vulnerability and psychological resource characteristics of the victims that mediate between disaster and psychopathology, Gibbs (1989) found that the 'search for meaning' is a particularly influential variable that influences coping effectiveness (p. 509).

Finding a meaning has been found to be a powerful contributor in the transformation of traumatic experience, for example, of HIV-seropositive men (Bower, Kemeny, Taylor, and Fahey, 1998; Schwartzberg, 1993), survivors of incest (Draucker, 1992; Silver, Boon, and Stones, 1983), bereaved college students. (Schwartzberg and Janoff-Bulman, 1991), parents of homicidal victims (Parappully et al., 2002), survivors of natural disasters (Thompson, 1985), and women with breast cancer (Taylor, Lichtman, and Wood, 1984). Bettelheim's (1979) comment on the significance of the search for meaning is worth noting in this context. He wrote:

> From time to time we cannot help wondering what life's purpose for human beings might be, if any. But it is not a problem that oppresses us greatly in the normal course of events. In times of trouble, however, the problem of life's purpose, or meaning, forces itself on our awareness. The greater the hardship we experience, the more pressing the question becomes for us. It makes good sense psychologically that we begin to worry about life's meaning when we already suffer from serious trials and tribulations, because our search for answers has a purpose. It seems that if we could just grasp life's deeper significance, then we would also comprehend the true meaning of our agony—and incidentally that of others—and this would answer the burning question of why we have to bear it, why it was afflicted on us. If in the light of our understanding of life's design our suffering is needed to achieve its

purpose, or is at least an essential part of it, then as all integral element of life's great design our affliction becomes meaningful, and thus more bearable (p. 3).

SPIRITUALITY, MEANING-MAKING, AND POSTTRAUMATIC GROWTH

Both spirituality and the search for meaning are significant factors in the transformation of trauma. Indeed, it appears that it is precisely by providing meaning and coherence that spirituality helps to transform trauma. There is a positive correlation between spirituality and finding meaning and coherence. Many people derive a sense of meaning and purpose from their spirituality. Religious world views propose answers to some of life's deepest questions and also evoke hope in the face of devastating setbacks, Spirituality and religious considerations provide a unifying philosophy of life that helps people make sense of who they are and how their life-stories provide over-all unity, meaning and purpose. They serve as an integrating and stabilising force in the face of the constant push toward fragmentation (Emmons, 1998; Myers, 2000; Pargament, 1996). Personality psychologist Gordon Allport writes: 'The religious sentiment...is the portion of the personality that arises at the core...and for this reason is capable of conferring marked integration upon personality' (in Emmons, 1998, p. 70).

In a study of parents who had lost an infant to sudden death syndrome, McIntosh, Silver and Wortman (1993) found that religion was positively related to processing and finding meaning in the death. They concluded, 'The more religious an individual is, the more prepared he or she may be to impose satisfactory meaning on a negative event. Furthermore, having found meaning, the more likely he or she may be to adjust success fully to the loss' (p. 814).

CONCLUSION

There is no doubt that traumatic experiences can fragment the personality, sometimes irreparably. But it is also true that healing from trauma is possible. Sometimes it is possible not only to heal, but also to make the traumatic experience the initial gateway through which one journeys toward growth and greater wellbeing. Trauma can be transformed into a gift. Spirituality and the religious sentiment, particularly in their capacity to provide meaning and coherence, are powerful resources in the transformation of trauma.

> So what was difficult or unimportant happened, only to give you for this daily living a thousand great comparisons through which you can powerfully grow.
>
> (Rainer Maria Rilke, 1938, p. 105)

REFERENCES

Adler, N. E., Epel, E.S., Castellazzo, G. & Ickovics, J.R. (2000). 'Relationships of subjective and objective social status with psychological functioning: Preliminary data in healthy white women.' *Health Psychology, 19,* (pp. 586–92).

Affleck, G. & Tennen, H. (1996). 'Construing benefits from adversity: Adaptational significance and dispositional underpinnings.' *Journal of Personality, 64,* (pp. 899–922).

Baumeister, R.F. (1997). *Evil: Inside human cruelty and violence.* New York: W.H. Freeman & Company.

Becker, E. (1968). *The Structure of evil: An essay on the unification of the science of man.* New York: George Braziller.

Bettelheim, B. (1979). *Surviving and other essays.* New York: Alfred A. Knopf.

Blake, D.D., Albano, A.M. & Keane, T.M. (1992). 'Twenty years of trauma: Psychological Abstracts through 1989.' *Journal of Traumatic Stress, 5(3),* (pp. 477–84).

Blankenship, K.M. (1998). 'A race, class, and gender analysis of thriving.' *Journal of Social Issues, 54,* (pp. 393–404).

Bloom S. L. (1998). 'By the crowd they have been broken, by the crowd they shall be healed: The social transformation of trauma.' In R.G. Tedeschi, C.L. Park & L.G. Calhoun (Eds), *Posttraumatic Growth: Positive Changes in the Aftermath of Crisis* (pp. 179–213). Mahwah, NJ: Lawrence Erlbaum.

Bower, J.E., Kemeny, M.E., Taylor, S.E. & Fahey, L.L. (1998). 'Cognitive processing, discovery of meaning, CD4 decline, and AIDS-related mortality among bereaved HIV-seropositive men.' *Journal of Consulting and Clinical Psychology, 66,* (pp. 979–86).

Calhoun, L.G., Cann, A., Tedeschi, R.G. & McMillan, J. (2000). 'A correctional test of the relationship between post-traumatic growth, religion, and cognitive processing.' *Journal of Traumatic Stress, 13,* (pp. 521–27).

Calhoun, L.G. & Tedeschi, R.G. (1998). 'Beyond recovery from trauma: Implications of clinical practice and research.' *Journal of Social Issues, 54,* (pp. 357–71).

Carver, C.S. (1998). 'Resilience and thriving: Issues, models, and linkages.' *Journal of Social Issues, 54,* (pp. 245–66).

Calhoun, L.G. & Tedeschi, R.G. (1998). 'Posttraumatic growth: Future directions.' In R.G. Tedeschi, C.L. Park & L.G. Calhoun (Eds.), *Posttraumatic growth: Positive changes ill the aftermath of crisis* (pp. 215–38). Mahwah, NJ: Lawrence Erlbaum.

Cordova, M.J., Cunningham, L.L.C., Carlson, C.R. & Andrykowski, M.A. (2001). 'Post-traumatic growth following breast cancer: A controlled comparison study.' *Health Psychology, 20,* (pp. 176–85).

Davis. C.G., Nolen-Hoeksema, S. & Larson, J. (1998). 'Making sense of loss and benefiting from the experience: Two construals of meaning.' *Journal of Personality and Social Psychology, 75,* (pp, 561–74).

Decker, L.R. (1993a). 'Beliefs, post-traumatic stress disorder and mysticism.' *Journal of Humanistic Psychology, (4),* (pp. 15–32).

———. (1993b). 'The role of trauma in spiritual development.' *Journal of Humanistic Psychology, 33(4),* (pp.33–46).

Draucker, C.B. (1992). 'Construing benefit from a negative experience of incest' *Western Journal of Nursing Research, 14,* (pp. 343–53).

Elliot, T.R., Kilpatrick, S.D. & McCullough, M.E. (1999). 'Religion and spirituality in rehabilitation psychology.' *Rehabilitation Psychology, 44,* (pp. 388–402).

Emmons, R.A. (1998). 'Religion and personality'. In H. Koenig (Ed.), *Handbook of religion and mental health* (pp. 63–72). San Diego: Academic Press.

Frazer, P., Conlon, A. & Glaser, T. (2001). 'Positive and negative life changes following sexual assault.' *Journal of Consulting & Clinical Psychology, 69,* (pp. 1048–1055).

Fahlberg, L.L., Wolfer, J. & Fahlberg, L.A. (1992). 'Personal Crisis: Growth or pathology?' *American Journal of Health Promotion, 7,* (pp. 45–52).

Gartner, J. (1996). 'Religious commitment, mental health, and prosocial behavior: A review of the empirical literature.' In E.P. Shafranske (Ed.). *Religion and the clinical practice of psychology* (pp. 187–214). Washington. DC: American Psychological Association.

Gibbs, M.S. (1989). 'Factors in the victim that mediate between disaster and psychopathology.' *Journal of Traumatic Stress, 2,* (pp. 489–513).

Greening, T. (1997), 'Posttraumatic stress disorder: An existential-humanistic perspective.' In S. Krippner & S.M. Powers (Eds.). *Broken images, broken selves: Dissociative narratives in clinical practice* (pp. 125–135). Washington: Brunner/Mazel.

Grotstein, J.S. (1990). 'Nothingness, meaninglessness, chaos, and the "black hole": I. The importance of nothingness, meaninglessness, and chaos in psychoanalysis. Harry Stack Sullivan Award Lecture on the Annual Scientific Day of the Sheppard and Enoch Pratt Hospital.' *Contemporary Psychoanalysis, 26,* (pp. 257–90).

Harvey, J.H. & Weber, A.L. (1998). 'Why there must be a psychology of loss.' In J.H. Harvey (Ed.), *Perspectives on loss: A source book* (pp. 319–29). Philadelphia: Brunner/Mazel.

Higgins, G.O. (1994). *Resilient adults: Overcoming a cruel past*. San Francisco: Jossey Bass.

Horowitz, M.J. (1992). 'The effects of psychic trauma on mind: Structure and processing of meaning.' In J.W. Barron, M.N. Eagle, & D.L. Wolitzky (Eds.), *Interface of Psychoanalysis and Psychology* (pp. 489–500). Washington, DC: American Psychological Association.

Jaffe, D. (1985). 'Self-renewal: Personal transformation following extreme trauma.' *Journal of Humanistic Psychology, 25(4)*, (pp. 99–124).

Ickovics, J.R. & Park, C.L. (1998). 'Paradigm shift: Why a focus on health is important.' *Journal of Social Issues, 54*, (pp. 237–44).

Janoff-Bulman, R. (1992). *Shattered Assumptions: Towards a New Psychology of Trauma*. New York: Free Press.

Janoff-Bulman, R. & Berg, M. (1998). 'Disillusionment and the creation of value: From traumatic losses to existential gains.' In J.H. Harvey (Ed.), *Perspectives on loss: A sourcebook* (pp. 35–47). Philadelphia: Bmnner/Mazel.

Janoff-Bulman, R. & Berger, A.R. (2000). 'The other side of trauma: Towards a psychology of appreciation.' In J.H. Harvey & E.D. Miller (Eds.), *Loss and trauma: General and close relationship perspectives* (pp. 29–44). Philadelphia: Brunner-Routledge.

Lantz, J. (1992). 'Using Frankl's concepts with PTSD clients.' *Journal of Traumatic Stress, 5*, 485–90.

Levin. J.S. & Chatters, L.M. (1998). 'Research on religion and mental health: An overview of empirical findings and theoretical issues.' In H. Koenig (Ed.), *Handbook of religion and mental health* (pp. 33–50). San Diego: Academic Press.

McAdams, D.P., Diamond, A., de St. Aubin, E. & Mansfield. E. (1997). 'Stories of commitment: The psychosocial construction of generative lives.' *Journal of Personality and Social Psychology, 72*, (pp. 678–94).

McIntosh, D.N., Silver, R.C. & Wortman, C.B. (1993). 'Religion's role in adjustment to a negative life event: Coping with the death of a child.' *Journal of Personality and Social Psychology, 65*. (pp. 812–21).

McMillen, J.C., Fisher, R.H. & Smith, E.M. (1997). 'Perceived benefit and mental health after three types of disaster.' *Journal of Consulting & Clinical Psychology, 65*, (pp. 753–39).

McMillen, C. Zuravin, S. & Rideout, G. (1995). 'Perceived benefit from childhood sexual abuse.' *Journal of Consulting & Clinical Psychology, 63*, (pp. 1037–47).

McCullough, M.E. (2001). 'Religion and morality.' In T.G. Plante and A.C. Sherman (Cochairs), *Religious Faith and Health—What do we know?* Symposium conducted at the 109th Annual Convention of the American Psychological Association, San Francisco, USA.

Myers, D.G. (2000). 'The funds, friends, and faith of happy people.' *American Psychologist, 55*, (pp. 56–67).

Parappully, J. (2002). 'Spirituality in psychotherapy: Emerging recognition of significance.' *Psychological Foundations: The Journal, 4(1)*, (pp. 22–30).

166 | Jose Parappully

Parappully, J. Rosenbaum, R., van den Daele. L., & Nzewi, E. (2002). 'Thriving after trauma: The experience of parents of murdered children.' *Journal of Humanistic Psychology, 42,* (pp. 33–70).

Pargament, K.I. (1996). 'Religious methods of coping: Resources for the conservation and transformation of significance.' In E.P. Shafranske (Ed.), *Religion and the clinical practice of psychology* (pp. 215–39). Washington, DC: American Psychological Association.

Pargament, K.I., & Brant, C.R. (1998). 'Religion and coping.' In H. Koenig (Ed.), *Handbook of Religion and Mental Health* (pp. 111–28). San Diego: Academic Press.

Park, C.L. (1998). 'Stress-related growth and thriving through coping: The roles of personality and cognitive processes,' *Journal of Social Issues. 54,* (pp. 267–77).

Park, C.L., & Folkman, S. (1997). 'Meaning in the context of stress and coping.' *Review of General Psychology, 1,* (pp.115–44).

Ramsey, J.L., & Blieszner, R. (2000). 'Transcending lifetime losses: The importance of spirituality in old age.' In J.H. Harvey & E.D. Miller (Eds.), *Loss and Trauma: General and Close Relationship Perspectives* (pp. 225–36). Philadelphia: Brunner-Routledge.

Rilke, R.M. (1938). 'The singer sings before a child of princes.' In M.D.H. Norston. *Translations of the Poetry of Rainer Maria Rilke* (pp. 99–105). New York: W.W. Norton.

Saakvitne, K.W., Tennen, H., & Affleck, G. (1998). 'Exploring thriving in the context of clinical trauma theory: Constructivist self development theory.' *Journal of Social Issues, 54,* (pp. 279–99).

Schaefer, J.A., & Moos, R.H. (1998). 'The context for post-traumatic growth: Life crises, individual and social resources and coping.' In R.G. Tedeschi, C.L. Park & L.G. Calhoun (Eds.), *Posttraumatic growth: Positive changes in the aftermath of crisis* (pp. 99–125). Mahwah, NJ: Lawrence Erlbaum.

Schwartzberg, S.S. (1993). 'Struggling For meaning: How HIV-positive gay men make sense of AIDS.' *Professional Psychology: Research and Practice, 24,* (pp. 483–90).

Schwartzberg, S.S. & Janoff-Bulman, R. (1991). 'Grief and the search for meaning: Exploring the assumptive worlds or bereaved college students.' *Journal of Social and Clinical Psychology, 10,* (pp. 270–88).

Shabad, P.C., & Dietrich, D.R. (1989). 'Reflections on loss, mourning, and the unconscious process of recognition.' In D.R. Dietrich & P.C. Shabad (Eds.), *The Problem of Loss and Mourning: Psychoanalytic Perspectives* (pp. 463–70). New York: International Universities Press.

Shafranske, E.P. & Maloney, H.N. (1996). 'Religion and the clinical practice of psychology: A case of inclusion.' In E.P. Shafranske (Ed.), *Religion and the clinical practice of psychology* (pp. 561–86). Washington, DC: American Psychological Association.

Silver, R., Boon, C., & Stone, M. (1983). 'Searching for meaning in misfortune: Making sense of incest.' *Journal of Social Issues, 39(2),* (pp. 81–102).

Simoni, J.M., Martone, M.G., & Kerwin, J.F. (2002). 'Spirituality and psychological adaptation among women with HIV/AIDS: Implications for counselling.' *Journal of Counselling Psychology, 49,* (pp. 139–47).

Taylor, S.E., Kemeny, M.E., Reed, G.M., Bower, J.E. & Gruenewald, T.L. (2000). 'Psychological resources, positive illusions, and health.' *American Psychologist, 55,* (pp. 99–109).

Taylor, S.E., Lichtman, R.R., & Wood, J.V. (1984). 'Attributions, beliefs about control, and adjustment to breast cancer.' *Journal of Personality & Social Psychology, 40,* (pp. 489–502).

Tedeschi, R.G., & Calhoun, L.G. (1995). *Trauma and Transformation: Growing in the Aftermath of Suffering.* Thousand Oaks, CA: SAGE.

Tedeschi, R.G., Park, C.L. & Calhoun, L.G. (Eds.). (1998). *Posttraumatic Growth: Positive Changes in the Aftermath of Crisis.* Mahwah, NJ: Lawrence Erlbaum.

Tennen, H. & Affleck, G. (1998). 'Personality and transformation in the face of adversity,' In R.G. Tedeschi, C.L. Park & L.G. Calhoun (Eds.), *Posttraumatic Growth: Positive Changes in the Aftermath of Crisis* (pp. 65–98). Mahwah, NJ: Lawrence Erlbaum.

Thompson, M.P. & Vardaman, P.J. (1997). 'The role of religion in coping with the loss of a family member to homicide.' *Journal for the Scientific Study of Religion, 36,* (pp. 44–51).

Thompson, S.C. (1985). 'Finding positive meaning in stressful event and coping.' *Basic and Applied Social Psychology, 6,* (pp. 279–95).

Thoresen, C.E. (2001, August). 'Science of spirituality and health.' In T.G. Plante and A.C. Sherman (Cochairs). *Religious faith and health—What do we know?* Symposium conducted at the 109th. Annual Convention of the American Psychological Association, San Francisco, USA.

Ulman, R., & Brothers, D. (1988). *The Shattered Self: A Psychoanalytic Study of Trauma.* Hillsdale, NJ: Analytic Press.

Ulmer, A., Range, L.M., & Smith, P.C. (1991). 'Purpose in life: A moderator of recovery from bereavement.' *Omega, 23,* (pp. 279–89).

Updegraff, J.A., & Taylor, S.E. (2000). 'From vulnerability to growth: Positive and negative effects of stressful life events.' In J.H. Harvey & E.D. Miller (Eds.). *Loss and Trauma: General and Close Relationship Perspectives* (pp. 3–28). Philadelphia: Brunner-Routledge.

Van der Kolk, B.A. (2002, December). 'Body keeps the score: Integration of body and mind in the treatment of traumatized people.' In *Psychological Trauma: Impact & Treatment.* Workshop organized by RAHI Foundation, New Delhi.

Van der Kolk. B.A., & McFarlane, A.C. (1996). 'The black hole of trauma.' In B.A. van der Kolk, A.C. Mcfarlane, & L. Weisaeth (Eds.), *Traumatic stress: The effects of overwhelming experiences on mind, body, and society* (pp. 3–23). New York: Guilford.

Volkan, V.D. & Zintl, E. (1993). *Life after loss: The lessons of grief.* New York: Charles Scribner's Sons.

Wertz, F.J. (1985). 'Methods and findings in a phenomenological psychological study of a complex life event: Being criminally victimized.' In A. Giorgi (Ed.), *Phenomenology and Psychological Research* (pp. 155–216). Pittsburgh: Duquesne University Press.

Wheeler. I. (1993–1994). 'The role of meaning and purpose in life in bereaved parents associated with a self-help group: Compassionate Friends.' *Omega: Journal of Death and Dying, 28*, (pp. 261–71).

Worthington, E.L., Kurusu, T.A., McCullough, M.E. & Sandage, S.J. (1996). 'Empirical Research on Religion and Psychotherapeutic Processes and Outcomes: A 10-Year Review and Research Prospectus.' *Psychological Bulletin, 119,* (pp. 448–87).

Wortman, C.B., Silver, R.C. & Kessler, R.C. (1993). 'The meaning of loss and adjustment to bereavement.' In M.S. Stroebe, W. Stroebe, & R.O. Hansson (Eds.), *Handbook of bereavement: Theory, research and intervention* (pp. 349–66). New York: Cambridge University Press.

Chapter 16

Trauma and Psychoanalysis*

Madhu Sarin

Madhu Sarin is a practising psychoanalyst based in Delhi. She has practised and taught in the US and India, done clinical work with political refugees and torture victims, and conducted many training workshops. She has a PhD from the University of Delhi, a Master's degree in clinical social work from New York University, and a diploma in psychoanalysis from The Institute For Psychoanalytic Training and Research, New York.

There are difficulties inherent in any attempt to produce a universally satisfactory definition of terrorism. As attribution theorists remind us, perspective is a critical element: one person's terrorist may very well be another's revolutionary freedom fighter, depending upon whether the focus is on the actor or the object (recipient) of the act.... Finally, in the international arena, we should appreciate that states, while they are often the objective of terrorism, have also been major perpetrators of terrorism, both against segments of their own population and, as third parties, against groups in other jurisdictions.

Richard V. Wagner, *Terrorism: A Peace Psychological Analysis*

Originally a Greek word meaning wound or bodily injury, trauma is commonly used to refer to an overwhelming experience, be it the

---

* This chapter was first published in *The Journal*, Vol. 7(2), December 2005, by the Psychological Foundations Trust, New Delhi.

collective experience of war, natural disaster, or deeply felt personal calamity. However, as with all such concepts, trauma resists easy definition and has changed along with shifts in history and culture.

Events in the 20th century such as the two world wars, the looming threat of nuclear war, the genocides in Germany, Armenia, Africa and Cambodia, natural and man-made disasters such as famine and earthquakes, which involved violence and the loss of life on a massive scale revolutionised the term and made it fundamental to contemporary thought. However, this shift surfaced into popular awareness only after the 1960s, in the wake of the Vietnam War and widespread social upheaval triggered by movements against the war, the experiences of war veterans and the emergence into the public domain of formerly taboo 'private' issues such as the sexual and physical abuse of children and domestic violence.

From its inception, the impact of trauma on mental functioning had been an intrinsic aspect of psychoanalytic theorising. With the shift mentioned above, clinical practice and theoretical formulations became increasingly complex, leading both to new investigations of psychic trauma and to its long-term effects.

FANTASY, REALITY AND PSYCHIC FUNCTIONING

The psychoanalytic understanding of trauma is dependent on underlying theories about the human mind and psychic functioning. We can broadly understand psychic trauma as a blow to the mind which engenders a state of helplessness, acute anxiety and regression, which affects the capacity to mentalise. Fantasy which structures the constellation of defences at both the level of individual and group functioning is an important component of mental functioning. Why is fantasy so important to psychoanalysts? Clinical and research evidence both indicate that a sense of reality is not a universal given but a developmental achievement, based on physiological intactness and contingent on a basic attunement between the growing mind of the infant and her caretaker.

The emergence of mentalising, the ability to symbolise and establish meaning, which depends upon an increasingly articulated sense of oneself and other, is deeply embedded in the child's primary early relationships, principally in the mirroring relationship with the care-giver. It is only the background structure of safety, stability, containment and understanding provided to a growing mind by a loving and patient caretaker, which allows for an intact sense of self and other. Without this, no sense of reality is possible and there is a reparative retreat into a fantasy world. Although analysts differ on a timetable for this, all agree that a growing sense of reality is a developmental achievement.

Fantasy is an organic and intrinsic part of every individual's defensive constellation. Contingent on a complex interplay of inborn constitutional factors and the environment—culture, history, temperament, physiology—it structures the psyche's adaptation and relation to reality. A barebone sense of reality is psychologically unacceptable without the illusion, if not outright delusion, of a kind of *maya* of everyday life. An ongoing sense of trust in everyday regularity and stability have their basis in fantasies of infantile omnipotence and self-idealisation, which are necessary background aspects of the mind. They echo childhood feelings of security brought about by early internalisation that 'no matter what happens, I will be protected.' Since much of experience is inextricably tinged with loss, disappointment, frustration and pain, life would be intolerable without the hope giving, reality undoing, gratifying daydreams and myths which imbue waking life and most of conscious experience. In research on psychoanalytic work with couples, it was found that relationships which were the most satisfying and enduring were based on the shared fantasy that the good times together outweighed the bad, rather than other factors such as better communication, spending more time together, etc. (as quoted in a report in the Science section of the *New York Times*, 2001).

A child's experience of psychic reality is an evolving one. It shifts from a view where there is no sharply demarcated sense of self and other, or of inside and outside, to an experience in which, there is as if, an exact correspondence between internal state and external reality. This mode is called 'psychic equivalence', to emphasise that for the young child, mental events are equivalent in terms of power, causality and implications to events in the physical world (a characteristic of magical thinking). Equating internal and external is inevitably a two- way process. The small child will equate appearance with reality (how it seems is how it is), but also thoughts and feelings distorted by fantasy (passionate libidinous and destructive wishes), will be projected onto external reality, unmodulated by any awareness of this distortion. At this stage in the infant's mind, an internal physical state and the psychic distress associated with the experience, like a pain in her stomach, might seem to be caused by mother who seems like a bountiful goddess if she is able to provide comfort, or else a demon attacking her entrails, in her inability to soothe.

DEFINITIONS OF TRAUMA

Over time, the multiple uses and blurring of distinctions within psychoanalytic usage aggravated by the growing use of this term in colloquial discourse, resulted in hybrid concepts that detracted from precise and technical meaning. As far back as 1967, in a symposium on trauma, Anna Freud bemoaned the fact that one of the consequences of the increasing use of psychoanalytic terms in popular parlance was the attendant loss of conceptual clarity. Increasingly, whatever had an adverse impact on mental functioning became identified with trauma and the precise psychoanalytic definitions of the term became obscured.

> We are in the position of witnessing this typical process with regard to the definition of trauma which extends at present from the original notion of the break through the stimulus barrier at one extreme to the notions of the accumulative, the strain, the retrospective, the screen trauma, until it becomes difficult at the other extreme to differentiate between adverse pathogenic influences in general and trauma in particular (Anna Freud, 1967).

Psychoanalysis started out with a concept of psychic trauma or traumatic neurosis, which was subsequently not clearly differentiated from other usages of the term, such as traumatic object loss or traumatic anxiety. Two of these were repeatedly discussed by Freud, namely, traumatic neurosis and traumatic (automatic) anxiety. A further distinction can be made by identifying a third condition which some have called a post-traumatic neurotic like state (Yorke, 1986). Each of these different kinds of traumatic experiences have specific neurobiological and psychological ramifications associated with them. Nowadays, trauma is generally equated with post traumatic stress syndrome (PTSD) and refers to the overwhelming experience of sudden or catastrophic events in which the response to the event occurs in the often uncontrolled, repetitive occurrence of hallucinations and other intrusive phenomena. It reflects the direct imposition on the mind of the unavoidable reality of horrific events, the taking over of the mind—psychically and neurobiologically—by an event that it cannot control. The syndromes of PTSD, uncomplicated by object loss (like a car accident), of traumatic bereavement (loss of a loved one at a very early age or as a result of natural disaster or violent conflict), of relatively non-traumatic bereavement (the death of a significant other at a timely age), of attachment patterns which lead to perversions of internalised objects causing inner feelings of abandonment and nameless dread and emptiness (through gross lack of attunement or other forms of abuse or neglect by caretakers early in life), though often interwoven and inseparable, are all different.

I will try and briefly disentangle some of these concepts so as to highlight their specificity.

Let us start with Freud's statement that 'the essence of a traumatic situation is experience of helplessness on the part of the ego in the face of an accumulation of excitation whether of external or internal origin' (Freud, 1926). A postulated stimulus barrier is breached which undermines normal ego functioning and engenders a state of helplessness. The traumatic state varies in intensity and duration from individual to individual with negligible consequences or what Freud called a full blown traumatic neurosis which manifests as total apathy and withdrawal or near panic and disorganised thought and behaviour. The postulated stimulus barrier is breached not only by stimulus coming from without, but also as a result of internal factors, i.e., intra-psychic conflict and constitutional factors. Although the common feature of 'reduction to helplessness' is held to characterise both, this serves to gloss over significant differences.

We can distinguish Freud's notion of traumatic neurosis from his psychoanalytic concept of traumatic anxiety as follows:

(1) What Freud called traumatic neurosis was the immobilisation of the ego and the consequent feelings of helplessness that arise due

to some external factor/s. A breach of the stimulus barrier initiates the traumatic neurosis.

Let us consider the impact on the psyche of stimulus coming from without and which can lead to a 'traumatic neurosis'. Freud's view of the nature of the traumatic neurosis was particularly clearly set out in *Beyond the Pleasure Principle* (1920/1955a) in the course of discussion of the significance of the compulsion to repeat. The disturbance arises when the ego is totally unprepared for a 'traumatising' event of an external kind and is what we now associate with PTSD (post-traumatic stress disorder). An example would be of a car crash coming totally out of the blue, (or an earthquake, or a tsunami) of which the driver had no anticipation and was therefore psychically unprepared for. Freud's view was that, in such conditions, the stimulus barrier broke down and the ego became helpless and was overwhelmed with a degree of anxiety it was unable to absorb or master, at the time. The ego was 'knocked out' and unable to function temporarily. This period of loss of functioning follows immediately on impact and continues for a short and slightly variable period. In the current example, an observer would see the victim as dazed, and would no doubt refer to her as suffering from 'shock'. We can assume that ego functioning is lost since the victim frequently clearly remembers the circumstances of the traumatic incident, but has little memory of the period immediately ensuing.

The subsequent clinical picture is well known. It is characterised by restlessness and variable but diffuse anxiety. A striking feature is the recurring dream in which the circumstances of the crash are vividly relived. These frightening dreams were, in Freud's view, not really 'dreams' at all in the sense in which these are understood psychoanalytically, i.e., disguised wish fulfillment (Freud 1920/1955a). They are a vivid re-experience of the disturbing event during sleep, in an attempt to absorb, digest or master the overwhelming and frightening affects involved, an attempt by the ego to restore equilibrium and function. The traumatic event may be re-lived in the form of daydreams or preoccupations during the day. The 'traumatic neurosis' can therefore be conceptualised in terms of Breuer and Freud's (1895/1951) pre-psychoanalytic notion of 'strangulated affect' and, indeed this was explicitly foreshadowed by Freud

(1893/1955b) who theorised it in the language of drive theory and in relation to the abreactive process.

(2) The second kind of helplessness Freud talked about was in connection with the psychoanalytic theory of anxiety reformulated by him in 1926 (Freud, 1926).

Anxiety functioned as a danger signal seated in the ego that warned of an impending situation of danger. The danger itself was such that, if the ego were unable to mobilise its defenses, it would be overwhelmed and rendered helpless by automatic anxiety in the face of a 'traumatic anxiety-situation'. (Freud, 1926 p. 148). The helplessness consequent on intra-psychic factors can itself be of two types: (a) One which comes early in individual mental development which some analysts have termed 'somatic vegetative excitation' (Yorke, 1986). This comes very early in development possibly at a pre-verbal state and when self-other differentiation has not occurred, is immobilising, is near psychotic, and diffuse. (b) The second condition arises at a later stage of development, when self-other differentiation has occurred within the psyche, and is identified by Freud as traumatic (automatic) anxiety which functions as a danger signal seated in the ego that warns of an impending situation of danger.

The earliest form of this anxiety (a), was distinguished by Freud from what he called (b) 'psychic' anxiety. Vegetative, somatic anxiety comes earlier in development (in fact he regarded the trauma of birth as a precursor and prototype) and precedes the child's capacity to experience psychic anxiety. It is this anxiety that is aroused in (1), when the stimulus barrier is breached by externally caused events. Although this condition shares with traumatic psychic anxiety the state of reduction to helplessness, there are, nevertheless, important differences. When the ego is overwhelmed such as in (a) it is not flooded or overwhelmed with pervasive anxiety but completely immobilised. When the ego encounters what it anticipates will be a danger and is unable to mobilise its defences such as in (b), pervasive anxiety floods the ego and overwhelms it.

When used in this sense, i.e. (b), trauma is a ubiquitous part of all development: for instance, every infant experiences 'traumatic' anxiety, when her needs are not met. However, if this is balanced by a reasonable amount of gratification, so that the balance between pleasure and pain is not seriously disturbed, the frustration is a motivating factor in development. So it is important to note that in this sense, traumatic anxiety is experienced by every child at all stages of development, is very often rapidly reversible, and, to that extent, is strictly not a traumatising experience as such. Freud identified common danger situations sequentially corresponding to stages in the developmental progression: (a) (i) When the very young child is threatened by a degree of pervasive anxiety with which she is unable to deal, this can only be alleviated by the ministrations of a mother or other caretaker in the parental role, who detects and attends to the source of that anxiety, or else this results in the prototype for later psychotic fears of annihilation (annihilation anxiety). (b) (ii) This is followed by anxieties associated with fear of loss of the object, (iii) fear of the loss of the object's love, (iv) castration anxiety, and (v) fear of loss of the superego's love or loss of self-respect/regard (Freud, 1926).

Once ego development is sufficiently advanced, through internalisations and identifications of nurturing functions out of love, fear and respect for those we are attached to as our caregivers and who form our overarching relational universe, when these basic danger situations are re-encountered in fresh form, they are re-experienced in a way such that a more resilient psychic structure can better ward off the threat and avoid the onset of traumatic anxiety. In other words, we develop better and more mature defences against different kinds of traumatic anxiety.

(3) The third condition refers to frequent entanglement of two levels of the so-called internal stimulus barrier that is breached by trauma. The breakthrough of the barrier against internal stimuli is often confused with an untimely breakthrough of the repression barrier, repression being a common psychic defence by means of which an idea associated with painful affects is excluded from consciousness. The two are distinct, though often interwoven in an individual's psyche such that later significant events, conflicts, and experiences are drawn into and entangled with early traumatic experiences. For

instance, as reported in a personal conversation, a senior analyst in New York who felt sure he had thoroughly plumbed all aspects of his personality in his own analyses, could not fathom the catastrophic sense of anxiety he experienced after 9/11 and couldn't shake off even after considerable time had elapsed after the event. It was only after he began to explore his associations to the latter, that for the first time this brought up memories of his family's response to a devastating fire in their home when he was very little, which had unconsciously enveloped his growing mind and which had never surfaced previously. Traumatic memories might also have a screening function where a 'screen trauma' like a screen memory, can serve either to cover another more significant trauma or else can stand for a group or series of traumatic events. For instance, Glover (1929), reports a patient who remembered how he burned his hand when he was about three and a half years, but had no recollection of a circumcision occurring at the same time. In their clinical work, analysts repeatedly come across similar phenomena and it requires considerable working through to reconstruct such data. One traumatic experience may function as a kind of organiser for others and serve to structure the patient's disturbances and anxieties in the form they assume when they re-emerge in analysis. The analytic task in a case such as this consists of the slow isolation of the trauma from all that goes before and all that follows. Yorke (1986) calls cases of this kind, post-traumatic neurotic-like states.

INDIVIDUAL FACTORS AND TRAUMA

Vulnerability to trauma varies from individual to individual and depends upon many factors, although the intensity of the precipitating stimulus in relation to the preparedness of the stimulus barrier is critical when considering specific episodes. It is well known, for example, that there are differences in the level of the threshold for pain. Constitution, past experiences, adaptive capacities, and concomitant ego strength, each have a role to play in determining individual response to trauma. Despite its pervasiveness, some forms of trauma have a greater impact than others, and create an adverse effect on development and heightened vulnerability in the ego. Repeated failures can have a pernicious cumulative effect which seriously hampers the maturation process and creates a predisposition to further trauma.

The environmental and psychic circumstances in which a trauma occurs, the meaning the individual attaches to the trauma/event rather than the event itself, the adaptive and primitive defences used to master it (which speak to constitutional factors, fixations and regressions in ego and superego development), the support given by self-esteem, by internalised as well as significant others in one's interpersonal world, all help to determine outcome.

PSYCHIC TRAUMA, FANTASY AND THE RELATIONAL CONTEXT OF THE EVOLVING SELF

Right from its inception, psychoanalysis elucidated both the fantasy distortion and elaboration of traumatic experience while retaining the importance of actual trauma. Psychic trauma has immediate effects as well as far reaching developmental consequences. When a child experiences a trauma, this event becomes intertwined with the growing child's, and subsequent adult's, unconscious fantasy life. Prior trauma can enhance vulnerability to subsequent trauma and to trauma linked to phase-specific unconscious conflict mentioned in 2(b). In the evolution of the child's psyche, the experience of affect (emotion, feeling) is the seed from which eventually mentalisation of affect (thoughts and judgements based on inner feeling and conviction) can grow, but only in the context of at least one continuing, and safe attachment relationship. The inability to tolerate an affect state cannot be explained solely, or even primarily, on the basis of the quantity or intensity of the painful feelings evoked by an injurious event. Developmentally, traumatic affect states have to be understood in terms of the relational systems in which they take form. Painful or frightening affect only becomes traumatic when the attunement that the child needs from caretakers, to assist in its tolerance, containment, modulation and integration, is profoundly absent.

Research and clinical observation suggest that perhaps, because it can be terrifying for thoughts and feelings to be experienced as concretely 'real', the small child develops an alternative way of construing mental states by starting out with a 'pretend mode'. In 'pretend mode', the child experiences feelings and ideas as totally representational, or symbolic, as having no implication for the world outside. At an earlier stage of development, child's play forms no bridge between inner and outer reality. Only gradually, and through safe closeness to an attachment figure, who can simultaneously hold together the child's pretend and serious perspectives, does the integration of these two modes give rise to a psychic reality in which feelings and ideas are known as internal, yet related to what is outside. This eventually leads to a more complex view which has as its hallmark the capacity to mentalise: to assume the existence of thoughts and feelings in others and in oneself, and to recognise these as connected to outer reality.

An outline of this process is as follows. The infant gradually develops and realises she has a separate and distinguishable self by slowly beginning to articulate, through the help of a caretaker, that she has clearly defined feelings and thoughts about herself, others, as well as the larger world beyond her, and slowly becomes able to distinguish these. This happens mainly through learning that her internal experiences are meaningfully related to by the parent/s or caregiver/s. When sexual, physical or verbal abuse, or repeated denial of a child's inner world is perpetrated by an attachment figure, it has been found that these traumas interfere with the developmental process described above. The following developmental glitches have been noticed in severely abused children and in their later adult selves:

(a) the persistence of magical thinking or a psychic equivalence mode of experiencing internal reality;
(b) a propensity to continue to shift into a pretend mode (dissociation); and
(c) a partial inability to reflect on one's own mental states and those of others.

If caretakers are unable to accept the reality of the child's experience (thereby rejecting her inner world and in that sense, rejecting her), or if they persistently ridicule or mock her, and insist upon the reality of their own viewpoint or neglect this aspect of mirroring back to the child that her own nascent productions have integrity and value, the child is left feeling traumatised. She has no way of validating her own thoughts and feeling and is left with an inner sense of abandonment, helplessness, inchoate nameless anxiety and humiliation for the rest of her life, unless modified subsequently by other factors. A child's sense of self and identity depends on being acknowledged and mirrored as does her sense of the external world—of other people's thoughts and feelings, as well as other aspects of external reality. Children can't form a robust, intact sense of self if they disavow reality, especially the reality of their own feelings, thoughts and opinions. I have found the following clinical picture quite widespread in my work with patients in India: it seems to be part of a cultural pattern that encouragement or praise is rare, and a child seems mostly to be put down and criticised, no doubt with a view to stimulate and challenge the child to grow and develop, but which more often than not, has the opposite effect of creating such enormous anxiety about her own internal productions that she is unable to make any realistic judgement about what might be good about herself. Instead there is a deeply internalised sense of herself as rotten, shameful or fraudulent.

If the message from parents is that we will only love you unconditionally if you do as we expect, or only if you can manage within the framework of our experience, expectations or values, this becomes what Betty Lifton (1996) has described as a Faustian bargain for a child who is left with little choice but to step out of her own narrative and adopt the narrative of her caretakers, if she is not to feel utterly wretched and alone at a stage in life when she is entirely dependent on them. If she wants to hold onto her parents, she must abandon her real self. A child in this situation feels compelled to identify with caretakers she is dependent upon, and adopt their viewpoint and relinquish her own, even if this is experienced as an assault on a sense of selfhood. Better to accept the aggressor's point of view than to experience inner abandonment. In fact, anything is more tolerable than to be left helpless and alone. This leaves the child with feelings of basic, overwhelming, traumatic anxiety about feeling isolated, abandoned and helpless, and inner feelings of rage and resentment at the choice forced upon her. A child who is put in such a predicament, is unable to develop feelings of self-worth or belonging and has little sense of validity or ownership about her own thoughts or feelings.

It also creates a split in the self between an artificial self and a forbidden self, neither of which is completely true or false. The artificial self becomes almost selfless in its desire to please. Wanting to fit in at any cost, it will deny its own needs for those of others because of a deep and primitive fear that if it expresses real feelings, it will lose the only person/s it can count/depend on. Real feelings are only available in daydreams and fantasy and are cut off from conscious awareness, including a deep sense of inarticulate resentment and rage at being put in this untenable position. The artificial self may behave like a perfect child but know itself to be an imposter. Having cut off a vital part of self, it may experience an inner deadness. The forbidden self holds on to the self that might have been, had it found acceptance. Refusing to disavow reality it goes underground for vitality and authenticity, harbouring a jumble of fantasies about life as it might have been, which are frequently sexualised and highly charged with a sado-masochistic flavour. Such a self also frequently acts out in anti-social ways when the unexpressed anger at suppressing aspects of self erupt as uncontrollable rage.

This fantasy world is an essential part of the developing self: the fantasies are attempts to connect with an internalised care-taking nurturing mother and provide a comfort zone that the real mother was unable to confer, and are also ways of expressing retaliative equivalence, pent up rage and upset. These fantasies are not only reparative but also a form of grieving, of conjuring up an absence, and of venting intense anger. But situated as they are in the psychic structure of the inner world of the child, they cannot connect with the outer world or become integrated into reality. If the parent cannot think about the child's mental experience, this deprives her of the basis for a viable sense of herself. The absence or distortion of this mirroring function may generate a psychological world in which inner experiences are poorly represented, and therefore a desperate need is created to find alternative ways of containing psychological experience and the mental world. Clinically this would mean that the child who has not received recognisable but modified images of her affective states, may later have trouble in differentiating reality from fantasy, and physical from psychic reality. This may restrict her to an instrumental (manipulative), rather than signal (communicative) use of affect. Fragmented and partial aspects of inner self states are projected onto aspects of external reality, and (self) control is sought by manipulating the latter, i.e. she becomes a 'control freak' manipulating other people or external events, as way stations to gain self-control.

Psychoanalytic research shows that trauma also plays a significant role in the psycho-genesis of violence. When children do not have access to their own internal states, i.e, when they are not able to feel themselves from within, they are forced to experience the self from without. Fragmented and partial aspects of inner self states are projected onto aspects of external reality, and (self) control is sought by manipulating the latter. Instead of being able to use their emotions and thoughts to communicate to others in symbolic representational mode, they are restricted to an instrumental (manipulative) mode. Here the psyche attempts to gain control of un-metabolised inner states by attempting to manipulatively control external aspects of reality which are experienced as projections of these disavowed, inarticulate, internal mental states. In other words, such people have little sense of why they are feeling as they do but feel an uncontrollable urge to give expression and vent intense inner feelings, often through acts of destruction or self destruction. These ways of thinking persist into adulthood, and play a vital role in acts of uncontrolled and enraged violence. The latter can be seen as ways to express and cope with such thoughts and feelings through physical action and involve various forms of self-harm or aggression towards others (Fonagy, Moran, & Target, 1993; Fonagy & Target, 1995).

Since the human psyche is capable of growth and flexibility, people in trouble can be helped to overcome the impact of prior trauma. The aim of psychoanalytic treatment is to recognise and work with individual deficit, fragility and strength in order to facilitate mental and emotional growth. Vulnerability is understood as arising from the impact of the trauma itself that leads to defences which are inadequate to deal with contemporary situations, or because of frailty in the character structure built around a specific defensive constellation, or some combination of both.

MASSIVE SOCIAL TRAUMA AND PSYCHOANALYSIS: INDIVIDUAL AND COMMUNITY BASED

Although analysts like Valmik Volkan (1988, 1990, 1999a, 1999b, 1999c, 2003) and Robert Lifton (1968, 1986, 1993, 1999) most notably, and a few others, had long drawn attention in their writing to large scale social trauma and its impact on individual, group and social functioning, it is only now, in response to recent events, that psychoanalysts have attempted to apply their substantial corpus of clinical, theoretical and research findings about trauma to such phenomena. This is reflected in the fact that trauma was the theme of the last International Psychoanalytic Congress held at Buenos Aires in 2005. Analysts in Latin America whose work is not well known in the English language, have long contended with the impact of repressive and brutal political regimes, those in Europe with conflicts in areas such as the former Yugoslavia, and more recently in North America, in the aftermath of 9/11, the Oklahoma city bombings and the killings at Columbine High school, many analysts have had to deal with issues of massive social trauma at first hand. Closer to home, Sudhir Kakar has used a psychoanalytic approach to understand similar material in his study of communal conflict and violence in Hyderabad in his *Colors of Violence* (1995), as has Asish Nandy in his ambitious and ongoing documentation of oral histories of perpetrators and victims of Partition violence. Younger scholars here have also used a psychoanalytic perspective to understand trauma such as Honey Oberoi in her doctoral work on the Tibetan refugee population in Dharamsala, also Manasi Kumar, in her study of survivors of the Gujarat earthquake of 2002.

Psychoanalysts have the advantage of having studied in great depth, the impact on the individual psyche, of various kinds of traumatic personal calamities. But does psychoanalysis have anything to offer toward an understanding of the massive social, political and natural disasters that seem to surround us at present? The typical post-traumatic stress disorder reactions seen in individuals subjected to socially circumscribed traumas seem inadequate in conceptualising the effects of massive social traumas of the type of armed conflict which affects children and family life such as in Kashmir, Nepal, and many other parts of the world, the reality and regularity of terrorist attacks on civilian populations, and natural disasters such as the tsunami or earthquakes.

In the Anglo-American world of psychoanalysis, the application of psychoanalysis to social problems often sparks debate because relatively few analysts have explicitly framed psychoanalytic interventions targeting community and social problems. Twemlow (2004) suggests that an analytic approach to work with terrorised or traumatised individuals who cannot think reflectively, let alone respond to an interpretive consultative clinical model, needs to be active-interventionist and group-focused. Although such an approach incorporates understanding of the transference-based expectations of group participation, it places greater emphasis on actively changing how the group functions than on interpreting its underlying dynamics. Despite being supportive rather than being insight-oriented, the method is nonetheless informed by a psychoanalytic understanding of large- and small-group unconscious dynamics.

Volkan was a pioneer who brought a psychoanalytic perspective to bear on such issues. He was one of the first analysts to point out that nations and communities must deal with unconscious processes if they are to forge lasting solutions to international and inter-ethnic conflicts. His work as consultant with the United Nations has led to a committee of analysts working regularly with that body. Using a group analytic approach, he works with the premise that the members of a community are best able to identify a community's most pressing concerns and so must be engaged in devising the nature of the intervention and in finding a point of entry for the most effective assistance. An analyst working in the community psychoanalyst mode is far less in charge than in the clinical context, and functions more as a stakeholder and collaborator in devising the solutions to problems about which the analyst may have little knowledge.

Stuart Twemlow (2004) is another contemporary analyst who has written and worked in a group mode. He proposes a potentially new role for psychoanalysis, one based on Freud's idea of psychoanalysis as a general psychology and significant social force. He reminds us that psychoanalysts have had a unique training that positions them to think about thinking and the unthinkable, and to make some sense of it— training that from a common sense perspective would suggest an obvious role for the analyst in the discussion of terrorism, violence and related matters. Psychoanalysts should be able to contribute significantly along the lines they are used to doing as part of their everyday work life: to understand and make meaning of what is apparently random and meaningless. Apparently senseless random acts of terrorism or violence could be reviewed from such a perspective. One factor that magnifies the traumatic impact of terrorism is its impersonal and apparently random nature in which innocent civilians are attacked rather than professional soldiers. Fonagy (2003), and Twemlow and Sacco (2002) have pointed out that the ontological terror promoted by such detached symbolic violence needs to be understood in its social context, especially if one is to reduce terror and restore the capacity to mentalise. To ignore this and instead address only the criminal, anti-social aspects of terrorist actions precludes a broader understanding of terrorism and its unconscious determinants.

The only way that apparently random symbolic violence can be made sense of, is if the viewpoint of perpetrators is heard and acknowledged, and not marginalised and degraded. Asish Nandy is attempting this in his ongoing unpublished research project, on the violence associated with the Partition of India and Pakistan at the Centre for Developing Societies, Delhi. Analysts have suggested the following in attempting to understand terrorism: Akhtar (1999, 2002) notes that the label 'terrorist' has historically been used to invalidate the project of a particular group. This implies disrespect and oversimplifies the group's views, which contributes to difficulties in considering responses to the terrorism. He points out that in times of turmoil, social groups and terrorists can unite against an enemy that has set itself up by adopting this attitude of disrespect. Volkan (2003) too shares similar views. Fonagy (2003) suggests that there is a certain rationality in the actions of terrorists as they try to bring about psychic equivalence—that is, bring their views and the outside world's closer to parity. The need is to understand this process rather than just react to it in a trigger happy mode. Jerrold Post (1990), who has hands-on experience interviewing terrorists, uses analytic thinking to suggest that we must be aware that the terrorist is trying to communicate a message representing a larger group identity. In his experience, since terrorists give up their lives wishing to be understood, it puts their idealism in a completely different category from that of antisocial personalities.

CLINICAL FINDINGS AND TREATMENT

To re-iterate: depending on individual capacity and its nature and intensity, trauma produces a state of fear, helplessness, regression, and prolonged and longstanding inner destabilisation. It affects the mind by impairing its symbolic capacities, disabling its capacity to mentalise and there by absorb or digest the experience in question. When a person is rendered helpless, then the mind's capacity to symbolise and create meaning can be significantly impaired, temporarily or permanently. If the emotional meaning of the event is lacking, then the individual may not be able to make sense of, or handle, a later situation of stress when strong affects may be aroused. If trauma is unresolved, it remains an insistent part of present psychic functioning, not only as a memory of a past event, but one which colours one's present perception of events and relationships to others and oneself. Some individuals may manage to integrate the traumatic experiences and find adjustment in spite of it; for others, this will result in lifelong disabilities and adjustment problems.

Whatever the individual response, trauma will never be forgotten and it is an experience which by definition, changes the person's perspective on life. The central problem in healing trauma relates to enhancing an individual's capacity to deal with the intense and difficult affects associated with it. Human beings and human minds are resilient and can recover, especially if there is a healthy and well-functioning ego in the first place, and if appropriate social and environmental conditions can be restored or created, which help survivors to move forward by being able to face and overcome the trauma.

Psychoanalysts work with the conviction that taking pre-morbid factors into account, it is possible to work with traumatised patients so as to give symbolic structure and form to the unmetabolised and horrific experience, so as to work this through, and achieve a restoration of the capacity to make meaning. Varvin and Volkan (2003) identify the following as goals to re-achieve equilibrium: for the individual, the important task is to overcome helplessness, to mourn the losses, and to regain control in life. For the group, the important task is to counteract the fragmentation and isolation of affected members, and to re-establish cohesion, leadership, and support within the group. The main task in individual psychotherapy and other related treatment is to attempt to enhance the mentalising capacity of the patient by connecting aspects of the patient's present life with the traces and derivatives of past trauma, and undergoing the complicated processes of mourning that are necessary to gradually repair and restore meaning and come to terms with loss.

In the case of traumas which have their origin in external events, two clinical points can be made. The first is that even the fully-blown picture tends to resolve itself without treatment, in somewhere around eight months, although there are exceptions. Psychoanalysts have learned that even a minor degree of anticipation can allow sufficient preparation for the 'shock' to be less pronounced and for recovery to take place within a comparatively short time. The second and related point is that the treatment situation or something equivalent to it, in which the victim is able to recollect and share the affects associated with the trauma over and over again, with an empathetic and concerned listener, effectively reduces the period during which the condition persists. In World War II, psychiatrists dealing with traumatic neuroses (as opposed to battle exhaustion) arising in the front line had found that medication using ether or pentothal, restored the victim to normal functioning within something like three weeks. We now know through clinical and research evidence, that the patient can be helped to work through the difficult affects experienced by means of all empathic and supportive psychotherapeutic relationship, without chemical assistance (Yorke, 1986).

When considering loss, absorbing all the feelings and thoughts associated with the loss, and undergoing a process of mourning and grief is the only way the psyche can recover and move on. In cases of loss, it becomes important to consider the age and stage of development when it occurs, the nature of the loss, its significance, socio-cultural factors, and the group process which influence individual responses to various forms of trauma and traumatic bereavement. For instance, in our own culture, the timely death of someone who has lived their full span of life is a cause for celebration. If to this, we add the idea of *varna ashrama,* or the various stages of life, where the later stages suggest a gradual withdrawal from material and social engagement, and the notion of rebirth, then our attitudes to death involve a gradual and accepting psychological preparation for it, and is relatively tranquil and stoic compared to say contemporary American cultural attitudes where the age for retirement has been abolished, where plastic surgery is increasingly popular and widespread, and where youth is valorised, and traditional definitions of old age are challenged thereby opening up all kinds of new possibilities for the elderly. All cultural choices and solutions to the universal issues of human existence come with relative sets of pros and cons and depending on orientation and values, one can find one or the other view attractive or repugnant.

Trauma transforms our usual experience of time as continuous and stable into a fragmented experience that is disconnected from the framework of biographical time and is a defensive regression to primitive internal states. In a traumatic condition, the usual chronology of narrative events is undermined and replaced by states akin to the inchoate fragmented existential time experience of dream states and fantasy known where the distinctions of past-present-future are hazy. Volkan (2003) calls this a form of 'time-collapse'. The temporal fragmentation allows the emotions of anxiety, aggression, and depression to dominate, and to a certain extent, destroys the effort of meaning-making and symbol formation.

When the capacity to mentalise becomes disturbed, it affects one's sense of basic trust and creates regressed, unstable internal states bordering, and reminiscent of, psychotic level annihilation anxieties. In addition, if the shattered sense of trust has not been worked on, then the possibility of relating with others, including getting help to alleviate such difficult emotional states, will also be vitiated. Other persons may be understood only in terms of one's own projected fear. For instance, a mental state in which I feel unsafe and think that others may harm me, becomes translated directly into the conviction that this will happen, irrespective of the reality of the particular situation. This mode of experiencing others may be so terrifying that it is split and dissociated, only to surface in conditions which resonate with the affect aroused earlier—some stress which arouses fear or helplessness. For some, this may happen quite frequently. The capacity to be self-reflective and maintain a sense of reality is undermined, and the person may resort to fight or flight behaviour or become paralysed with anxiety.

From a relational perspective, the trauma represents the loss of internal protection related to a good internal object, primarily affecting the necessary feelings of basic trust and mastery. It also affects infantile omnipotence and self-idealisation. This may be experienced as the loss of the protective and empathic other, or as damaged relations to internalised others who otherwise give meaning to thoughts and actions. When this internal linking is broken, damaged or destroyed, attachment to others may be perceived as dangerous. An interpersonal encounter becomes potentially fraught, frightening, confusing and overlaid with power struggles. Relating to the internal or external other (including the therapist), may trigger a greater risk of re-experiencing the original helplessness and re-emergence of a feeling of being left alone in utter despair. This may result in a pattern of withdrawal and inner feelings of inner abandonment, helplessness and despair. Ulman and Brothers (1988) have utilised a unique clinical research population of rape and incest victims and Vietnam combat veterans to argue that trauma results from real occurrences that have, as their unconscious meaning, the shattering of 'central organising fantasies' of self in relation to self-object.

Massive disasters undermine this basic sense of trust and induce childhood danger signals of anxiety, especially anxiety over loss of mother, her love, and the security she provides. Henry Krystal (1971; Krystal, van der Kolk, Greenberg, & Boyd, 2005), an analyst when reflecting upon his own war time experiences and the research he did on survivors of the Nazi Holocaust found 'the essential function of primary childhood narcissism' resulting from the 'programming' of the child in a state of secure attachment to the mother that he was loved and lovable, was 'the most important single asset' in promoting survival in Holocaust victims. 'My mother's loving and caring response and her rescuing and "guarding" me helped me to turn the trauma experience into something I could live with and reflect upon' (1971). If large members of a group share the experience of a natural disaster such as an earthquake, when both literally and symbolically, the ground and surround around them suffer disruption, large-scale group regression occurs, such as increased magical belief. Volkan (2003) reports how in the aftermath of the earthquake in Turkey, followed by 4,000 aftershocks, many people in Istanbul built or thought of building iron cages to sleep in.

What primarily differentiates a disaster caused by enemies from other catastrophes is that the former creates an extreme sense of humiliation and helpless rage associated with a frustrating wish for revenge. The blow felt to the self and to the feeling of self-worth further complicates the situation. The effect of being subject to de-humanisation leaves traces of lasting and profound feelings of shame, humiliation and worthlessness. This may have to do with acting in ways that are incompatible with the person's usual ego-ideal or superego standards, so as to ensure survival in extreme circumstances and not just with being treated inhumanely. If circumstances do not allow members of the affected group to work through their humiliation, to mourn their losses, and to turn their passivity into activity, then a sense of shared victimisation begins to attach to their large group identities which can be intergenerationally transmitted and reverberate down the centuries. Note Al Qaeda's recent identification of the Queen of England as a major enemy because of the Christian Crusades against Islam, led by her ancestor, Richard the Lionheart, nine centuries ago!

Psychoanalysts' specialised knowledge of individual psychic functioning under stress, of group dynamics and their corpus of interpersonal skills can be of use in understanding and responding to conflict, violence, terrorism, other natural and man-made disasters, and their effects. Their ability to understand and handle large and small group dynamics including those in which there is intra- and inter-group hostility and to re-frame unanswerable questions into workable strategies are psychoanalytic skills which can be put to use in interventions such as those described.

REFERENCES

Akhtar, S. (1999). The psychodynamic dimension of terrorism. *Psychiatry Annals* 29, 350-5.

———. (2002). Forgiveness: Origins, dynamics, psychopathology, and technical relevance. *Psychoanalytic Quarterly* 71, 175–212.

Breuer, J. & Freud, S. (1951). *Studies on hysteria.* In J. Stratchey (Ed. and Trans.). *The Standard Edition of the Complete Psychological Works of Sigmund Freud* (vol. 2). London: Hogarth Press. (Original work published 1893–1895).

Fonagy P., Target, M., Steele, M. & Steele, H. (1997). The development of violence and crime as it relates to security of attachment. In, J. D. Osofsky (Ed.), *Children in a Violent Society* (pp. 150–77). New York: Guilford.

Fonagy, P. (2001). *The Psychoanalysis of Violence,* Paper presented to the Dallas Society for Psychoanalytic Psychotherapy. March 15, 2001.

————. (2003). The violence in our schools: What can a psychoanalytically informed approach contribute? *Journal of Applied Psychoanalytic Studies,* 5, 223–238.

Fonagy, P., Moran, G. & Target, M. (1993). Aggression and the psychological self. *International Journal of Psychoanalysis,* 74, 471–485.

Fonagy, P. & Target, M. (1995). Understanding the violent patient: The use of the body and the role of the father. *International Journal of Psychoanalysis,* 76, 487–501.

Freud, A. (1967). Comments on trauma. In S. S. Furst (Ed.) *Psychic Trauma* (pp, 235–245). New York: Basic Books.

Freud, S. (1926). Inhibitions, symptoms and anxiety. In J. Stratchey (Ed. and Trans.). *The Standard Edition of the Complete Psychological Works of Sigmund Freud* (Vol. 18). London: Hogarth Press.

————. (1955a). Beyond the pleasure principle. In J. Stratchey (Ed. and Trans.). *The Standard Edition of the Complete Psychological Works of Sigmund Freud* (Vol. 18, pp. 7–64). London: Hogarth Press. (Original work published 1920)

————. (1955b). On the psychical mechanism of hysterical phenomena. In J. Stratchey (Ed. and Trans.). *The Standard Edition of the Complete Psychological Works of Sigmund Freud* (Vol. 3, pp. 27–39). London: Hogarth Press. (Original work published 1893)

Glover, E. (1929). The screening function of traumatic memories. International. *Journal of Psychoanalysis,* 10, 90–93.

Kakar, S. (1995). *The Colours of Violence.* New Delhi: Penguin.

Krystal, H. (1971). *Psychoanalytic approaches to trauma: A forty-year retrospective 11,* 54–88.

Krystal, H., van der Kolk, B. Greenberg, M. & Boyd, S. (2005). Inescapable shock, neurotransmitters, and addiction to trauma: Toward a psycho biology of post traumatic stress. In C. L. Figley (Ed.), *Mapping Trauma and its Wake.* New York: Routledge.

Lifton, B.J. (1996). The adopted self. In C. Strozier & M. Flynn (Eds), *Trauma and Self* (pp. 19–29). Rowman and Littlefield publishers, Inc.

Lifton, R.J. (1968). *Death in life: Survivors of Hiroshima.* New York: Random House.

————. (1986). *The Nazi Doctors: Medical Killing and the Psychology of Genocide.* New York: Basic Books.

————. (1993). *The Protean Self: Human Resilience in an Age of Fragmentation.* New York: Basic Books.

————. (1999). *Destroying the World to Save it: Aum Shinrikyo, Apocalyptic Violence and the New Global Terrorism.* New York: Metropolitan Books.

Post, J. (1990). Terrorist psycho-logic: Terrorist behavior as a product of psychological forces. In W. Reich, (Ed.), *Origins of terrorism: Psychologies, ideologies, theologies, states of mind* (pp. 25–40). Cambridge: Cambridge University Press.

Twemlow, S.W. & Sacco. F.C. (2002). Reflections on the making of a terrorist. In C. Covington. P. Williams, J. Arundale & J. Knox. (Eds) *Terrorism and Political Violence* (pp. 97–123). London: Karnac.

Twemlow, S.W. (2004). Psychoanalytic understanding of terrorism and massive social trauma. *Journal of the American Psychoanalytic Association.*

Ulman, R.B. & Brothers, D. (1988). *The Shattered Self: A Psychoanalytic Study of Trauma.* Hillsdale. NJ: The Analytic Press.

Volkan, V. (1988). *The Need to have Enemies and Allies: From Clinical Practice to International Relationships.* Northvale, NJ: Jason Aronson.

———. (1990). *The Psychodynamics of International Relationships.* USA: Lexington Books.

———. (1999a). The tree model: A comprehensive psycho–political approach to unofficial diplomacy and the reduction of inter-ethnic tension. *Mind and Human Interaction 10,* 142–210.

———. (1999b). Psychoanalysis and diplomacy: Part I Individual and large group identity. *Journal of Applied Psychoanalytic Studies 1,* 29–55.

———. (1999c). Psychoanalysis and diplomacy: Part II Large group rituals. *Journal of Applied Psychoanalytic Studies 1,* 223–47.

Varvin, S. & Volkan, V. (2003). *Violence and Dialogue: Psychoanalytic Insights on Terror and Terrorism.* London: International Psychoanalytic Association.

Yorke, C. (1986). Reflections on the problem of psychic trauma. *Psychoanalytic Study of the Child, 41,* 221–236.

Chapter 17

Terror, Trauma and Transformation*

Rajat Mitra

Rajat Mitra is a clinical psychologist and he received the Ashoka fellowship for working on criminal justice reforms in India. He holds a PhD in psychology and has worked extensively with victims of abuse, violence and trauma. He has interviewed hundreds of sex offenders over several years to understand the motivation behind their attacks. He works with non-profit organisations that provide counselling and support to victims of violence in the immediate aftermath of the event.

As I begin to pen down my thoughts on the topic of Trauma and Transformation, I am overwhelmed by the vastness of the subject and wonder if I can, in the space of one essay, condense for the reader, my own journey towards an understanding of trauma and its transformation. I am still in the process of understanding it in depth and putting it into words and creating meaning. This turns out to be much more challenging than I thought it would be.

---

*This chapter was first published in *The Journal*, Vol. 7(2), December 2005, published by the Psychological Foundations Trust, New Delhi. Despite best efforts to contact the author of this chapter, Rajat Mitra, the editors have been unable to reach him. The chapter is being reproduced here in good faith.

I am working as the head of an organisation that works with victims of heinous crimes and violence, accidents and other overwhelming events. The service is in operation seven days a week, twenty-four hours a day and connected to the police helpline. The service is mandatory vide a police order that explicitly states that all victims need to be referred for counselling, without delay.

I had never intended to work with trauma victims in the first place. It happened quite accidentally. Seven years ago, a chance event brought me to a police station where I had to wait in one of the few empty spaces available. I was quite preoccupied with myself as I was flying off to the United States for a bone marrow transplant for someone. My preoccupation was rudely jolted by the aggressive confrontation of a burly policeman sitting nearby, who was shouting at a family of three children and their father. The policeman was yelling at them, saying 'tell me what you know otherwise you all are staying here the whole night.' The children, all in their early teens, were crying and their father was sitting in a numb state. Finding it difficult to be a mere witness, I asked the policeman what had happened. What I could gather is that their mother was murdered a few hours ago and the policeman was trying to get a statement out of them, which he was finding very difficult to do. I volunteered to be a counsellor for them and was granted permission by his senior officer. Just being a good listener and empathising with their sorrow was all I could do. The children calmed down and the father looked less numb. After nearly an hour, they gave their statement. The policeman got what he needed and before I left told me in chaste Haryanvi, 'Saab, aise har situation mein ek psychologist ko jaroor hona chahiye.' (Sir, in every situation like this, there should be a psychologist).

That was seven years ago. Subsequently, I had gone to the then police commissioner, narrated this incident and asked him if a psychological service could be offered, through which families undergoing emotional crises after an overwhelming event, could be attended to without delay. He had agreed and given us two police stations to start with, on an experimental basis.

We started dealing with every conceivable atrocity that could befall a human being. We worked with a ten-year-old boy who was beaten so badly that one arm and leg had multiple fractures. He would wake up in the night screaming. A teenage girl, who was raped, burnt and left to die, whom we counselled in the burns ward till the moment of her death. A family that was inconsolable after their five-year-old was raped and killed. A family where the father had killed all his children aged 2, 4 and 5. A family whose two infant children were brutally slaughtered by their uncle. These were the kind of people we were being asked to counsel.

Designing a programme that would cater to the needs of this population was most challenging. Their grief was overwhelming and they were inconsolable. Each person's needs were different and required careful analysis. A programme was needed that would be evidence-based, humane and able to negotiate with the criminal justice system. Evolving and designing such a programme became a team effort and involved taking the help of a number of experts at different stages. Having worked in this field for the last seven years, I can now say that trauma arises from the experience of an inescapable stressful event that overwhelms people's coping mechanisms.

RETRAUMATISATION

According to Judith Herman (1992), 'to study psychological trauma is to come face to face with both human vulnerability in the natural world and with the capacity for evil in human nature.' Trauma involves a victim and a perpetrator. Dr Leo Bitinger, a psychiatrist, who studied the victims of concentration camps, describes the cruel conflict of interest between the victim and bystander, the issue the community wants to detach itself from and erase from memory. The victim remains the losing party in this silent and unequal dialogue. In order to escape accountability, the perpetrator does everything in his power to promote forgetting. Secrecy and silence are his first line of defence. The second is his attacking the credibility of the victim. The victim, according to him is a liar, invited it up on herself.

As our work increased, we came across such attacks on the credibility of the victim again and again. Protecting the victim against the accusations levelled against her also became part of our work. In one of our earlier cases, we had just begun to talk to a victim of sexual assault in a police station. She had been traumatised and was explaining the situation when suddenly a police officer walked in and requested me that my colleague and I come out and talk to someone urgently. Can it not wait? What we had been called for urgently was a meeting with a political leader, who told us that the girl was lying and trying to frame someone. Completely disgusted, we told him off and went back to our session. The girl meanwhile had become more closed. In between, two more people had walked in and demanded to know from her what had happened. We had to reassure her again that we trusted her and wanted her to continue. Slowly she continued with her story, which was very poignant and alarming. She asked us, 'do you believe me as no one else believes me?' In the sessions that we had with her, we understood the gamut of issues she was dealing with. In her family everyone believed she brought the rape upon herself. In the weeks following the rape, she went through flashbacks, nightmares, would get scared if she was alone, and then showed severe withdrawal. She also contemplated suicide which her family got to know and, instead of providing support, beat her up and locked her up. She would call us up at all times, sob on the phone and want to know why she should carry on. Therapy with her involved listening, believing in her and reconnecting her to her self-worth. After seeing a few thousand cases, we realise that the experience of this girl is what nearly all the female victims of sexual assault go through. We, as a society, are still far from providing support and compassionate care to the rape victim.

In another case, a fifteen year old was assaulted in west Delhi. She was disposing garbage at night, when two men dragged her to one side and assaulted her. When we went to see her on her third visit, she had returned to her garbage disposal job. Why was there no one else in the house to do it, we wondered? There were four grown up men but holding garbage and throwing it out was something no man in their family would ever do. In a similar vein, we discovered that a large percentage of women get raped when they go to the community toilet or open the toilet early in the morning or late evening. Going to the toilet is fraught with risk for women all over India and a large percentage of this form of sexual traumatisation is never reported by the women.

Trauma survivors also encounter difficulties with social judgement. Beyond the issues of shame and doubt, they also have to find a balance between unrealistic guilt and denial of all moral responsibility. At *Swanchetan* (a non-profit organisation that works with victims of abuse, violence and trauma), we have come across hundreds of women who report that they have been blamed for the rape and told that it will make it difficult for them to get married in the future and therefore they would prefer to deny that it ever happened with them. It is not uncommon for us to lose many people in therapy because they would rather choose not to think, talk or mention their traumatic experience to anyone.

I have known a father who chose not to talk about his teenage daughter's sexual assault, as he feared that the publicity around it may affect his chances of getting an impending promotion.

As counsellors, one of our responsibilities is that we have to draw attention to the suffering of the victim again and again and not judge her character or antecedents. Condemnation of the victim's character is widespread, It often cripples the victim's psyche and weakens her capacity and willingness to fight her case. In a recent incident, during the test identification parade for a rape victim, a woman judge remarked, 'If women drink they will get raped.' Since that remark, the victim has refused to pursue her case any further. In another case of sexual assault, the issue was raised as to why a girl goes out late in the night and the whole debate centred around whether women should go out late in the night. Such debates only help to make the perpetrator's argument more irrefutable and completely ignores the trauma of the victim.

TRAUMA AND SOMATIC MEMORIES

One of the key issues involved in talking to victims is retrieving their memories of what happened after the trauma. The nature and reliability of traumatic memories have been controversial issues in mental health for over a century. Traumatic memories have been difficult to study because the profoundly upsetting experiences that may give rise to PTSD (Post Traumatic Stress Disorder) and other trauma-related outcomes cannot be approximated in a laboratory setting. It is now believed that traumatic memories are encoded differently than memories for ordinary events, perhaps via alterations in attentional focusing, because extreme emotional arousal interferes with hippocampal memory functions (van der Kolk, 1996). We came across a situation where we had to help a woman reconstruct the face of her assaulter through the computer. She was sexually assaulted by two men whom she met during a transaction for obtaining a visa. I remember her words 'I am very good with faces. If a person applies to me for a visa and I refuse it, I remember his face. Even if he applies after a year again with changes in his face, I would recognise him. This has happened so many times. But this man who assaulted me only a few hours ago, I cannot remember anything about his face. Why is this happening to me?' She was finally able to reconstruct his face using sensations she had undergone during the sexual assault. This behaviour of hers and that of many others and that of many others we have worked with support the premise held by many theoreticians in this field that traumatic memories cannot be integrated on a semantic/linguistic level, they tend to be organised more primitively as visual images or somatic sensations. From the experience of many victims, we find that the persistence of intrusive sensations related to trauma, even after the victim has built up her narrative, supports the premise that learning to put the traumatic experience in words does not help to erase flashbacks by the victim. A century ago, based on his clinical observations, Janet stated that, 'traumatic memories are highly state dependent and cannot be evoked at will. That they are invariable, consist of sensations and cannot be condensed in time.'

In a recent case, a ten-year-old girl was brutally assaulted during Ramlila. She could not recall anything of her assaulter but kept on saying 'hair'. Finally we could conjecture that she had a lot of small strands of hair on her body alerting us to the fact that her assaulter may have been to a barber shop. He was subsequently caught because of this information. In another case, a mentally challenged girl of eleven was raped. She could only utter the word 'tarwa' and point to our feet. As she could hear and speak only a limited range of frequencies, the word turned out to be 'jalwa' meaning being burnt. It subsequently narrowed the search for the offender who was found to have burnt feet. He was subsequently caught and confessed to the crime.

NEED FOR A REDEFINITION

Psychological trauma affects the powerless more than the powerful. It was once thought that such events are uncommon. In 1980, when the term Post Traumatic Stress Disorder was coined, the American Psychiatric Association defined traumatic experiences as being outside the range of normal human experiences. Yet, rape and other forms of domestic and sexual violence are such a common part of women's lives in our country, and perhaps everywhere too, that they can hardly be described as outside the range of ordinary experience. And in the same vein, considering the number of people killed in war, riots and terrorist attacks in the past century, trauma related to these too must be brought under the domain of ordinary human experience.

The severity of the traumatic experiences is perhaps difficult to measure on a single scale. Reductionistic efforts to quantify trauma can lead us to comparisons of horror and helplessness. Yet certain elements increase the likelihood of harm done to the victim.

These include being taken by suddenness and surprise, trapped, exposed to the point of emotional and physical exhaustion, witnessing extreme violence or death. In each event, the salient feature for the victim is to inspire helplessness and terror. According to Judith Herman (1992), the main symptoms of Post Traumatic Stress Disorder fall into three categories. They are hyper arousal, intrusion and constriction. According to her, hyper arousal reflects the persistent expectation of danger; intrusion reflects the deep imprint of the traumatic moment; and constriction reflects the numbness felt by the victim.

Traumatic events also confront us with our basic notions of human relationships. They disrupt and often destroy our attachment to family, friendship and our sense of belonging to a community. In a moment, they can shatter our self-esteem that we may have built over the years, formed and sustained over years. They violate our basic sense of trust and can cast us into a crisis where it is difficult to find meaning.

TRAUMA AND EVIL

An article on terror would be incomplete without a mention of evil. As a psychologist, along with providing emotional support to victims, I also come face to face with serial killers, mass murderers and those who rape and kill children, people who in the eyes of society personify evil. I have to answer questions raised by victims and their families on how somebody could be so brutal. Above all, I have to answer myself as to why a person could deny all the vicissitudes of normality and act so barbarically against a helpless human being?

The problem of evil is a big challenge to psychology. It does not easily submit itself to reductionism. To me, evil has to do with destroying and killing not just the body, but, by and large, all those attributes that give life meaning, such as growth, autonomy and will. We are working with a ten-year-old boy who was kidnapped nearly four years ago, kept in captivity and almost killed for ransom. Though he was rescued after a week, he changed completely after the incident and, as his parents put it, there is something that just died in him during the ordeal and it will take a long time for him to come back to his normal self.

I have just finished creating a behavioural profile of a man, accused of having raped and murdered a five-year-old and then thrown her body in a tank. As I began to delve into his history, he told me that he had done this before to other children. He had done so in a planned, calculated manner and he was never found out. He told me he was himself the victim of sexual abuse in childhood and used to be beaten mercilessly by his father. I am reminded of the statement made by a well known psychotherapist, 'When a child is confronted by significant evil in his parents, he will most likely misinterpret the situation and believe that the evil resides in himself.' This observation used to be deeply unsettling to me in the beginning.

Eric Fromm saw the genesis of human evil as a developmental process. According to him, we are not created evil or even forced to be evil, but we become evil slowly over time through a long series of choices. His emphasis on choice and will is something that affected a generation of psychologists working in this field.

Swanchetan, the organisation I work for, is carrying out a study on the psyche of severely violent offenders. While the initial study to some extent does confirm Fromm's view, yet for many offenders, evil is something that made them feel most alive for as long as they can remember. More work is necessary to understand this complex psychological phenomenon.

HEALING AND RECOVERY

Having dwelt upon terror and trauma in victims in the earlier part of the article, I would like to share with the reader, my experiences of what causes healing and recovery.

What causes recovery in trauma? Having worked with nearly a thousand victims, I must say that the answer is still not fully clear. We use approaches that are evidence-based and scientific, yet a large number of victims just respond to our trying to create new connections to them. I have observed that working with victimised people requires a committed moral stance. It involves understanding the fundamental injustice of the traumatic experience and yet be aware that the therapist is not there to provide justice but rather first and foremost, to provide safety. Time and again we have to tell our victims that safety comes before justice. It is deeply healing for many to know that justice is not under their control and that they may never get it, but they can create an island of safety which is their own.

The subject of trauma and recovery is a vast one and I have been a late entrant in this field. I have realised it is important to set very realistic goals in this field. Though there have been dramatic recoveries, most people going through an overwhelming event heal rather slowly. I would like to share the history of Suneeta (name changed). I have chosen her not because her story is extraordinary but because many of the elements of her story are so common. Suneeta was thirteen years old when her mother got into an extra marital affair with a man running a gang. Under his influence, she and her lover killed her husband and then her older daughter who was a witness to the murder. Suneeta and her brother knew a lot of details and could get her mother into trouble and were witnesses for the police. The mother, again on the advice of her lover, transferred them to a distant place where they were locked up for six months before they managed to run away and were rescued by the police.

Suneeta was referred to us for counselling. When we first saw her, she was lying in a corner of the police station and refused to move. She looked very dishevelled and was mute, had a vacant look in her eyes and kept on staring into space. She would not answer any questions that the police asked her.

In our first meeting, she described feeling suicidal (she had attempted suicide in her captivity) and that she had not slept for several days. She would get startled easily and was not able to listen to anything for long. Even if accidentally touched, she would turn violent. Above all, her family wished to have nothing to do with her, as she was a girl, was dark and they believed that she carried her mother's evil spirit inside her. Our first task was to provide her with a shelter where she could live anonymously. It was not as easy as no shelter would take her, seeing her disturbed state. Finally one shelter did agree on the condition that in case she gets more depressed or suicidal or anything happens to her, she would be immediately asked to leave and we would have to take over her responsibility. Further, she would stay in shelter for six days and on Sundays she would work on her issues with the therapist. Initially we worked with symptoms through some selective exercises. She found them highly beneficial. Suneeta also developed an intense transference to the therapist working with her.

Suneeta has carried on like this for three years. She is by and large free of her symptoms, has worked through her transference towards her therapists and, most important, is able to structure her day by going to school after a gap of three years. But she still keeps on having flash-backs and when something reminds her of her past, she is unable to get back to the present for a long time.

From Suneeta, I would like to take the reader to our work with victims of mass violence. Though we have worked with victims from both Kashmir and Gujarat and the trauma of both are nearly the same, I will use the case of Gujarat as it was a more detailed and exhaustive study we did. At the request of the National Human Rights Commission, we worked with children at different camps. This was the most horrible, the most poignant and the most diabolical situation that we had ever encountered. People, specifically women and children, had been butchered and killed in a most sadistic manner. Individual counselling was nearly impossible and we had to take in groups of ten to twenty and work on their problems. I remember one situation very poignantly. We were having a group session in the night. Suddenly the lights went off in the camp and everybody started screaming and yelling hysterically On a quick impulse, we asked everyone to hold each other's hands and calm down while another person ran and switched on the headlights of a car parked nearby and turned its direction towards the shelter camp. That helped in calming everyone down. People spent the rest of the night like that till the first rays of the morning sun came, and then everyone went off to sleep.

As we worked with hundreds of children in the camps, what struck us was the brutality that everyone had witnessed and how deeply it kept on intruding on their consciousness. There was a mother whose whole family was slaughtered in front of her. She sat with the dead bodies and refused to leave them. There was a father who kept running with his son till he died as no doctor would treat him. But most poignant was our finding a half-burnt baby boy in the ill-fated bogey where 56 people perished so tragically.

There are many myths about working with trauma victims. One is that working with them in states of high distress and letting them confront what has happened to them, is the way to resolve traumatic issues. Nothing could be further from the truth. The primary need of a trauma survivor is to feel safe once again and begin to recover his or her self-esteem. The survivor needs the therapist to separate past from present, danger from safety and this can be done by slowly learning to differentiate again and finding one's roots. The survivor defines oneself once again and learns to negotiate the new reality that he or she needs to integrate within themselves. As a survivor told me recently,

All what I had known to be normal has been wrested away from me. Along with my beliefs about what can happen anywhere, how unsafe I am anywhere, anytime, the people around me who don't seem the same anymore and how I will have to live my life day to day. And the challenge is to convince myself every moment that there can be a certainty within the new uncertainty that has suddenly gripped my life and finding the path to find that out.

REFERENCES

Herman, J.L. (1992). *Trauma and Recovery: The Aftermath of Violence—from Domestic Abuse to Political Terror*. San Francisco: Basic Books.

Van der Kolk, B.A. (1996). Trauma and memory. In B.A. van der Kolk, A.C. Mcfarlane & L. Weisaeth (Eds), *Traumatic Stress: The Effects of Overwhelming Experience on Mind, Body and Society* (pp. 279–302). London: Guilford.

Chapter 18

A Child's Act*

Sanjay Kumar

Sanjay Kumar is the Founder and President of pandies' theatre. He has been directing theatrical performances and the workshops conducted by pandies since its inception in 1993. He also co-authors the scripts of the plays performed by the group. His work speaks from the margins and represents diverse 'minorities'—slum dwellers, children, women and religious/caste minorities. He has been teaching English literature at Hansraj College, University of Delhi, since 1984. His areas of expertise include twentieth-century drama and contemporary literary theories.

This essay is an attempt to graph the tenuousness of the experience of working with Kashmiri Pandit and Kashmiri Muslim children in Jammu and Kashmir. Child stories are located in the midst of adult strife. In the region, violence and hatred define the matrix of adult perception. Operating within that are the fears and also the hopes and desires of the child story. The essay catalogues; it catalogues attempts to cope with trauma and attempts to make enabling sense of the trauma.

My intervention comes in the form of an activist group—pandies' theatre, that has been working in schools, colleges and slums for over a decade—doing intensive and extensive work with children. The group

---

* This chapter was first published in *The Journal*, Vol. 2(2), December 2005, by the Psychological Foundations Trust, New Delhi.

works in Delhi and outside. It does theatre 'workshops' with children. It prioritises themes of gender, class, religion, caste and now region and religion together. In adult constructions of these concepts, the child's perspective is regarded as insignificant. The group penetrates the child's marginality in the adult world. It goes beyond to work with children who are further marginalised (the poor, the girl–child, the lower caste, the other religion and the mentally challenged) and works on these very themes of marginality (with 'marginalised' and 'mainstream' children).

The participant groups, then, proceed to 'make plays'. Each group first makes a small two–minute skit around the short story they had created earlier. The instructor's intervention is strictly on demand and the children work largely by themselves. Over a period of time and using more ideas from the workshop, these plays are built into performances of about twenty minutes each.

Theatre is the methodological tool. The term Theatre is used in an extended sense—not only as performance but also as a flowing experience, where often the actor/activist begins as performer and ends as audience. At the initial stage and in extreme cases the effect on the child is cathartic. However, the impact of the workshop usually goes beyond to reveal the limitations of the cathartic process and empower the child with the belief that his or her views (including fears and desires) hold the key to possible solutions. In its workshop mode, theatre is not only penetrative but often becomes subversive of hegemonic adult conceptualisations. What one gets are multiple, at times discordant, but often enabling engagements with psychosocial realities.

The experience that this essay draws upon is part of a larger children's project against communalism in the post Gujarat scenario. It focuses specifically on the child in Jammu and Kashmir and narrativises experiences since 2002. If on the one hand, it relates the healing process of the diverse children involved and their contributions to the process, it is also the story of the growth of the narrating voice. The narrating voice grows in its endeavour to grapple with the convoluted aspects of the Jammu and Kashmir 'reality' and in its attempt at understanding alternate strategies of coping. The 'I' is subjective but representative. Cannibalising from four years of work and diverse interactions, it derives from collective experience. The first person singular represents all my colleagues, some of whom have been participants in the entire experience and many for the diverse parts. It is truly a pandies 'I'.

The adult story comprises the tale of two communities with a combined history—the Kashmiri Muslim and the Kashmiri Pandit. As the articulation spells out, the 'Kashmiri' unites and the 'Muslim-Pandit' separates. Centuries of living together, of combined landscapes and mindscapes are interwoven with feelings of hatred, of suffering at each other's hands. There are attempts at adult reconciliation, rationalisations that attempt to bridge the gaps but core problems remain. And it comes out of the mouths of adults in unguarded moments in the form of suspicions and resentments.

'Peace process—what about the 80,000 jehadis who have died?'

'What about us being forced out of our homes for no fault of ours?'

Tolerance, peace—these have become dirty words. What are the other words? Where are the other vocabularies, other languages?

The political imbroglio compounds the problem. Caught in an actual tug of war between India and Pakistan, a visit to Kashmir reveals a vanquished land where all are victims, all losers.

My story covers four years of involvement—fulfilling, dissatisfying. Four chosen highlighted experiences spread over three and a half years:

2002 November—Recce visit to Jammu
2003 March–November—Workshops in Jammu and Srinagar
2003 December—The festival at Dilli Haat
2005 June—Workshop in Gulmarg culminating in a performance in Srinagar

Pandies' Theatre

pandies theatre was formally registered in 1993 (though many of us were working together informally from 1987). The name is a British expletive and used for the first time in the wake of '1857'. It continued in the lexicon of the British commanders for over fifty years. Deriving from Mangal Pandey, 'pandies' was used to describe Indian soldiers employed in the British army who showed potential for dissent and subversion. From incipience, we saw ourselves in a subversive relationship with what is seen to constitute the 'mainstream' of our society. We were first seen as a 'feminist' group working in the proscenium. From 1996, we became purely 'activist' converting 'plays' into projects and workshops. The first focus was gender and related areas of sexuality. Pioneering work was done on issues of rape, HIV, prostitution, the Mental Health Act, *Dayan hatya* (killing 'witches'), institutions of love and marriage (transgender issues including gay and lesbian rights have also been targeted though the group did not come up with a full production on the issue). Even at this stage the child, especially the girl-child, was a special focus and we did sensitising workshops on most of these issues in schools and slums.

Gujarat changed our course. We decided to include gender, class and caste within the ambit of an anti-communal tirade. Keeping an eye ahead, the child has become the prized focus. The canvas is vast—rural child, urban child; schools, slums; Hindus, Muslims, Christians, Sikhs; Delhi, Punjab, Haryana, Jammu and Kashmir. We proceed through our workshops sensitising, teaching and above these, learning.

Pandies' methodology for workshops with children

The workshop begins with standard theatre exercises for physical coordination and getting the bodies and minds of the children in focus. Exercises also help to remove peer hierarchies because anyone can perform well. The children then participate in making images and machines where they are given a word that they express through their body and face. Words are weighted: hatred, love, enmity, Muslim, Christian, etc. Next we divide them into small groups and each group collectively makes images and machines that are collectively discussed.

Creative writing

Next, the group is given the beginning of a story. The children work collectively and present their stories. This time each presentation is followed by a question/answer session where everybody else asks questions and the group answers.

Theatre

Theatre pandies prepares small theatrical pieces for each set of workshops carefully creating scripts pertaining to the highlighted themes. These piece(s) are generally presented after the creative writing session to elicit further discussion and throw theatre ideas at the participants before they prepare their own skits. At times, especially if the discussion after the image exercises has not been satisfactory, pandies theatre-pieces are presented instead/also before the creative writing session. Multiple methods are used to make the participants express themselves on the issues. Apart from discussions, the facilitators often narrate anecdotes (real and fictional) and ask the participants to share like experiences. Forum mode (where a participant is asked to come on stage and replace an actor specially if the participant feels that the actor's action was not acceptable in the given situation, the participant/actor then performs instead of that actor and the rest of the players go along and help him/her in the search for a better solution without allowing him/her to change the parameters of the situation) is often used.

My story seeks its contexts in the socio-political happenings in Kashmir. In Kashmir's history these are the years of Mufti Muhammad Syed's taking over the government reins, these are also the years that follow the increased militancy in the valley—brutal violence and brutal suppression. In India's political history, these years chronicle the stranglehold of the BJP-led NDA over national politics and the emergence of UPA. It also seeks its co-ordinates in the pandies' increasingly aggressive position against right-wing fundamentalism—three productions on the trot, condemning majoritarianism, work in schools and slums asking for understanding difference. My story, however, is intervened upon by children's stories. And the markers become less relevant as these stories often move away from adult reality into fantasy and desire.

The saga begins in November 2002 with a recce visit to Jammu. Courtesy my friends from the valley, (informally a group *Yakjah,* comprising Kashmiris of diverse hues—Hindus, Muslims, Sikhs—inside Kashmir and outside) I was visiting the area after 1988 and it was not even a visit to the valley but only to Jammu. The city took me by surprise. My memory was of a small, beautiful town but what I saw was an almost total Hindu takeover of the place. The old Jammu existed, as I found later, small and in the innards, in the little bazaars, in the famous Tourism Department's Wazwan restaurant that serves extremely good Kashmiri and not Jammu cuisine. The town, however, at first sight, seemed more like an extension of and a preparatory halt towards Vaishno Devi. Reeling under the Hindutva rhetoric echoing across the country, my antennae were up, was I over-reacting? But the signs were there, unmistakable—saffron-coloured deities staring down from across the walls of the city. Was the saffronisation of Jammu a result of the Islamisation of Srinagar? Was it the reverse? It was difficult to say but in my imagination I was sure that the two would be linked. I became somewhat fearful of what to expect in Srinagar. While in Jammu, I visited Pandit migrant camps and schools where the students were mainly from Hindu families that had left Kashmir. What stories, what experiences lay behind those faces? At the moment, we could only talk about how and when the workshops would take place and enlist their participation and support.

March 2003 is characterised by long workshops together with my colleagues, first in Srinagar and then Jammu. The children in Srinagar were almost exclusively Muslim and those in Jammu, exclusively Kashmiri Pandits. In Jammu, we had chosen migrant children from the lower middle and middle classes. The class levels were the same in Srinagar, though there were some children from elite Muslim families. Like Jammu, my Srinagar too had been lost somewhere. Miles before the city we saw, at a distance of fifty meters each, soldiers with carbines. It was almost like working in a foreign country, more so one that is hostile and feels itself under siege from 'our' army. The beauty was there, submerged, in the sunrise from a houseboat in the backwaters of Nagin Lake. We worked in a small school in the Nagin region.

We gave them situations from their personal experience—Srinagar today, how I would ideally like it to be, elections in the valley. Left to work by themselves, images of violence, terrorist instigation, unfair polls and army brutality followed with unwavering velocity. The children were opening up, their exercises in image-making portrayed what their words could not articulate. There was an aura of distrust, of hostility and it stood out stark as the discussion started. A lot of grown-ups, teachers from diverse schools, started to participate. Child voices were getting drowned. Anecdotes, direct questions, imaginative tasks—we tried to keep the focus on the children. My first interceptive story is of a distinctly upper class, twelve-year-old Shia girl, Zaheera:

These Dilliwalas—they asked me to play being the prime minister of India for a day. What would I do? Where was the need to examine such a situation? Just yesterday my brother was slapped for holding a toy gun. No, it's not as if my parents are unfeeling, not even as if the family is beset with hardships and so the need to restrict. We play act, we deny. Television sets are switched off or children sent out of the room when talk of terrorism or news of anti-terrorist operations comes on. Why should I pretend playing prime minister, it's your bloody state that has reduced the inhabitants of Srinagar to animal modes of living. I raise my hand and say unflinchingly, 'Sir, remove the army and there would be no terrorism.' Stunned silence. They all agree, feel pleasure but have to disagree.

'What about the blasts in the markets, who would control them?' Asks a toady from another school. I rejoin hotly:

'How do you know they aren't planted by the army with a view to take action against the local people?' Smiles of approval from our people.

My teacher tells them: 'If this was shown on TV, these children would be taken away by the army, "your" army.'

Where do I put this story, it is obviously an attempt to mock centrist, state-sponsored peace attempts. It seeks to unmask even my endeavour. It's a subversive voice. But it's also a mimic. It echoes the sentiments of many adult segments in the valley. It also moves away from it all to express a dominant desire for a cessation of the existing situation.

There was a set of students who joined us late. Given the special circumstances under which we were working, violating usual theatre discipline, we allowed them to participate and create a play outside the holistic workshop. My next voice is of the middle class 14-year-old, Samer:

It had been stressful; I had not been able to come for the first day of the workshop. These Delhi VIPs have tight schedules; they had to have it on a festival when our school was closed. Create a skit. What skit? I will direct.

They had had their parents killed at the hands of either/both sides. I remember my little Nasser. Sweet child, barely above ten, sat quietly for one whole day in the corner while workshop was going on. And then he spoke, a small sentence. It was celebrative. Nasser had found his tongue again. He had seen his parents slaughtered before his eyes and had been unable to speak since. Arrangements had been made and he was taken away to a hospital for psychotherapy. Amidst sundry other child voices in Dilli Haat is the voice of these children. The next intervening story is the eleven-year-old Gulzar's:

> I came with these rich Hindu boys. I was scared, I had been warned. Association with them would defile me. They were unclean and dirty. I stayed with them for three days. I may have been from anywhere but Srinagar is mine. I told them after the performance, 'The problems of Kashmir stem from unscrupulous politicians who make big promises and do not honour them. The way is total cleansing, cleanse the administration of such people and problems can be solved. 'We, all of us, Mudassar, Muhammad, have to move together forward. I asked the other children: 'Can success be found by sticking to those who belong to your religion, or to your region only? Srinagar, Kashmir, India must move forward.' And what about these boys, the Jammu ones? They appear much better after three days together. We talked together and on the way back I... I shared my lunch box with them.

In the festival, finally three plays arrived from Kashmir and four from Jammu. The plays built on original themes 'migrancy' and loss (Jammu) and administrative corruption (Srinagar) but the real drama was happening around the festival. It was in the haunting ghosts of adult discourses of mistrust, in the growing bonding and friendship, in the interaction with children from Delhi, in the story of the young boy and girl from Jammu who got 'left' behind to steal an extra day of romance in Delhi.

My last and most significant stop is a six-day workshop in Gulmarg in June 2005. The group—fifty-five children between ten and sixteen years of age. An almost even split of Kashmiri Pandit and Kashmiri Muslim children, of girls and boys. The Pandit children were from migrant camps in Delhi and Jammu and areas around Jammu. A handful of them had worked with me before, the rest were new to the experience. The Muslim kids were from diverse parts of the valley, from camps, schools and orphanages in Brijbehara, Baramullah and areas around Srinagar. Most were poor and many had lost their parents. I had a target to have a production involving all the children ready for a performance in Srinagar on the seventh day. A unique experiment of putting the two communities together, literally in a 24 × 7 format, it was fraught with danger. The situation was volatile as all the children carried baggage. A daunting creative task too, made twice difficult by the physical hardship of it being a nature camp. The pandies' methodology of individual followed by collective exercises, of short story writing, of creating twenty minute skits, culminated this time in tying these short skits into a holistic mode of a final play of about ninety minutes' duration. While splitting them into five groups, great care was taken to see that children from diverse areas were there in each group. Given the nebulous situation, as facilitators, we took the decision to avoid a direct steering into the political, to focus on other relevant areas and allow the children to take us into the conflict zones as and when they desired.

The beginnings of the short stories (that would later become skits and then episodes) were provided by the chief short story facilitator. The beginnings indicated thematic choices among love stories, class (a poor boy in a dhaba), gender (a stepdaughter's story) and physical and mental disabilities. Each group was under the charge of one facilitator. As work started, drama was happening not only in the workshop but also around it. This was a set of unusually good-looking young people; many of them were 'free' for the first time. Romance was in the air, in the campfire dance (unfortunately disallowed by the security personnel after the first night). The Jammu boys (especially those from Mutthi) were older and dominating. The Kashmir children, especially the boys, were traumatised and repressed—many of them going and spending the night with *Yakjah* members rather than in their own tents. There are many stories; arbitrarily I pick one, Ishfaq Ahmad Bhat from Baramullah.

This whole work seems suspect. Why have our teachers brought us here? They tell us that play-acting is bad in Islam. And still we are here. No I will not participate in the theatre activity and I'll tell my group

214 | Sanjay Kumar

instructor so.... But I like it here. My teacher also wants me to participate. They see it as a process of learning, of getting exposure and
improving our chances in future. I will take part. But I feel uncomfortable with these older Jammu boys; they are so volatile, ready for
violence. 'Sir,' I told the instructor from Delhi, 'Why do we need to
go to Srinagar; whatever we had to learn we learn here, that is just a
performance.' He kept quiet.... Well, I'll go for the performance.

The stories and the subsequent skits that emerged were all Srinagar-
centric. I held one group back to create a meta-narrative tying up the
various episodes. This group and I decided to exploit the factual situation
and locate the story in the milieu of a children's camp.

They all say they love Srinagar. 'I hate Srinagar.' I tell them, 'If my father
was to die, I would never bury him in the valley.' India, yes, but it is
important only as a passport for a better future, I want to get away from
it all, go to the west. And these terrorists—I hate them. This city is sold
out to them and the Pakistanis. In my play, I tell them: 'They have to
die, they hide behind trees and shoot us innocents. Pakistan Murdabad.'
The story ends with two slaps across my face from my schoolteacher.

'But sir,' I moan, 'Isn't this the truth? Or rather what you asked us to
say before them—the Dilliwalas?'

Two voices: girl, boy; Shia, Sunni; brave, disturbed. Lots of submerged
stories here. There is an important common point—change the situation. Forty other voices, deistic to nationalistic. One meeting point—
desire for change.

The prolonged three-day workshop ended strangely, I stood in the
principal's room attempting to prove my credentials before him.
The blame of Samer's play had been put on us by the teacher who had
slapped him. The situation had been compounded by some casual
remarks made by one of our instructors. My friends from the valley,
Hindu and Muslim stood and argued. Long discussion and finally
shaking of hands. Peace had been amicably restored.

But we lost. We could not continue our work into the second leg.
In the succeeding weeks, we got diverse reasons. We were suspected
of being western agents with the mission of converting the children.

We were state agents. Extremists had threatened the principal of the school. The threat was real, it was our safety that they were bothered about. The principal's child was kidnapped and let off after paying ransom and a promise that such projects would not be allowed in future. And so on. The timorous, tentative conclusions:

The child of our 'heavenly' valley is mute; he is supposed not to feel. It is true, parents get uncomfortable if s/he carries a toy gun. S/He is not supposed to participate in discussions on Kashmir, Pakistan or India. Pray, I wanted to know, what else is s/he supposed to talk about? The intense hatred for the army was manifest. There is sympathy for the terrorist, but muted and so qualified that in their mind's eye, he is not violent and ceases to be terrorist. These children need the avenues to express. They are in a hateful situation; they are being bombarded by contradictory, hostile discourses. Their stories and short skits focused on militancy, satirised electoral processes and government inefficiency. All Srinagar stories and skits ended in desire: reconciliation, lasting peace and collective advance.

The children in the Jammu camp were marginally older than the children in Srinagar. Nearly fifty in number, they were extremely talented, ambitious and embarrassingly saw us and the workshop as keys to future success. Extroverted and friendly, one of them took us to their house in the Mutthi camp. My memory is of a low-roofed, semi-pucca house where one had to stand bent and soon had the desire to move out and stretch. The makeshift, cramped environment became emblematic of the cramping of dreams and desires and of the imper-manence in which these children find themselves placed. The absence of Srinagar became the dominant theme of the Jammu workshop. The next story is Deepak's, phenomenally talented, his byte appeared on Star TV when they came to cover the workshop, it was so good that it became a part of the promotion campaign when Star branched into NDTV.

I want to go back to Srinagar. I am 13 years old. No, it does not matter that I was born in Jammu not even that I have never been to Srinagar. It is embedded in my mind. I hate those of the opposite faith, those who betrayed our trust, were responsible for the deaths of so many in my family. Must return to Srinagar.

The irony escapes Deepak. His family left Srinagar a year and a half before he was born. Apart from four students of the tenth class, all the participants have been born here. However, they all desire to 'return'. All the stories and skits focussed on migration or, to use Jammu parlance—'migrancy' (the word encompasses not only the migration but also all the problems that led to it and ensue from it till today, it's like the exodus really). And they all culminated in fantasy—a jubilant, welcome return to Srinagar.

The first interaction, Srinagar or Jammu, showed that the child's desire is to obliterate the violence of the adult world. Its Srinagar is prelapsarian.

The next stop of my narrative is December 2003, Dilli Haat, New Delhi. It is in the midst of a children's theatre festival against communalism organised by pandies' theatre with over a score of plays from Delhi, Jammu and Srinagar. The majority of plays are from Delhi. A lot has happened since March. The right wing government is on an amazing high. Genocide has actually procured a pat on the back for Modi in Gujarat as he emerges victorious in the state polls. The army action is hitting new highs in Srinagar. November 2003—the famed Ghazi baba has been shot dead in Srinagar near his support base in Safa Kadal. I was there then doing another workshop in an orphanage—*Yateem* trust. I was working with children who had been orphaned in diverse parts of the valley—children from Jammu, Srinagar and Ladakh. From this epicentre, various episodes would evolve as narratives of experience of the participants. Interludes and three songs would be used to tie things up. A quick look at the four stories that got translated into skits and then episodes in the final play.

The first was a love story: Rich boy-poor girl, a decoy Pandit to make the girl fall in love, rich parents' objection and finally elopement. Unashamedly Bollywood, it worked with its humour and constant references to Nishat and Shalimar gardens and the Dal Lake. The next interventionist story is of Aksa, a pretty thirteen-year-old from Baramullah:

Our Kashmiri song was a real hit. It's a song about love. Everyone liked it; we'll dress up in our Kashmiri dresses and sing the song before the love episode. I sing the song and then play the lead in the love story. While doing the workshop, the lady facilitator asked me if someone like Vipin really loved me and his parents objected what would I do? 'If he has the guts to propose,' I replied, 'I would run away with him.' And that became the climax of our episode. Vipin yes, but Neeraj pursues me too. When Tariq sir did not allow us girls to take part in the evening dance, Neeraj repeatedly asked him. I was looking at them through the tent. Tariq sir was really angry, he would have slapped him had it not been for the presence of the Delhi people. Neeraj, does he really care? Should I go behind the tent and meet him?

Here we were talking about love and defiance among teenagers in the most customary manner—within and without the play. Somebody needed to pinch and remind me. These were hostile, almost warring communities, weren't they?

The next story/episode was about a poor boy working in a Srinagar dhaba. He wants to study but his father refuses to educate him. Latching on to a few words in the facilitator's beginning ('people like us do not get work'), the group had contextualised the father's refusal in the lack of opportunity and hurtful mistrust of Kashmiri Muslims in mainstream India. Tapering away from regional/religious margins, the story moved into fantasy with the use of a deux ex machina in the form of the boy's employer who funds his education. The boy becomes a doctor and returns to Srinagar in the service of his community.

The third was a story of a widower with a young daughter. He remarries, a woman with a mentally disabled child. Cinderella-torture ensues. Cinderella triumphs, not by upstaging the stepmother but by taking her along. She saves the life of the disabled child and the two lead to a 'realisation' in the mother. There was a lot in the nuanced warm scenes between the siblings, in the desire at the end to not locate and hate the oppressor, but abjure hatred itself.

The fourth episode was the real engagement. Its dynamics could be seen to epitomise the dynamics of the entire workshop. The group was dominated by two boys from Mutthi. They were older, they had worked with me before and they were also good actors. The story was of polio-hit lame girl (Kashmiri Pandit) who lives in Srinagar. Her father is threatened by militants (aatankwadi) and asked to cough up money if he wants to live. Unable to pay he is killed. Living in fear, the family finally moves to Jammu to her maternal uncle. Historical, temporal correctness was maintained. They migrate in 1993 and the girl is at that time 9 years old. She grows up in Jammu. Now twenty years old, she returns to Srinagar en route to Amarnath. This is not the Srinagar of adult constructions. Loved and welcomed, she settles here. The story raised a furore in the group itself. The younger Muslim children wanted to know how they could say with certitude that the killers were terrorists (aatankwadi). They could be dacoits or state goons. Also, it was unfair to put the blame for the happenings in the valley on one community. The problem was resolved by referring it back to the group and asking particularly the young Muslim kids from the valley to suggest alternate endings. This is what they came up with: the murderers should be dealt with like common criminals and without any glory! So when the Pandit girl returns to her village from Jammu, it's her brother (yes the masculine bias was there), who together with his Muslim neighbours from the past, apprehends the second of his father's murderers. An important change was to make the inspector who helps the Pandit children a Muslim; this was ideologically stronger and also correct in the sense that policemen inside the Kashmir valley are more likely to be Kashmiri Muslims.

Despite the Kashmiri Pandit bias and blaming the Muslims for their exodus (adult stories), the Jammu boys had expressed their desire in the warm welcome return. While casting off blame and valorising the Jehadi (adult stories), the Muslim boys had welcomed the Pandits with open arms and wanted to re-establish them, ferreting out criminals from their own ilk. A new Srinagar landscape had been created, was it an augury for the return of the mindscape that had for centuries connected the two communities? I hoped.

My last interventionist story is of Neeraj Gautam, a fourteen-year-old boy from Jammu in my group:

I had come here full of apprehensions, prejudices created by my parents in Jammu. Hatred was just below the surface. But what we got was unqualified love, best expressed in the song we sang together at the end of the performance. 'Iss desh ko Hindu na musalman chahiye/agar chahiye to ek achha insaan chahiye.'

Valorised though it is, the peripeteia of Neeraj's story cannot connote the truth of the experience. Secular, but again an adult voice, it is cliched and jargonised. The greater truths of the stories lie elsewhere. They are in the mesmerising (despite glitches) performance in Srinagar, in the streaming tears and standing ovation of the three hundred strong adult audience—Pandits and Muslims. They are there in the Srinagars created in the episodes; spaces where the gardens and Shikaras are back as cuddle spots for young lovers, spaces where deux ex machina still exist, where Cinderella's step mother is a vulnerable, loving person. And above all, for me, truth lay in the creation of a landscape where Kashmiri togetherness can elbow out the Hindu–Muslim separateness.

Chapter 19

In Giving We Received
Working with Survivors of the Gujarat Carnage*,†

Mahamaya Navlakha and Kanika Sinha

Mahamaya Navlakha and Kanika Sinha were Psychology honours students from Lady Shri Ram College, Delhi, when this essay was written. They took a year off from further studies to work with voluntary agencies after the Gujarat Carnage. Mahamaya Navlakha now leads the research and development vertical at Arthan Foundation, Delhi. Kanika Sinha is Director, Partnerships and

---

* This chapter was first published in *The Journal*, Vol. 4(2), December 2002, by the Psychological Foundations Trust, New Delhi.

† Gujarat Carnage took place in 2002. The carriage of a train was set on fire by a few miscreants, allegedly Muslims, at Godhra (Gujarat), killing the passengers. The passengers were devotees of Rama (an epical hero, now worshipped by many Hindus) and were returning from Ayodhya where they were involved in the building of a temple devoted to him at a spot reputed to be his birthplace. This was the same spot where the Babri Masjid (mosque) originally stood and had been demolished in order to build the temple. This event set into motion Hindu reprisals in the form of killing and raping of Muslims and burning of their homes, shops and businesses in several places within the state of Gujarat. It has been widely reported that the state government and police connived in this carnage rather than control it. The violence, which was intense for four days continued for well over three months and stray incidents occur to date. The surviving people, mostly belonging to the Muslim community, were rendered homeless and temporarily put in camps of varying sizes and conditions.

Outreach, ComMutiny–the Youth Collective, Delhi. Both Mahamaya and Kanika have master's degrees in social development from University of Sussex.

'River Sabarmati, not just a physical divide.' This statement has now become an inside joke among the volunteers, but the truth behind it becomes glaringly obvious as one drives from Ahmedabad Junction in Kalupur (Old Ahmedabad), to Navrangpura (new Ahmedabad). The famous C.G. Road with its international chains of stores and fast cars is far removed from the reality of the small *paan ka gallas* and *phat phatiyas* of the Vatwa area in Old Ahmedabad. This is not just because of the economic disparity characteristic of these two areas, which is common to almost all large cities. 28 February 2002, and the weeks that followed it, had vastly different implications for the two areas. While life in new Ahmedabad was punctuated briefly by the calm caused by the curfew, life in Old Ahmedabad was thrown into turmoil by the extensive violence and destruction that pulverised the atmosphere there.

We arrived in Ahmedabad in June, four months after the riots had begun, by which point the violence had stopped, but its effects could be seen everywhere. The killing, looting, burning and raping was over, but the destruction had left thousands of people homeless, orphaned, widowed and wounded. Camps had been set up all over Old Ahmedabad, and our work was distributed between the Vatwa and Gomtipur areas. There were five fully functional camps spread out in these two areas, only a couple of which were recognised by the government.

As we walked towards the camps, our first reaction was, 'it's better than I thought it would be.' Having heard gory reports of the kinds of violence that had taken place during the riots, we expected to meet only injured, burnt, invalid people, but what we saw was a dusty patch of ground, with a makeshift tarpaulin roof, and a hundred-odd people sitting around. It almost seemed like a picnic, except that this 'picnic' never ended. People never went back home. They sat on that dust-ridden ground through the heat of the day, and slept on the very same spot through the untimely rains at night. The life that they had led previously had no meaning anymore, and now their very existence was defined by that patch of dust, which had been their home for the last four months.

The conditions at the camps varied from terribly hard to unbearable, yet the inmates were living through it with the hope that at some point they would be able to put it all behind them, and restart their lives with whatever degree of normalcy possible. Every day there were threats from politically-motivated quarters to shut down the camps. Every time the supplies arrived, they would fall short. The compensation that had been provided to the lucky few was a pittance, compared to their actual losses. Despite the seeming lack of improvement, the camp members smiled, prayed, and most of all, hoped; everyone hoping that he might he one of the few lucky recipients of the next hand cart or sewing machine being gifted by an NGO.

A great source of inspiration, not just for the victims, but also for the volunteers, was the group of Aman Pathiks. These individuals were those who had themselves suffered grave losses during the riots, but had volunteered to help with relief work. Being a part of the same community, living under the same adverse circumstances as the rest of the inmates, the Aman Pathiks formed the link between the victims and the NGOs that were involved with their rehabilitation. Putting aside their own trauma, they worked towards a better future, not just for themselves, but hundreds of other families.

Before leaving for Ahmedabad, the volunteers went through an orientation session. It was during such a briefing that we were warned that we might be at the receiving end of negative outbursts from the inmates. Due to the severe emotional trauma, it was quite likely that some amount of resentment may be directed towards us, owing to the religious and social communities we belonged to, or simply because some people might need an emotional vent. Our experiences during the seven weeks (over a period of four months) in Ahmedabad, proved anything but. Frustration was evident through the spats that the inmates had with one another or the arguments with the camp organisers that ensued after the distribution of any kind of supplies. But not once did these survivors of violence show any kind of resentment towards us. In fact, they looked at us with hope, as people who might help them out of their misery. Each time that we left Ahmedabad, we left with the love and blessings of the members, who now treat us as their own.

A major part of the work that we did at the camps especially during the period from June to July involved filling out compensation forms.

This required us to sit down with each family and fill out details of the kind of losses they suffered during the riots, and the kind of compensation (or the lack thereof) they have received since then. Many of the bonds that we formed with the camp members began with this work. Each form could take up to forty-five minutes, as we would ask for details of personal history, personal possessions and the like. This was also an opportunity for the survivors to talk. It was perhaps the first time that these people were being asked to share their experiences. They would reminisce about the good old days, and break down as they narrated the events of the night that changed their lives. They did not know if we would be able to help them out, and we made sure not to give them any false hopes; but they did know that we were there to listen, and that we wanted to hear them. It was this that formed the foundations of the relationships that the volunteers made with the camp members.

During our second visit to Ahmedabad, we focused on medical needs. This was an area that had so far been neglected by the NGOs involved with rehabilitation work. We initiated a health care system, that was carried out with and often without organisational support. Medical attention was urgent, and expensive. Epidemics of jaundice, typhoid and malaria were on the rise, and there were many severe cases of TB and epilepsy. The camp members were desperate for medical attention. Taking people to the hospital every day, getting them examined, bringing to them the required medication, and following up to make sure that patients were recovering adequately, all served to strengthen the rapport that we had already established with the people. It was rewarding to see that improvement of physical health made the people stronger and more committed to start their lives again, and to face their current situation with greater strength.

Amongst our closest relationships were the ones that we formed with the children. Even those of us who were not directly involved with the children, formed very close bonds with some of them following just one visit to their school. Every time the children would then spot us on the roads, they'd call out to us, sit with us, talk to us, and continued looking out for us every day. Clearly, the children needed attention, something that they had been deprived of for too long after a great trauma.

It wasn't till four months after the riots that the needs of the affected children were looked into. Since their arrival at the camps, the children had spent their time loitering around with nothing constructive to do. No one had been able to address the trauma that they had gone through, not even their own parents, who were themselves unequipped to cope with their children's problems. They had pressing survival issues to deal with first. The children had, till this point, found their own ways of coping with the trauma that they had gone through during the riots and the situation after.

In June, a small school was set up with the help of an academician who formulated a module based on which teachers could be quickly trained. Ladies from nearby houses, who had time to spare, volunteered to teach at this school, following the guidelines that had been established. At last the children were getting some of the attention they badly needed, and their energies positively channelled. The activities of the school ranged from creative to academic, so as to be educational as well as therapeutic. The school has grown from being a temporary place where the children could constructively use their time, into an establishment that is now being supported by an NGO called Sahyog, on a more permanent basis. Sahyog provides the study material, the salaries of teachers, and even an afternoon snack for the children. This school, in the Vatwa area is one of the bigger success stories from among the work that the volunteers have been involved in.

Lately volunteers have begun focusing on livelihood support measures for the camp members, which are activities now fully preoccupying NGOs working there. This involves rebuilding of houses, relocation of families and distribution of livelihood kits. Goods like handcarts and sewing machines have been distributed, so as to provide families with some means to earn a living, and thus, regain a bit of economic independence. These efforts have begun to show results.

Ten months after the carnage there are fewer people in the camps, many have found homes, many have become financially independent. On our third visit to Ahmedabad, we had the opportunity to visit them in their new homes, share meals with them, and be a part of their newly built lives; a very heart-warming experience. A faint glimpse of what their lives once were, can now be had, but we would be foolish to believe that things have returned, or that they ever would return, to a state of normalcy. Elections are round the corner, stray incidents of communal violence continue, and public apathy is as apparent as before. On the surface, life in Old Ahmedabad may appear to be what it might have been ten months ago, but can we expect things to normalise when, even in their own homes, people live under the constant shadow of fear?

Chapter 20

Psychosocial Interventions in Conflict Situations*

Shobna Sonpar

Shobna Sonpar is a clinical psychologist and psychotherapist in private practice, and was a Trustee of Psychological Foundations. Her research interests have been in gender, social justice and political violence. She has been associated with projects in Kashmir that build capacity for psychosocial support and with women's peacebuilding initiatives, and has researched militant lives and the role of psychosocial programming in Kashmir.

Batticaloa on Sri Lanka's eastern coast lies in an area ravaged by many years of violent conflict and by the tsunami that struck in 2004. On the surface it seems like any small town with busy people going about everyday lives. It is a charming place with great tracts of tranquil lagoon separated from the restless ocean by narrow strips of sandy land. We are told that the picturesque fishing hulks that on closer look are quite decrepit are the misguided bounty of some humanitarian agency that donated hundreds of sea-going fishing vessels after the tsunami not realising that they were catering to a lagoon fishing community. Indeed

---

* This chapter was first published in *The Journal*, Vol. 9(2), September 2009, by the Psychological Foundations Trust, New Delhi.

the international humanitarian community has a marked presence with an entire street of bungalows facing the lagoon bearing their boards. We are told about the big wave, the bodies that littered the beaches and the buildings that were destroyed, the camps for those displaced and the concerted efforts by a team of Sri Lankan humanitarian workers whose conflict-related experience in the preceding years helped to devise a coordinated plan of action to bring relief and begin the process of material and psychosocial reconstruction. We see the almost 100-year-old lighthouse that withstood the onslaught of the tsunami in its spectacular location where the lagoon meets the ocean, and the casuarinas that were torn to the ground but have burst back to form a thick green edging to the beach. There is colour everywhere—the green of palmyra, coconut, and spreading jackfruit trees, bright blue churches, walls telling stories in murals, exuberantly decorated temple *gopurams,* and exquisite cotton weaves in the dingy showroom of the moribund handloom industry.

It is only gradually that we become aware of the grim realities of people's lives—the disappearances, the thousands displaced, the atmosphere of fear and suspicion. We learn that the region is known for its highest rates of suicide and child recruitment to militant groups. We learn that ethnic conflict simmers in the region which comprises Tamil Hindus and Christians as well as Muslims, and recall the drab Muslim villages we crossed on the road to Batticaloa. We are no longer sanguine as we encounter the many security personnel on the bridge across the lagoon and at checkpoints on the road. And one evening on Kallady Beach we pause in our frolic as severe-faced young men bristling with machine guns gather around their boss, an erstwhile militant leader, who has also come to enjoy the breeze. After some time they jump into their cars and roar away as everyone scatters to the side of the road.

We were a group of people—Pakistani, Indian, Nepalese, Sri Lankan, Maldivian and Palestinians from Lebanon—who have been doing psychosocial work in conflict areas and had come together for a collaborative learning course on mental health and psychosocial support conducted by the Peace-building & Development Institute in Sri Lanka. We included psychologists, counsellors, doctors, humanitarian aid workers and anthropologists. Batticaloa was the site of our field visit.

Several aspects made an impression. What we saw was a model of expanding, interlinking and coordinated psychosocial programming that evolved to meet psychosocial needs of particular sections of the population as these emerged. A case in point is the work around gender-based violence and child protection. The Gender-Based Violence (GBV) Desk was established by the GBV task force, comprising government and non-government members in 2005 following the observation that many victims of domestic violence came to the Batticaloa Teaching Hospital with burns and other injuries, suicide attempts, somatic complaints and sick children. The GBV Desk liases closely with the hospital with which it has an excellent rapport, a legal support centre, a crisis refuge for women, the child protection unit and a shelter for children. It is staffed by community workers who have had training in counselling and case management along with gender sensitisation and communication skills. It does community outreach in the surrounding villages and when need arises it liases with village level functionaries, the police and also with organisations working with men who have substance abuse problems. The nature of their engagement is such that they are able to have an overview of the many issues connected to GBV and to respond accordingly.

Secondly, professionals worked alongside community level workers without deference or arrogance, each valuing and respecting the others' realm of knowledge.

Thirdly, there was a quality of leadership that helped create new leaders, so essential to sustainability of programmes. This seemed to happen through a combination of modelling of problem-solving and calculated risk-taking, of encouraging staff to take new initiatives while taking responsibility for errors.

Fourthly, it was demonstrated that funding factors need not become imperatives guiding policy and intervention and that low-budget options, as well as local resources including public-private partnerships were credible options.

Some initiatives illustrated an integrated approach to psychosocial work in that they provided 'psychosocial accompaniment' rather than any specific psychosocial intervention. One of these was by a group of people, largely women, who got together when they realised that the 'culture of fear' was causing such social atomisation that people in tragic circumstances were abandoned to their grief. It was felt crucial to struggle with one's own fear and 'do the thing that makes us human'. They broke the isolation by meeting with and sharing the pain of families who had a member who had been killed or had disappeared. Certain activities evolved from this, such as planting a tree in memory of someone lost, and painting the surface of roads with colourful assertions of 'Life'. Mothers of children who had been 'taken' connected deeply in their anguish across ethnic and political divides and their sharing became a book of poems, *Parents Life Pulse*. One poem was entitled *Hungry Amma*:

> The gate at the fence
> Will be flung open
> Forgetting to close it
> In his hunger
> My child will come
> During the day...
> Amma waits,
> Alert

> Night comes
> The rice is cold
> New rice is cooked again, it is hot
> The cold night creeps in...
> I must keep awake
> To serve him...
> At the break of dawn
> The cock crows
> I must have nodded off
> I wake up suddenly, shaken
> It is well past dawn
> His plate of old rice
> Must be washed and dried
> For my child who will come during the day
> Must have hot rice on the plate.

Another poem:

> I called for my child
> By the name I gave
> Studying dates, planetary positions;
> No one there they told me By that name.
> Only fighters
> Fighting for rights
> In the names they had given
> No one in the name I gave...
> Yet that is my child!
> Today
> My child has no rights.
> And for me
> No rights even to his name.

Other psycho social initiatives are driven by psychological therapeutic principles but adopt methods that are innovative, creative and culturally congruent. One such is the *Butterfly Garden,* a programme for trauma healing at the level of the child and for peace-building within the community. The Garden which began in 1996 is an oasis of imagination and creativity bringing together animation artists, peace-workers, ritual healers and children aged 6–16 years from various ethnic and religious groups. The children are drawn from about 20 communities around Batticaloa and are transported to the Butterfly Garden in a large white bus that has itself become a symbol of peace. Approximately 150 children affected by the armed conflict attend a weekly after-school and weekend programme for 6–9 months to engage in a variety of activities— clay work, drawing, storytelling, arts and crafts, and healing rituals—facilitated by local trained animators from different communities. For those who require additional individual attention, there is a trauma healing programme using storytelling, innovative games, genograms and interview methods.

MAPPING THE 'PSYCHOSOCIAL' FIELD

A definition of the term 'psychosocial' which has come into popular usage since the UNICEF described it in 1997 holds that,

The term 'psychosocial' underlines the close relationship between the psychological and the social effects of armed conflict, the one type of effect continually influencing the other. By 'psychological effects' is meant those experiences that affect emotions, behaviour, thoughts, memory and learning ability and how a situation may be perceived and understood. By 'social effects' is meant how the diverse experiences of war alter people's relationships to each other, in that such experiences change people, but also through death, separation, estrangement and other losses. 'Social' may be extended to include an economic dimension, many individuals and families becoming destitute through the material and economic devastation of war, thus losing their social status and place in their familiar social network. (UNICEF, 1997, p.12)

Although the need for psychosocial intervention in contexts of violent conflict is rarely disputed, the conceptual principles that should guide intervention are a matter of debate. For a long time, the dominant conceptualisation of suffering has been in the idiom of psychopathology, especially post-traumatic stress disorder (PTSD). Indeed, trauma has become synonymous with PTSD in popular and scientific thought. But the biomedical model applied to suffering arising from violent conflict and disaster has been the subject of much controversy. It has been criticised on various fronts: It ignores sociopolitical context and reduces complex and varied human responses to clinical phenomena; it tends to be individual in focus and neglects the wider social impact of conflict on communities; it ignores cultural expressions of suffering, community strengths and ways of coping, and people's own priorities (Bracken, Giller & Summerfield, 1997; Ager, 1997; Summerfield, 1999, 2004; Breslau, 2004; Pedersen, 2002).

Alternatives to the dominant trauma conceptualisation emerging from the field of medical and social anthropology include 'social suffering' (Kleinman, Das & Lock, 1997) and 'cultural bereavement' (Eisenbruch, 1991). The former is a term invested with a moral rather than clinical tone, capturing the experiential dimension of suffering while anchoring it in social adversity and injustice. It allows for collective levels of analysis that link local problems with global issues, community-grounded responses with professional responses, and health with social problems. 'Cultural bereavement' is a concept that emerged from the subjective experience of Cambodian refugees and gives primacy to what the trauma meant to them, their cultural idioms of distress and cultural strategies for overcoming their pain. The increasingly accepted framework today is that of psycho social well-being where the emphasis is on the domains of well-being which are affected by conflict.

The opposition between the biomedical and the constructivist perspectives associated with social and medical anthropology has typically taken the form of competing discourses on trauma and resilience. The resilience discourse is associated with interventions that recognise the capacity and resources of people and which respect and protect the rights of local culture and traditions, while the trauma discourse is associated with the application of western, medically oriented or psychological interventions. On the ground this has often taken the form of an opposition between counselling approaches and community-developmental approaches (Samarsinghe, 2002).

An issue of concern has been the extent to which concepts from the Western world have infiltrated the core of professional and academic thinking in the countries of the third world (Samarasinghe & Galappatti, 1999). This has resulted in the domination of an international therapeutic model that constructs war-affected populations as inevitably traumatised and subject to dysfunctions that sustain new cycles of violence; this new form of 'external therapeutic governance' becomes a form of cultural imperialism imposing western models on other societies (Pupavac, 2002). The systems of meaning used by sufferers, the cultural forms of signalling distress, and cultural practices for coping and healing are ignored.

Apart from conceptual and disciplinary controversies, the plethora of interventions that huddle under the umbrella term 'psychosocial' adds to the confusion. A remarkably varied range of interventions such as counselling, befriending, trauma healing, psycho-education, interpersonal skills development, conflict mediation, communication, expressive activities including play, theatre and drawing, mobilisation of social networks, supportive practices for child development, vocational training, livelihood support, micro-credit, spiritual work and human rights interventions are included. These diverse activities are loosely associated with different disciplinary fields—psychiatry, counselling psychology, social psychology, developmental psychology, cultural anthropology—each having its own theoretical frame of understanding psychosocial impacts of violent conflict and disaster and thus of problem definition, choice of intervention and desired outcomes.

As described by Galappatti (2003), most psychosocial interventions fall broadly within the mental health, community-developmental and social justice/human rights domains of intervention. The mental health approaches use frameworks borrowed from psychiatry, clinical psychology and counselling, and focus on the explicitly psychological consequences of violent conflict and aim to support survivors on this basis of understanding. These activities constitute the first-generation of psychosocial projects and remain the most widely recognised form of psychosocial intervention.

Community-developmental approaches draw on social anthropology and social psychology and employ strategies to support psychosocial resilience and wellbeing through fostering changes in the material and social environment of communities affected by conflict. In a more recent trend, they attempt to integrate supportive or therapeutic principles into diverse mainstream development and reconstruction activities such as building infrastructure, developing livelihoods, supplying material relief, mobilising communities and so on (Galappatti, 2003). Based on the understanding that people's conflict-related experiences affect them on material, social and psychological levels, it is suggested that all interventions should be informed by and incorporate a working understanding of the relevance of psychosocial issues (Williamson & Robinson, 2006).

Poverty-reduction programmes are ideally suited to enhance psychosocial well-being in the aftermath of political violence according to Salih and Galappatti (2006) who described a resettlement programme where psychosocial principles were integrated into economic-developmental interventions. The involvement of psychosocial workers on a daily basis to facilitate group meetings, understand group dynamics, avert group conflicts, advocate on vulnerable members' behalf, model perspective-taking, and in general be involved in a genuine but non-intrusive way in the lives of people was found to be very useful though not entirely devoid of problems. Weyermann (2007) described something similar in Nepal. A psychosocial approach was applied in five ongoing projects, three of which dealt primarily with economic betterment of the target population. The staff working on these projects was taught to use an empowerment tool that assesses the disempowerment process at social, material and psychological levels so as to identify the unique needs of each beneficiary and to devise helping strategies accordingly. The staff thus gained insight into the inner life of people and the complexities of individual families while psychologists learned about economics and livelihoods.

The explicitly social justice/human rights orientation to psychosocial programming is not as common since most organisations take pains to avoid activities that are overtly political. This is so partly because of the very real dangers faced by organisations in conflict areas, and partly due to a failure to grasp the significance of the social justice/human rights facet of conflict-related experience. A major exception is psychosocial work accompanying activism on issues of disappearances, torture and displacement (Galappatti, 2003). However, since violent conflict is often found to be rooted in structural factors of deprivation and social injustice, current approaches to psychosocial intervention increasingly emphasise issues concerning collective action for social transformation and resistance against injustice and oppression (Wessels, 2008).

It should be noted that the trajectory of psychosocial programming has been completely different in Latin America. Sales and Beristain (2008) described how the first psychosocial teams in the mid-1970s were part of organisations defending human rights so that therapeutic attention and 'psychosocial accompaniment' were integrated into the wider legal and social processes right from the start. They openly rejected clinical models based on diagnoses like PTSD, viewed victims as subjects of social transformation who opened spaces for denouncing the abuse of power, questioned the classic idea of therapeutic neutrality and conceptualised harm in social rather than individual terms. They accompanied processes of reparation like the exhumation of the bodies of those forcibly 'disappeared' by providing psychosocial support to families, opening spaces for dialogue in the community, and also by keeping the local and national debate on disappearances alive so as to maximise the potential for social transformation. The psychosocial accompaniment for resistance included generating spaces for consciousness-raising about political realities and internalisations as well as emotional mobilisation that dealt with fear and with grief over loss.

FOCUSING THE FIELD

The rapid expansions of the field of humanitarian psychosocial intervention and the conceptual and disciplinary controversies have made urgent the need for a comprehensive framework. Such a framework representing the joint efforts of a large number of humanitarian and academic institutions is offered by the Psychosocial Working Group (2003). Within this framework the concept of psychosocial wellbeing replaces the narrow construct of mental health. Psychosocial wellbeing is defined with respect to three core domains: human capacity, social ecology, culture and values. Each of these domains can be mapped in order to determine the impact of the events and circumstances of conflict situations, to identify the domain-specific resources of people and communities and to design psychosocial interventions accordingly. The value of a framework such as this is that it can be used to trace casual factors and psychosocial effects, plan interventions and evaluate them within the relevant domain.

A significant gap in psychosocial work has been the absence of a multi-sectoral, interagency framework that enables effective coordination, identifies useful practices and flags potentially harmful practices. The Inter-Agency Standing Committee (IASC) Guidelines on Mental Health and Psychosocial Support in Emergency Settings (2007) aims to fill this gap. These guidelines are based on the consensus that psychosocial concerns involve all sectors of humanitarian work because it is the manner in which aid is being implemented that affects psychosocial wellbeing. They are therefore meant for a wide range of actors in diverse sectors. In place of the trauma idiom, the guidelines identify a holistic conceptualisation of psychosocial wellbeing that centres on risk, resilience and protective factors and highlight the primacy of social interventions over counselling and other clinical interventions. In describing the nature of psychosocial problems that may need attention in emergencies, the IASC guidelines divide these in terms of pre-existing, emergency-induced and humanitarian-aid induced problems. The structure of the guidelines includes recommendations for emergency preparedness, minimum responses to be applied during the acute period and comprehensive responses to be implemented during the stabilised and early reconstruction period of the emergency. The guidelines are based on certain core principles: the promotion of human rights and equity, the maximisation of local participation and local capacity, and 'do no harm' by ensuring cultural competence, local knowledge, evidence-based practice and awareness of power dynamics.

The IASC (2007) suggested a pyramid model of multilayered supports to populations affected by emergency. At the base of the pyramid, catering to the largest section of the population, are the supports addressing basic needs for shelter, food, water, security and basic health care. At the next level are community and family supports that help preserve the integrity of family and community networks otherwise disrupted due to loss, displacement, separation and social distrust such as family tracing, mourning ceremonies, livelihoods and educational activities. At the next level, those who require more focused individual, family or group intervention such as victims of gender or sexual violence, widows, orphans, may receive more focused non-specialised support for basic mental health care and psychological first aid. The topmost level represents the support required for the small percentage whose suffering warrants specialised psychiatric and psychological support.

In India, the National Disaster Management Authority (NDMA) has recently brought out Guidelines for Psychosocial Support and Mental Health Services in Disasters (2009) which draws on the IASC Guidelines as well as on local expertise on psychosocial interventions following natural and man-made disasters.

IN THE FIELD

Among the many issues that concern practitioners in the field, the assessment of psychosocial functioning and the impact on the self of the practitioner of working in difficult and sometimes dangerous conditions need special mention.

Assessment

The development of participatory methods for assessment of psychosocial needs and evaluation of interventions has been significant. Most epidemiological studies in war and disaster-affected populations have focused narrowly on PTSD without considering its utility in specific cultural contexts. There has been a heavy reliance on measures developed in Western contexts, a failure to distinguish between normal distress reactions and actual mental disorders, and little attention to culturally specific indicators and idioms of distress (Miller & Fernando, 2008).

Psychosocial wellbeing must be understood within the social and cultural context where the intervention is taking place. The purpose of participatory methods is to learn from the target population about those experiences which are important to them, what they consider to be positive and negative psychological and social states, and their understanding of their resources and risks. The participatory approach thus views the population as social actors with important insights into their lives and an important role to play in enhancing their own and their community's wellbeing (Hart et al., 2007). Participatory methods could also be used to generate culturally grounded categories that may then be used to develop quantitative measures (Miller & Fernando, 2008).

The methods include mapping exercises and diagrams such as risk/resource maps, body maps, spider diagrams and problem trees (Hart et al., 2007) as well as ethnographic methods such as free listing and key informant interviewing to arrive at the priorities within a population (Bolton & Tang, 2004). The Psychosocial Assessment for Development and Humanitarian Intervention (PADHI, 2009) framework developed in Sri Lanka is another approach. It incorporates five domains so that people are said to experience wellbeing when they can build social connections, exercise participation, access physical, material and knowledge resources, enhance physical and psychological wellness and experience competence and self worth. The model includes the role of power and identity in mediating wellbeing, and the role of institutions and systems in being facilitative or obstructive.

Self care

It is well-known that working in the context of conflict and extreme human suffering is very frustrating and stressful. Psychosocial workers try to alleviate suffering amid circumstances that are tragic, frightening, chaotic and often characterised by grave social injustices. Their experiences in the field can take a toll on their emotional wellbeing and personal life. Recognising this, humanitarian agencies incorporate guidelines for good practices in managing stress for their staff. Such guidelines include a written policy about preventing or mitigating stress, screening and assessing the current capacity of staff members, ensuring that all staff members have appropriate preparation and training for assignments, monitoring the stress of staff on an ongoing basis, and providing ongoing training as well as psychological support (Antares Foundation, 2006).

There are also several steps that humanitarian workers can take to reduce the risk of burn-out including taking breaks, taking care of physical health, maintaining some separation of work and personal life, making and keeping relationships outside of work, accepting that it may not be possible to change everything while validating the worth of one's work, realising that feelings of anger and despair about the situation are legitimate, taking psychological support if available, and having a belief system that gives meaning to existence.

REFERENCES

Ager, A. (1997). Tensions in the psychosocial discourse: Implications for the planning of interventions for war-affected populations. *Development in Practice,* 7(4), 402–07.

Antares Foundation (2006). *Managing Stress in Humanitarian Workers: Guidelines for Good Practice.* Author.

Bolton, P. & Tang, A. (2004, January–March). Using ethnographic methods in the selection of post-disaster, mental health interventions. *Prehospital & Disaster Medicine,* 97–101.

Bracken, P., Giller, J. & Summerfield, D. (1997). Rethinking mental health with survivors of wartime violence and refugees. *Journal of Refugee Studies, 10*(4), 431–42.

Breslau, J. (2004). Culture of trauma: Anthropological views of post-traumatic stress disorder in international health. *Culture, Medicine and Psychiatry. 28,* 113–26.

Eisenbruch, M. (1991). From post-traumatic disorder to cultural bereavement: diagnosis of Southeast Asian Refugees. *Social Science & Medicine, 33*(6), 673–80.

Galappatti, A. (2003). What is psychosocial intervention? Mapping the field in Sri Lanka. *Intervention, 1*(2), 2–17.

Hart, J., Galappatti, A., Boyden, J. & Armstrong, M. (2007). Participatory tools for evaluating psychosocial work with children in areas of armed conflict: a pilot in eastern Sri Lanka. *Intervention, 3(1)*, 41–60.

Inter-Agency Standing Committee (2007). IASC Guidelines on Mental Health and Psychosocial Support in Emergency Settings. Retrieved from www. humanitarianinfo.org/'iasc

Kleinman, A., Das, V. & Lock, M. (1998). Introduction. In A. Kleinman, V. Das & M. Lock (Eds), *Social Suffering* (pp. ix–xxvii), New Delhi: Oxford University Press.

Miller, K.E. & Fernando, G. (2008). Epidemiological assessment in emergency settings: Recommendations for enhancing a potentially useful tool. *Intervention, 6(3/4)*, 255–60.

National Disaster Management Authority (2009). *Guidelines on Psychosocial Support and Mental Health Services in Disasters.* Retrieved from www.ndrna.govinjndma/ guidelines /PSSMHSGuidclines.pdf

PADHI (2009). *A Tool, a Guide & a Framework: Introduction to a Psychosocial Approach to Development.* Colombo: Social Policy Analysis & Research Centre, University of Colombo.

Pedersen, D. (2002). Political violence, ethnic conflict and contemporary wars: Broad implications for health and social well-being. *Social Science& Medicine, 55*, 175–90.

Psychosocial Working Group (2003). *Psychosocial Interventions in Complex Emergencies: A Conceptual Framework.* Edinburgh/Oxford: Author. Retrieved from www.forcedmigration.org/ psychosocial

Pupavac, V. (2002). Therapeutising refugees, pathologising populations: International psychosocial programmes in Kosovo. *New Issues in Refugee Research,* UNHC Working Paper No. 59. Geneva: UNHCR. Retrieved from www.unhcr.org

Sales, P. & Beristain, C.M. (2008, September). *Trauma, development and peace-building: A Latin American perspective.* Paper presented at INCORE & IDRC Conference on Trauma, Development & Peace-building, New Delhi.

Salih, M. & Galappatti, A. (2006). Integrating a psychosocial perspective into poverty reduction: The case of a resettlement project in northern Sri Lanka. *Intervention, 4(2)*, 127–45.

Samarasinghe, G. & Galappatti, A. (1999). *PSE Survey Report.* Unpublished manuscript, Social Scientists' Association and IWTHI Trust, Colombo.

Sarnarasinghe, G. (2002). *Counselling vs. community-based approaches.* Paper presented at National Conference on Mental Health, Sahanaya, Colombo.

Sununerfield, D. (1999). A critique of seven assumptions behind psychological trauma programmes in war-affected areas. *Social Science & Medicine, 48*, 1449–62.

———. (2004). Cross-cultural perspectives on the medicalisation of human suffering. In G. Rosen (Ed.), *Post-traumatic Stress Disorder: Issues and Controversies* (pp. 233–45). London: John Wiley.

UNICEF (1997, April). *Cape Town Principles and Best Practices: Adopted at the Symposium on the Prevention of Recruitment of Children into the Armed Forces and Demobilization and Social Reintegration of Child Soldiers in Africa*. Cape Town, South Africa, 30 April, 1997. Retrieved from www.unicef.org/emerg/files/Cape_Town_Principles(1).pdf.

Wessells, M. (2008, September). *Trauma, peace-building and development: An Africa region perspective*. Paper presented at INCORE & IDRC Conference on Trauma, Development & Peace-building, New Delhi. Retrieved from www.incore.ulst.ac/research/projects/trauma/

Weyermann, B. (2007). Linking economics to emotions; Towards a more integrated understanding of empowerment in conflict areas. *Intervention, 5(2)*, 83–96.

Williamson, J. & Robinson, M. (2006). Psychosocial interventions or integrated programming for wellbeing? *Intervention, 4(1)*, 4–25.

About the Editors

Shobna Sonpar is a clinical psychologist and psychotherapist based in New Delhi. In addition to her clinical practice, she has helped set up the counselling service at IIT Delhi and the training programme in clinical psychology at Tribhuvan University, Nepal. Her research interests are gender, social justice and violence. She has been involved with projects in Jammu and Kashmir that build capacity for psychosocial support and peace building. She has also undertaken research on militancy in Jammu and Kashmir and on the transformative impact of social programming.

Neeru Kanwar is a practising psychotherapist and counsellor based in New Delhi. Her area of interest is social psychology. While her work has been primarily with persons suffering from anxiety and depression, she has held a particular interest in areas of childhood trauma, sexual abuse, communal conflict and couples' conflict. The overall guiding focus has been development of resilience and compassion in persons attending to social distress. Dr Kanwar is one of the founding members of the Indian Association of Family Therapy.